A WORLD *of* NATIONS

DANKWART A. RUSTOW

A WORLD *of* NATIONS

Problems of Political Modernization

THE BROOKINGS INSTITUTION
Washington, D.C.

SBN   8157   7641-1 (paper)
SBN   8157   7642-x (cloth)
Library of Congress Catalogue Card Number 67-26139

To the memory of

ALEXANDER RÜSTOW

1885–1963

THE BROOKINGS INSTITUTION is an independent organization devoted to nonpartisan research, education, and publication in economics, government, foreign policy, and the social sciences generally. Its principal purposes are to aid in the development of sound public policies and to promote public understanding of issues of national importance.

The Institution was founded on December 8, 1927, to merge the activities of the Institute for Government Research, founded in 1916, the Institute of Economics, founded in 1922, and the Robert Brookings Graduate School of Economics and Government, founded in 1924.

The general administration of the Institution is the responsibility of a self-perpetuating Board of Trustees. The trustees are likewise charged with maintaining the independence of the staff and fostering the most favorable conditions for creative research and education. The immediate direction of the policies, program, and staff of the Institution is vested in the President, assisted by an advisory council chosen from the staff of the Institution.

In publishing a study, the Institution presents it as a competent treatment of a subject worthy of public consideration. The interpretations and conclusions in such publications are those of the author or authors and do not purport to represent the views of the other staff members, officers, or trustees of the Brookings Institution.

FOREWORD

PROCLAMATIONS OF INDEPENDENCE in some sixty new states and the new prominence of Asia, Africa, and Latin America on the world scene are among the most portentous events of the mid-twentieth century. The resulting problems of political and economic development have for some years been the subject of study by the Brookings Institution. The Institution's work, in this as in other fields, has been based on the premise that the scholar's theoretical perspective can broaden the outlook of the official policy maker, just as the practical problems confronting the government official can give sharper focus to the scholar's generalizations. A study group conducted at Brookings in 1960-61 was one of the first efforts to identify political development as a key problem in the emerging countries and one which required more governmental as well as scholarly attention.

Dr. Dankwart A. Rustow became a senior staff member of Brookings in 1961 and actively participated in the work of the Foreign Policy Studies Program until 1963 when he returned to Columbia University as Professor of International Social Forces. The present work is an outgrowth of his association with Brookings; it also draws freely on his earlier and later research in the fields of comparative politics and international relations.

Much of the literature on the developing countries has been concerned with economic questions and with such related political problems as the diplomacy of foreign aid or the role of government planning. Dr. Rustow believes that the political problems of

ix

the newly developing countries deserve systematic attention in
their own right. Modernization and the nation-state are the two
central concepts of his analysis. At every stage in his argument,
the author contrasts the recent experience of the late-modernizing
countries of Asia, Africa, and Latin America with the earlier history of the countries of the West. His analysis is sustained by a
clear theoretical perspective as he examines the quests for authority, identity, and equality as the central political aspects of modernization, as he analyzes the dynamic features of political leadership within charismatic, military, and single-party regimes, and
as he discusses the rival appeals of democracy and communism to
peoples in the throes of late modernization.

Dr. Rustow had the benefit of the views of an advisory commit-
tee at various stages in the planning and execution of his work.
Members of the committee included Robert E. Asher of Brookings;
Leonard Binder of the University of Chicago; Major Michael
Dunn, U.S. Army; Rupert Emerson of Harvard University; Robert
Good of the Department of State; Samuel P. Huntington of Har-
vard University; Wynne James of the Department of Defense;
Vernon McKay of the School of Advanced International Studies,
The Johns Hopkins University; John N. Plank of Brookings; Wil-
liam R. Polk of the University of Chicago; Ronald Schneider of
Columbia University; Kalman H. Silvert of New York University;
Philip B. Taylor of the School of Advanced International Studies,
The Johns Hopkins University; Andrew F. Westwood of Brook-
ings; and Howard Wriggins of Columbia University. Huntington,
Plank, and Wriggins acted as a reading committee. During Dr.
Rustow's residence at Brookings, Walter F. Weiker and Peter
Ranis assisted him. The project was conducted under the general
supervision of H. Field Haviland, Jr., Director of the Foreign Pol-
icy Studies Program.

The Institution also joins the author in expressing appreciation
to Conrad M. Arensberg of Columbia University, Reinhard Bendix of the University of California at Berkeley, Luigi Einaudi of
the RAND Corporation, Manfred Halpern of Princeton Univer-

sity, Albert O. Hirschman of Harvard University, and James O'Connell of the University of Ibadan, for critical reading of parts or all of the manuscript at various stages of drafting; to Mrs. Mary Lynne Byrd for research assistance, particularly in the compilation of the tables of the appendix; and to the Institute of War and Peace Studies at Columbia University and its director, William T. R. Fox, for support during the final stages of writing. Evelyn Breck edited the manuscript; Adele Garrett prepared the index.

The Institution is grateful to the Ford Foundation, whose grant for general support provided the funds for this study.

The views expressed in this book are, of course, those of the author and do not necessarily represent the views of those consulted during its preparation, nor of the trustees, the officers, or other staff members of the Brookings Institution or the Ford Foundation.

KERMIT GORDON
President

July 1967
Washington, D.C.

CONTENTS

CHAPTER ONE

INTRODUCTION:
NATION AND MODERNITY

O le bon temps que ce siècle de fer.
VOLTAIRE

We are caught between the millstones of . . . two revolutions.
NASSER

NATION AND MODERNITY are among the most potent ideals of the twentieth century. They are distinct in concept but often reinforce each other in practice. Scientific discovery, new technical skills, and industrial production are among the tools of modernity; among the emotions of nationhood are common purpose and mutual trust. Nationality can lay the social foundation for the division of labor in modern science and industry; and the desire for modernity can bring national loyalties into focus. Nations, as Cyril Black has suggested, have been human communities that have ventured jointly upon the major tasks of modernization.[1] Together nationalism and modernity form an arena of tacit assumptions in which the vocal battle between political ideologies such as democracy and communism has been fought.

Modernization began in Europe in the Renaissance and spread overseas in the wake of Europe's expansion. The result always was a dynamic blend of traditional and Western influences, and before long Western ideas were turned against the West's own

[1] Cyril E. Black, *The Dynamics of Modernization: Essays in Comparative History* (Harper, 1966), pp. 27, 75, and passim.

1

imperialism. The nation-state, like modernization, has European roots, having grown out of the dynastic states of the twelfth to eighteenth century. But Western nationalism did not burst forth fully until the American and French Revolutions, and in that same period it became linked to modernization. Since then, in Latin America, Asia, and Africa, nationhood and modernity have appeared as two facets of a single transformation—a dual revolution loudly proclaimed and often ardently desired but never accomplished quickly or with ease.

National and modernizing motifs blend in the rhetoric of postcolonial leaders in Asia and Africa and of revolutionaries and reformers in Latin America. The same themes echo in the appeals by which Americans, Russians, and Chinese try to direct the ferment in the southerly regions of the world. Democracy and communism themselves today appear as the major alternatives of modern government, and whereas democracy revealed its nationalist affinities in the days of Jefferson and Robespierre, communism came to terms with nationality in the days of Lenin and Stalin. Today in local wars in Asia or Africa, Americans can support their allies in the name of national independence and the communists theirs in the name of national liberation.

Nonetheless, the foreign relations among democrats and communists, and between their blocs, sharply reveal the latent tension between modernity and nationhood. In Europe, economic and technical progress is bursting through the narrow boundaries drawn by monarchs and nationalists in the eighteenth and nineteenth century; hence democratic Europeans have been thrown into a protracted crisis of supranational unification. Among the communist states, the nationalist passions released by the Sino-Soviet dispute have undermined Marxist claims to universality and infallibility. Where once nationhood was the proud achievement of a few peoples isolated from the rest of humanity, it now has become the vocal aspiration of 130 peoples all linked tightly through modern means of communication and transport. Where once the nation-state was the symbol of sovereign power and unfettered independence, today it means interdependence and common peril. Sometime in the nineteenth century in Europe, modernization was wedded to the nation-state, and in Asia and Africa that alliance is being consummated anew in the present day; but unless the marriage contract is renegotiated or dissolved in voluntary separation, it may well turn into a suicide pact.

The Changes of Modernity

Modernization is a term that has gained currency among American social scientists and historians to designate the grand transformation of society and culture that began in Europe toward the fifteenth century and that by now has engulfed the rest of mankind. Its currency, however, is still not universal even among scholars, and its meaning is not always made precise by those who accept the word. Modernization as here understood denotes rapidly widening control over nature through closer cooperation among men. It transforms both man and society, but most of all man's mind.

The modern man seeks empirical, not magical knowledge. Truth to him is not the unchangeable content of a final revelation; it is the latest in a never-ending series of approximations. His curiosity makes him thirst after variety and go in quest of the exotic. But he seeks change not merely for change's sake. One of his most cherished assumptions is that the new is likely to be better than the old; that man, through purposeful action, can improve his lot on this earth. Modernization, therefore, is antithetical to any concept of human history as moving in cycles from perfection to decay and regeneration, or as a predicament which man escapes only in the hereafter. It is human history conceived as a history of progress.

Modernization implies an intellectual, a technological, and a social revolution. It transforms three of man's most fundamental relations: to time, to nature, and to his fellowman. Time to modern man is not repetitive or cyclical, but a process—a pattern at once of coherence and change. He enjoys reading novels which unfold the continuing interaction of personality and circumstance, rather than ballads or epics which array a loosely joined sequence of episodes. Keenly conscious that human history does not repeat itself, modern man laments that he has not "world enough and time." As geographic contact among modern men increases, regional differences are obliterated, and the prevalent social and intellectual styles change more rapidly. Standardized fashions of dress, for example, tend to displace the wide variety of traditional local costumes. Only the livelier pace of change relieves the drab uniformity from place to place.

In the vagaries of fashion, few would see more than a temporary illusion of improvement. It is in the realms of scientific discovery and of technical innovation that the possibility of progress, of cumulative rationality, is most readily apparent. Modern man assumes that the natural universe constitutes a single pattern, orderly and comprehensible. His scientific research is designed to explore that universal order, his technology to shape it to his human ends. The results of science and technology have borne out that initial assumption and have led researchers to cling to it steadfastly in the face of any temporary setbacks.

Scientific and technical progress is closely linked to the third aspect of the modern revolution, the changed relationship of man to man. The link holds in both directions. The effect of science and technology is to change the lives of human beings in society as well as the natural environment. "Engineering is the application of rationality and authority to material things; modern social organization is its application to human beings and social groups."[2] The precondition of science and technology is specialization within a social division of labor. The growing understanding and control of the environment are not attained by individuals in isolation. Robinson Crusoe, alone on his island, controls pre-

[2] Gabriel A. Almond and Sidney Verba, *The Civic Culture* (Princeton University Press, 1963), p. 4.

ciously few of the forces of nature. Rather, collective control is wielded by social man as he becomes part of an ever more complex and powerful web of social organization.

Modernization, as here defined, is a comprehensive term, and it is ethically neutral. Although it is clear as a concept, the historical phenomena corresponding to it shade off at the edges. It may be considered uniform or diverse, depending on the observer's viewpoint. And it has important political implications. Each of these considerations may be spelled out in more detail.

MODERNIZATION AND THE SOCIAL SCIENCES

The revolution of modernization comprises many specific changes, and the tendency of most scholars has been to concentrate on the aspects of immediate interest to them. Historians have described successive phases of the over-all process, such as the Renaissance, the Reformation, the Age of Enlightenment, and the Revolutionary Era. Changes from subsistence agriculture and barter to monetary exchange, to the accumulation of capital, and to industrial production have concerned the economist. Legal scholars have noted that contract has replaced status as the principle of social obligation. Historians of ideas have recorded the development of sacred into secular thinking and of speculative metaphysics into empirical science. The transition from ascription to achievement as the basis of social status and from the "extended" to the "nuclear" family have attracted the attention of sociologists and social anthropologists. Political scientists have examined the expansion of bureaucracies, the intrusion of the masses on the political stage, and the replacement of empires by nation-states.

In the real world outside the scholar's study, all these changes are of course closely connected and tend to reinforce each other. It is possible to select any particular aspect of modernization and to subordinate all others to this one aspect as causes or effects or concomitants. Theologians, for example, may find the key to all other changes of the modern age in man's loss of revealed faith and the disintegration of a universal church. A generation after Freud, some theorists have concentrated on psychological changes, such as the heightened desire for achievement or the capacity for wider empathy.[3] Similarly, Karl Marx, who conceived the first grand theory of modernization without using that term, chose certain economic aspects—the material means of production and their ownership—as the central ones. Many other thinkers who reject the Marxist political creed, including figures as diverse as Charles A. Beard and Walt W. Rostow, have proposed their own variants of an economic interpretation of modern history. More recently, Karl W. Deutsch has advanced an explanation of modernization based on changing patterns of communication.[4]

Modernization, then, includes all the more specific changes such as industrialization, rationalization, secularization, and bureaucratization. The more comprehensive term has the advantage that it does not assign priority to any specific aspect, that it does not commit the student at the outset of his inquiry to a narrow view of causation in human affairs. Unlike the other terms that pick out single threads, modernization draws attention to change throughout the social tapestry.

The present inquiry will also concentrate on a single strand, namely the political, but it will relate politics to the broader context of modernization. This political focus may surprise readers who have come to think of economic development—the growth of industry, the improvement of agriculture, the raising of per capita incomes—as the only "real" problem in Asia, Africa, and Latin America today. Yet it well accords with the recent work of economists who have become increasingly conscious of the noneconom-

[3] David McClelland, The Achieving Society (Van Nostrand, 1961); Daniel Lerner et al., The Passing of Traditional Society (Free Press, 1958).

[4] Beard, An Economic Interpretation of the Constitution (Macmillan, 1913); Rostow, The Stages of Economic Growth (Cambridge, England: University Press, 1960); Deutsch, Nationalism and Social Communication (Wiley, 1953), and "Social Mobilization and Political Development," American Political Science Review, Vol. 55 (September 1961), pp. 493-514.

ic factors that condition economic development, including education, social structure, and political institutions.

The leaders of the newly independent and economically underdeveloped countries may be invoked to the same effect. They leave little doubt about their priorities. "We for our part," Touré of Guinea insists, "have a single and indispensable need, that of our dignity. There can be no dignity without freedom. Therefore, we prefer poverty in freedom to riches in slavery." Nasser of Egypt, speaks of self-government, of justice, and of national unity. Nkrumah in even more sweeping language exhorted his followers: "Seek ye first the political kingdom and all things else shall be added unto you."[5]

A political scientist, it is true, has recently affirmed that the aspirations of the "developing countries" are more economic than political, that they "seem to want economic development more than freedom" in the form of democratic institutions.[6] But he overlooked that national independence, power for individual leaders or parties at home, and prestige for the nation abroad are intensely political goals. Nor does this preoccupation with politics subside when independence is achieved. Such recent events as the Iranian oil crisis of 1951-53 and the nationalization of the Suez Canal in 1956 show that even independent countries will suffer short-run economic losses for the sake of long-run political gains. The communists, too, for all their professions of economic determinism, have been acutely aware of the political nature of their struggle.

But no apology is needed for the theme of this book beyond the most obvious one. Whatever the comparative importance of the economic, intellectual, or psychological dimensions of mod-

[5] Sékou Touré, *Expérience guinéene et unité africaine* (Paris: n.d.), p. 6; Kwame Nkrumah, *Ghana* (Nelson, 1957), pp. 162ff. Cf. Kenneth W. Grundy, "Nkrumah's Theory of Underdevelopment," *World Politics*, Vol. 15 (April 1963), pp. 438-54, esp. pp. 439ff., "Pre-Eminence of Politics." Cf. Gamal Abdul Nasser, *Egypt's Liberation: The Philosophy of the Revolution* (Public Affairs Press, 1955); the motto from Nasser at the beginning of this chapter appears on p. 41.

[6] Joseph LaPalombara, ed., *Bureaucracy and Political Development* (Princeton University Press, 1963), p. 41.

ernization, the political one is significant enough to merit systematic study; and the author is a political scientist.

MODERNIZATION, DEVELOPMENT, AND PROGRESS

Modernization is preferable not only to narrower terms such as industrialization, rationalization, or secularization, but also to the vague and currently fashionable term "development." Development may mean any sort of gradual change: the barbarian invasions of Rome, the growing alienation of modern city life, and the erosion of top-soils in the Middle East each had their phases of development. Development can also mean desirable change, as when United Nations officials proclaim a "decade of development," or when writers in the United States equate political development with growth of democracy.

But modernization is less than change as such, and it includes changes that may or may not be desirable by plausible standards of evaluation. It is an open question that will be taken up in a later chapter whether the late modernizing countries will develop toward democracy, or totalitarianism, or in other directions. A recent author, moreover, has suggested that modernization may lead to political decay as well as political development—development in his definition being institutionalization, that is, the growth of political organization.[7] In any case, the task of understanding the process of change in the modern world is distinct from that of evaluating it, the role of the participant from that of the observer. Society as a whole cannot engage in modernization without accepting its ingredients as beneficial or its totality as inevitable, but the student of modernization need not concur in either of these judgments. Modernization as an analytical concept has the advantage of being ethically neutral.

The modern attitude, it was suggested earlier, assumes that man can improve his lot through systematic application of

[7] Samuel P. Huntington, "Political Development and Political Decay," *World Politics*, Vol. 17 (April 1965), pp. 386-430.

science, technology, and social organization. This vision of history as human progress proved especially alluring in the early stages of European modernization, attaining its brightest glow in the eighteenth and nineteenth centuries. Voltaire spoke as a proud modernizer when he extolled "le bon temps que ce siècle de fer" —"this good Iron Age"—and in the following verses proceeded to ridicule both the Greek myth of the Golden Age and the biblical myth of the Garden of Eden.[8]

As the age of iron and steel has evolved into the age of space missiles and nuclear bombs, the confident optimism of Voltaire's generation has become tinged with considerable apprehension among its descendants. Even before atomic weapons conjured up the nightmare of wholesale destruction of human culture, critics of modern life were conscious of many of the shortcomings of industrial civilization and of mass society. Modernization, together with unprecedented benefits, brings inevitable hazards and deprivations. Every day we pay for the comforts of technology with sacrifices of privacy, of intimacy, and of leisure. And every few decades humanity as a whole has paid for its technical advances in holocausts of ever more barbarous slaughter. A mid-twentieth-century observer, therefore, can hardly avoid the conclusion that the effects of modernization are morally ambiguous. As modern man interacts more intensely with his fellows, he may interact with them for greater material comfort, for wider spiritual exchange, for more insidious exploitation, and for more savage physical destruction.

Like any other historical concept, modernization must reconcile the precision of abstract logic with the fluidity of human and social phenomena. Modernity has been defined here as a phenomenon of potential universality, a cluster of attitudes that might be developed or adopted in any society. In fact, of course, these patterns first developed in one particular time and place; yet in a

[8] Voltaire, "Le mondain" (1756) as quoted by J. B. Bury, *The Idea of Progress* (Macmillan, 1932), p. 151. This paragraph and the next borrow from R. E. Ward and D. A. Rustow, eds., *Political Modernization in Japan and Turkey* (Princeton University Press, 1964), pp. 3ff.

study concerned mostly with present-day non-Western countries, one need not inquire why modernization began five or six centuries ago and why on the shores of the Mediterranean and the Atlantic. It would be best, at any rate, to think of modern European and Western civilization since the Renaissance as combining two sets of elements. The first comprises those traits that are essential to modernization, and the second comprises all other aspects of the Western heritage with its Greek, Hellenistic, Roman, Judaeo-Christian, and medieval contributions. It is easier, however, to draw such a distinction in the abstract than to apply it to the world of historical phenomena.

Once modernity spreads beyond its initial locale, the cultural mixture in the settings of secondary modernization may be thought of as including not just two sets of elements but three. First, there will be modern cultural traits developed or adopted as a result of the modernizing impact; these will spread by virtue of their rationality and instrumental efficiency. Second, there will be traditional or parochial traits retained by the original modernizers and taken over by others on the strength of the prestige of those pioneers. Third, there will be traditional elements of the indigenous culture surviving even after the modern impact. Some of these may even be reasserted more strongly as psychological counterweights to imported modernity. The discussion in Chapter Two of the historical consciousness of nationalism and of the timing of political modernization will furnish numerous illustrations in this last category.

Among the cultural traits that are essential to modernity and potentially universal are the desire for higher material standards and habits of punctuality and precision. These may be contrasted with those traditional features that inhibit the growth of modernity or that are compatible with it without being essential. It is best to think not of a clear-cut distinction, but rather of a continuous scale from the most essential to the indifferent and to the most antithetic. Even in this graduated form, the distinction is more easily formulated than applied. For example, it is one of the more controversial questions of contemporary political theory, and one that will be touched on later, where along such a spectrum a multiparty system and competitive elections are to be placed.

It might be thought that among the indifferent features (those that are neither essential to modernity nor antithetical to it), a rich tradition of variety would survive into the modern age. But even here there is a tendency toward global uniformity as modern man's love of the new and the exotic leads him to adopt tastes and habits from all parts of the world. Coffee from Arabia, tobacco from America, porcelain from China, and syncopated rhythms from Tropical Africa have become ingredients in Western civilization, as much as the combustion engine, electricity, and aspirin have become parts of modern civilization outside of Europe. Modern society is equally adept at disseminating and at absorbing cultural influences. Together these two qualities have transformed what once was a European or Western culture into a world civilization.

Although modernization, then, has often been tantamount to Westernization, the former term is more widely applicable. One can speak of the Westernization of the Ottoman Empire and of Egypt since the late eighteenth century. But it would be incongruous to speak of the Westernization of Europe itself in the fifteenth to nineteenth centuries, or to label as Westernization the Japanese influences on Korea or current cultural changes in Latin America. The term modernization also leaves room for the hypothesis advanced by recent historians that Tokugawa Japan (1603-1868), even prior to any Western impact, displayed many of the characteristics of modernity, including popular education, an empirical outlook, and a vigorous business class.

TRADITION A RESIDUAL CONCEPT

One further point in the foregoing discussion should be made explicit. Modernity, though a broad concept, can be positively defined. Not so its opposite, tradition. Modernizing societies all resemble each other in that an influential and growing proportion of their members embrace the characteristically modern attitudes toward time, toward the physical environment, and toward other men in society. Beyond this, the propulsive and expansive force of modernization ensures a broad uniformity not only in essentials but even in accidentals.

Traditional societies, by contrast, offer no obvious similarities. The tribes of camel herders in the Arabian desert; the villages of Tropical Africa; and the imperial civilizations once governed by the Manchus in China and the Ottomans in Turkey—all become similar only as they are confronted in fact or contrasted in concept with modern civilization. Traditional societies are non-modern societies. Beyond this, traditional cultures all tend to react in a number of similar ways to the uniform impact of modernity. But when this impact occurs, the modern transformation already is under way. The similarity of response is part of an early, reactive phase of modernization. Whereas modernity can be affirmatively defined, tradition remains largely a residual concept.

It is often assumed that traditional societies are all alike in that they are inherently static; but this assumption needs to be cautiously stated. Modernization is always highly dynamic. It does not follow that tradition is sluggish or inert, that modern Western civilization is the only dynamic force injected into a scene of immutable tradition. Pre-modern history is replete with accounts of the rise and fall—at times gradual, at times rapid—of empires and civilizations; and this traditional dynamism also continues into the era of modernization. The conventional view of Chinese history is one of cycles of barbarian invasion, absorption of the invaders into a reinvigorated stream of civilization, gradual decay, and renewed invasion. The Arab expansion in the seventh and eighth centuries A.D. and that of the Ottomans some seven hundred years later proceeded more rapidly and produced more lasting cultural consequences—proved more dynamic, that is—than most comparable historic episodes. The Bantu migrations to southern Africa and the spread of Islam to West Africa and Indonesia occurred or continued long after the first arrival of Europeans in those regions, and in independent interaction with it. In short, it is only ignorance of other histories and a certain ethnocentric pride that make us disregard the cultural diversity and the social dynamism of non-Western traditions.

Nor should the contrast between modernity and tradition be overdrawn. Control over nature and social division of labor are accomplishments common to all human societies. It may well be argued that such prehistoric discoveries as the planting of cereals, the domestication of animals, the making of fire, the use of the wheel, and the art of navigation were more decisive steps in man's conquest of nature than any innovations since the Renaissance.[9] Nonetheless, it may be argued (and use of the term modernization must be justified by some such argument) that at a certain stage the increase of human control over nature became so rapid as to produce a qualitative and not just a quantitative change, that the transformation became henceforth self-sustaining and self-propelling.

It is probably true, moreover, that even the most dynamic traditional societies were dynamic in only a few respects. The cycles of Chinese history were mere oscillations around a constant mean. The Muslim Arabs were the dynamic protagonists of a revelation held to be final and unchanging. Most traditional empires aimed at stability, and most traditional religions were based on some intuition of eternal truth. Modern societies, by contrast, expect to change; and modern changes in science and technology, in social organization, and in the art of government all support and propel one another. The modern age, above all, is the first in which all parts of humanity have made contact with each other, in which the self-sustaining revolution has therefore become world-wide.

[9] For a succinct historical account emphasizing the interplay of technology and social organization from the rise of civilization in Mesopotamia to the present, see William H. McNeill, *The Rise of the West: A History of the Human Community* (University of Chicago Press, 1965).

This world-wide spread was brought about by some of the dynamic forces inherent in modernization—forces that would have had a similar dispersive effect wherever and whenever they first appeared. An outward, searching cast of mind and new means of transport were sure to bring the earliest modernizers into contact with peoples in more remote regions of the globe. Greater control over nature and habits of closer social cooperation would enable them to overwhelm one by one any non-modern societies or to force them into emulating modern ways as the price of their continued independence. If modernization occurred first in a world region divided into separate political entities, such as post-Renaissance Europe, competition among these might be expected to accelerate the outward spread.

But there is not only propulsion but also receptivity. In Europe since the Renaissance and in other continents more recently, there have been many critics and opponents of modernization. Yet aside from some of the utopian communities of the nineteenth century, few of the European critics made any concerted attempt to return to the social customs or methods of production of a bygone age. Lately, moreover, there have been no remote open spaces left for such dissenters to settle undisturbed. The strictures of many other critics have been incorporated into the mainstream of modernity, and thus enhanced its force. The aristocratic critics of nineteenth century Europe did much to shape representative institutions in an age of egalitarianism; and the socialists, who protested against the gross iniquities of early industrialization, promoted the later development of the industrial welfare state.

In the non-Western countries, there has been a recurrent tendency to reassert traditional values in the face of the modern impact; and more recently one suspects that proclamations by some of the Asian and African leaders about economic development and social reform are tinged with some hypocrisy. Yet the only successful strategy of resistance to the modern impact has been defensive modernization—that is, an adoption of the very tech-

niques of modernity that threaten traditional values. As for hypocritical endorsements of modernization, they are perhaps the
most eloquent testimony to its widespread appeal.

The evidence, then, suggests that an overwhelming majority of
men have reacted similarly to the challenge of modernization,
whether in the Europe of the Renaissance and the Industrial Revolution or in Asia and Africa in the ages of colonialism and
postcolonial independence. Whether in peace or in war, they
have preferred the products of machines to those of human or animal labor; they have insisted on the benefits of mass organization; and they have succumbed to the lure of mass entertainment.
It is the cumulative effect of such preferences that has given
modernization its irresistible force. What may appear as the inevitability of modernity is merely human choice writ large. John
Plamenatz has stated the relationship succinctly:

> Progress is not inevitable in the sense that it will go on forever
> without leading to catastrophe, or in the sense that men are bound
> to be happier or wiser or better on account of it, or in the sense that
> it would happen whatever men did; but it probably is inevitable in
> the sense that those who are against it cannot now stop it because
> of its very nature it adds to the power of those who are for it.[10]

GRADUALISM, UNIFORMITY, AND VARIETY

Ubiquitous as is modernization, its beginnings cannot usually be
established with precision. Such dramatic events as the French
and Russian Revolutions or the Meiji Restoration in Japan make
it convenient to date a new era from 1789, 1917, or 1868.
Significantly, all these were upheavals in the political sphere; yet
even political control does not as a rule pass suddenly and irrevo-
cably from unregenerate defenders of tradition to out-and-out
modernizers. Did the political modernization of Germany begin
with Luther's alliance with the territorial princes, with the Peace
of Westphalia in 1648, with the Prussian reforms of 1807, with

---

[10] Plamenatz, *On Alien Rule and Self-Government* (London: Longmans, 1960),
p. 169.

the abortive revolution of 1848, with the unification of 1871—or even in 1918, 1933, or 1945? Or that of Russia with Peter the Great, with the emancipation of the serfs, or with the Bolsheviks? The gradualism that pervades politics is even more obvious in other spheres of culture. The scientific discoveries since the Renaissance, the new methods of production of the Industrial Revolution, the Westernization of the Ottoman Empire represent so many series of accretions.

Modernization typically proceeds by degrees and stages and allows for wide margins of coexistence between traditional and modern cultural features. Peasant families survive within an industrial society. Ancient religious beliefs retain their power in an era of secular, scientific education. Age-old artistic themes remain valid in an age of mass entertainment. In politics, traditional symbols are used even, or perhaps especially, in the most modern societies—witness the American cults of Plymouth Rock and Williamsburg, the restorations of the Japanese Emperor in 1868 and 1945, and the annual award of honors at Buckingham Palace.

Modernization is by definition a continuing process, so that no society can claim to be completely or definitively modern. Like the modern conception of truth, modernization itself is a series of approximations. Within this overall process, it would seem that science, technology, and economic production leave indefinite room for cumulative rationality. But in society and politics, in art and religion, modernity remains at every stage linked to tradition. The most durable links are forged by man's biological endowment, by his need for pomp and ceremony, and by his search for meaning in a transitory existence.

If the beginnings of modernization cannot be dated precisely, there is even less profit in sweeping statements about its outcome. Marx and Engels, in their theory of modernization, looked forward to a fixed if vague goal of social change. In a world-wide proletarian revolution, history as mankind had known it (or rather as Marx and Engels had analyzed it) would come to an end. There would be a "leap from the realm of necessity into the realm of freedom."[11] But with this turn in the argument, the Marxian scheme made a leap of its own—a leap from the realm of scientific analysis into the realm of chiliastic prophecy. In his highly original way, and despite his scathing critique of contemporary society, Marx, too, shared the boundless optimism of the nineteenth century.

According to a more current prophecy of doom, technology will destroy society, and civilized man will have modernized himself out of existence. If this prediction should prove true, any scattered survivors of the holocaust are likely to look back on "modernization" as a temporary and disastrous episode in man's history: the continuity and desirability of modernization will have turned out to be a macabre illusion.

While modernization continues, is it a uniform process in all societies or does it vary in each setting? Does it follow an inevitable sequence of "stages of growth" or does it offer choices of alternative directions? These are not strictly empirical questions. In the eyes of his beloved, any man is unique and incomparable; in the eyes of an omnipotent god, all men are alike. Comparability, that is to say, is an attribute dependent more on the observer's perspective than on the nature of the phenomena. Much the same holds for inevitability and choice. The astronomer tracing the orbit of a star, the biologist raising a culture of bacteria, the chemist testing the composition of a molecule—indeed any outside observer—may meaningfully search for laws of inevitability. But the social scientist is an observer from inside society, and within those confines his task becomes more modest and more difficult. In presuming to predict mankind's inevitable bliss or doom, he is forsaking his vocation. The social scientist's proper function is to ascertain the margin of choice offered by man's social condition and to clarify the choices in that margin.[12]

[11] Friedrich Engels, *Anti-Dühring* (1877-78, 3rd ed., 1894), Pt. 3, Chap. 2. Also in his *Socialism: Utopian and Scientific* (1880).

[12] For a study of modernization that consistently emphasizes this element of choice, see David E. Apter, *The Politics of Modernization* (University of California Press, 1965).

The inside viewpoint has, of course, its compensations. The present condition of society reflects past human circumstances and past human choices; hence the human observer has a chance of understanding them more directly than he can the natural environment. "Whoever reflects on it," remarked Vico, the eighteenth century proponent of a *New Science*, "cannot but marvel that the philosophers should have bent all their energies to the study of the world of nature, which, since God made it, He alone knows; and that they should have neglected the study of the world of nations, or civil world, which, since men had made it, men could come to know."[13]

The definition of modernization given earlier, like all definitions, has singled out the uniformities of the phenomenon. Any societies which by some such criteria are modernizing resemble each other, at least to that extent. In later chapters, the viewpoint will shift. No longer concerned with the common features that distinguish all modernizing from all traditional societies, the inquiry will turn to the differential features that distinguish some modernizing societies from others. The analysis will avoid the myopic extreme of regarding every society and every historical situation as unique. Rather, it will dwell, at an intermediate level of generality, on the differences between early and late modernizers, between conservative and radical proponents of modernity, and among various political regimes in modernizing societies.

MODERNIZATION AND POLITICS

It remains, in this introductory chapter, to identify some of the specifically political aspects of the modern revolution. The chang-

---

[13] Giambattista Vico, *Scienza Nuova*, 3d ed. (Naples, 1744), para. 331; translated by Thomas Goodard Bergin and Max Harold Frisch as *The New Science of Giambattista Vico* (Doubleday, 1961), p. 53. "This aberration," Vico goes on to explain, "was a consequence of that infirmity of the human mind by which, immersed and buried in the body, it naturally inclines to take notice of bodily things, and finds the effort to attend to itself too laborious; just as the bodily eye sees all the objects outside itself but needs a mirror to see itself."

ing time perspective of modernization broadens and sharpens the political aspirations for the future. It is also reflected in a reinterpretation, now more conscious and now less, of the political history of the past. The differential attainments by various societies in control over nature, in intensity of communication, and in social cohesion are readily converted into power and thus become a decisive factor in their external relations. Foreign wars, in turn, have always been one of the chief forces for the further expansion of domestic functions of government and for the elaboration of political institutions.

The change most significant for politics is, of course, man's growing dependence on other men. Modern man has an unprecedented need and an unprecedented capacity for organization, and tighter organization invariably entails a widening of the scope of political power. The last two centuries provide significant landmarks of this increase, such as the spread of conscription on the European continent after Carnot's *levée en masse* of 1793; the adoption of universal public education in the early nineteenth century; the shift in public revenue from customs and excises to income taxes, first level and then steeply graduated; the development of governmental welfare services and of central economic planning in this century; and the enormously expanded use of the means of public information and propaganda. If freedom is taken to mean the absence of governmental regulation, then the course of modern politics clearly belies Tennyson's view of English history (still enshrined in many high school textbooks) as one "Where freedom slowly broadens down"/"From precedent to precedent."[14]

This vast organizational power in modern society may be concentrated in the sole hands of the government or it may be shared by autonomous institutions such as private corporations, trade unions, and other associations. In the government itself, it may be wielded by a narrow self-perpetuating circle of men, or it may be dispersed among central and regional authorities, parliaments, cabinets, independent agencies, government corporations, an au-

[14] Alfred Lord Tennyson, "You ask me why, though ill at ease . . . ," lines 11-12.

tonomous judiciary, and the like; and the exercise of power may
further be checked by periodic appeals of competing parties to a
mass electorate. These alternatives, indeed, measure the vast distance between modern democracy and modern totalitarianism.
Yet under either form, modern government wields a formidable
power over the lives and fortunes of its citizens—a power far beyond the reach of most traditional despots. In traditional society,
the inadequacy of transport and communication and the small
scale of social and economic organization provide more inexorable guarantees against governmental control than do any modern
laws or constitutions. In the nation-state, which has widely come
to be accepted as the normal form of modern government, close
interaction based on a common loyalty multiplies the total
amount of power at society's disposal.

The Ideal of Nationality

A century ago, John Stuart Mill offered the following classic
definition. "A portion of mankind may be said to constitute a Nationality, if they are united among themselves by common sympathies, which do not exist between them and any others—which
make them co-operate with each other more willingly than with
other people, desire to be under the same government, and desire
that it should be government by themselves or a portion of themselves, exclusively."[15]

Two decades later, Ernest Renan celebrated the sentiments of
nationhood in the following famous passage: ". . . A nation is a
great solidarity brought about by the feeling of the sacrifices that
one has made and that one is prepared still to make. It supposes a
past, but it is contained in the present in a tangible fact: the common feeling, the clearly expressed desire to continue life in common. A nation (if you will allow the metaphor) exists by virtue of

[15] John Stuart Mill, *Considerations on Representative Government* (1861),
Chap. 16.

a daily plebiscite—*l'existence d'une nation est un plébiscite de tous les jours.*"[16]

What Mill called a "Nationality" later usage would tend to term a nation; otherwise his definition well accords with the views of Renan and of contemporary Asian and African leaders. To put it even more succinctly, a nation is a self-contained group of human beings who place loyalty to the group as a whole above competing loyalties. A nation-state, of course, is an independent state whose membership coincides with that of a nation. And nationalism is the desire to create, maintain, or strengthen such a nation-state.

Although "nationality" in Mill's day was a new word, the word "nation" had had a long history, and for two generations had become a chief weapon of political polemics. Ever since the French in the 1790's proclaimed themselves *"la grande nation,"* opposing factions have celebrated the national principle as one of the greatest boons to mankind or condemned it as one of the greatest evils. The idealists of 1919, for example, blamed wars on the suppression of nationality and tried to secure peace by redrawing the European map on national principles. The idealists of 1945, by contrast, blamed wars on unfettered nationalism and yearned for a world government that would tame the bellicose nations.

THE COMPLEXITY OF THE CONCEPT

Some confusion arises from the widespread legal or euphemistic use of the word "nation" as a synonym for "independent State" and from the pejorative use of the term "nationalism." It would seem that to Western journalists "nationalism" is almost any strident or truculent political activity in "backward" countries—or, as

[16] Ernest Renan, *Qu'est-ce qu'une nation?* (Paris: Calman-Lévy, 1882), p. 27, my translation. For slightly different translations see Renan, "What Is A Nation?" in Alfred Zimmern, ed., *Modern Political Doctrines* (London: Oxford University Press, 1939), pp. 186-205, which gives the whole essay, and in Louis L. Snyder, ed., *The Dynamics of Nationalism* (Van Nostrand, 1964), pp. 9-10, which gives excerpts.

in the case of "Black Nationalism" in the Negro slums of New
York City, in "backward" parts of their own. Nationalism thereby
always turns out to be something that the other fellow does, and
something quite reprehensible at that. Yet in serious usage, it
should be clear that nationalism is a term applicable to white
Americans, to Frenchmen, and to Russians, as much as to Bolivi-
ans, Sinhalese, or Nigerians.

The classical writings of the nationalists themselves have done
little to clarify the basic concepts. As Elie Kedourie has noted,
the philosophic content of this literature has been surprisingly
meager.[17] From Fichte and Mazzini to Nasser and Nkrumah, it
has generated more emotional heat than intellectual light. One
obvious reason is that the talk about the nation has been loudest
where the sense of nationality has remained weakest—among
nineteenth century Germans and Italians and among twentieth
century Arabs, Asians, and Africans, rather than among English-
men, Frenchmen, or Japanese.[18]

Until the appearance some years ago of the works of Karl W.
Deutsch (of which more will be said in the next chapter), scholars
often added to the confusion: few of them, at any rate, improved
on Mill's definition or Renan's characterization of a nation. One
writer, for example, confesses in a spirit of weary resignation that
"A century of study of . . . nationalism has produced no precise
and acceptable definition" and modestly entitles his chapter "Toward a Definition of Nationalism."[19] Another, after a lifetime of
investigation of the subject, concludes in some bewilderment that
"Nationalities are groups . . . of the utmost complexity. They defy
exact definition."[20]

One major source of bewilderment has been the dubious dis-

---

[17] Elie Kedourie, *Nationalism*, rev. ed. (Praeger, 1960), p. 9 and *passim*.

[18] Although Renan's essay "What Is A Nation?" is unusual for its clarity and
perception, it is no exception; for his address was delivered under the impact of
the loss of Alsace-Lorraine—of the failure, that is, of a major French national aspiration. See the veiled allusion in Renan's final paragraph and cf. Boyd C. Shafer,
Nationalism: Myth and Reality (Harcourt, 1955), p. 243, note 12.

[19] *Ibid.*, p. 3. Italics added.

[20] Hans Kohn, *The Idea of Nationalism* (Macmillan, 1948), p. 13.

tinction between so-called "objective characteristics" of nation-hood—such as geography, political history, and economic structure—and so-called "subjective characteristics"—such as consciousness, loyalty, or will. The distinction carries echoes both from German metaphysics and from Marxist sociology, and the resulting confusion is deepened when these "objective" and "subjective" factors, singly or together, are introduced into the definition of terms. To give one example, a leading American political scientist has proposed that "the nation may be defined . . . objectively" as a community "which manifests cultural uniformity, spiritual union, institutional unity, and material unification to the highest possible degree and subjectively as one with which the members consciously identify themselves."[21] The so-called "subjective" formulations generally are genuine attempts at definition, although they often suffer from vagueness. The "objective" definitions in truth are not definitions at all but are attempts, usually less than adequate, at explanatory hypotheses; for a definition must aim at simplicity, whereas an explanation must account for the complexities of the real world.

The spurious distinction between subjective and objective factors, that is to say, obscures a valid one between definition and explanation, between the analytic characteristics of nationhood and its empirical causes. There is no point in asking "What makes a people into a nation?" unless one has an answer to the prior question "By what signs do we recognize a nation when we see it?" One can only hope to explain a phenomenon if one knows which phenomenon is to be explained. Common language, common history, prolonged self-government—these and other conditions are likely to promote feelings of nationality, but they are not among the defining characteristics of a nation. The Swiss are a nation although they speak three or four different languages; Is-

---

[21] Quincy Wright, A Study of War (University of Chicago Press, 1942), Vol. 2, p. 992. Often, however, authors who use the objective-subjective dichotomy do not make it clear whether they are defining or describing. For example: "Although some of these objective factors are of great importance for the formation of nationalities, the most essential element is a living and active corporate will. Nationality is formed by the decision to form a nationality." Kohn, op. cit., p. 15.

rael is a nation even though Jewish communities had very different histories in two thousand years of diaspora; and Poland remained a nation through a century and a half of partition.

Even Renan leaves some ambiguity with his allusion to sacrifices of the past, although his emphasis clearly is on the willingness to make sacrifices in the present and the future. "A nation," he said choosing his words, "supposes a past, but it is summed up in the present in the . . . desire to continue life in common." The search for empirical antecedents points to the past; the definition of nationhood must rest on a stable present intention with regard to the future.

Giuseppe Mazzini, life-long conspirator and most exuberant of the nationalist writers, rejoiced that "Nationalities are sacred and providentially constituted. . . ."[22] Renan, historian of religion and no less a nationalist, took the soberer view that nations are as transient as any other works of man. "The desire of nations to be together," he said, "is the only real criterion that must always be taken into account. . . . Human desires change; but what does not change on this earth? Nations are not something eternal. They have begun, they will end." Speaking at a time when nationalism had spread as yet little beyond Europe, he added: "They will be replaced, in all probability, by a European confederation. But such is not the law of the century in which we live."[23]

THE FLUIDITY OF ALLEGIANCE

Here a genuine difficulty comes to the fore, and one that "nation" shares with "modernization" and other historical concepts—that of reconciling logical clarity with the variety and change of social phenomena. If a nation is conceived of as a group of people bound together by common loyalty, it follows that nationhood, like loyalty itself, is a matter of degree. A given people at a given time may be more or less of a nation; and none fully approxi-

[22] Quoted in Crane Brinton, *Ideas and Men* (Prentice-Hall, 1950), p. 420.
[23] Renan, in Snyder, ed., *op. cit.*, p. 10.

mates the ideal type. Nation-states are also a matter of degree in the further sense that a state's boundaries may not coincide with the limits of national consciousness—may include ethnic minorities that do not feel the same national allegiance and exclude national groups beyond the borders (or irredentas) that do.

Taking both variables into account, it is fairly easy to agree, by a series of intuitive judgments, that Malaysia today is less of a nation-state than Algeria, Algeria less than Turkey, Turkey less than Belgium, and Belgium less than Sweden; but circumstances might arise that would reverse some of these rankings. Any such assessment implies a series of predictions that under certain conditions, loyalty will prevail, under others, break down; hence many different measures might be devised, their accuracy in each case depending on foresight. Still, once nationality is acknowledged to be a matter of degree, there is little profit in drawing a line somewhere across the sliding scale and insisting that all peoples above that line are nations and below that line are not.

Naturally, the intellectual and political leaders of new nations tend to rank their peoples higher along the scale of more perfect nationhood than they may in fact belong. Often, indeed, these leaders assume the solid existence of a nation that is still to be created. Many nations thus had their origin in the vision of thinkers and statesmen rather than in any historical tradition of loyalty. Before Jinnah and the Muslim League at Lahore in 1940 called for the formation of a "Pakistan," even the name of the future nation was scarcely known. When Mustafa Kemal, the future Atatürk ("Father of the Turks") was born in 1881, his Turkish-speaking countrymen thought of themselves as Ottomans rather than Turks. And Fichte, in his *Speeches to the German Nation*, was addressing a hypothetical community that his oratory helped call into life.

The temptation is to project future hopes into the present and the past, to persuade oneself that one is discovering what in fact one is trying to create. Nationalism, defined as the desire to form or maintain a nation-state, thus has often preceded the emergence of a nation—or rather its ascent on the scale of nationhood. Yet the early nationalist in complete sincerity will see his program as one of the effects rather than one of the causes of the existence of a nation. In this, he resembles the reformers of revealed religions, such as Christianity and Islam, who do not commonly proclaim deliberate innovations but see themselves as recapturing lost meanings from the sacred scriptures of the past.

National loyalty, like any other loyalty, may newly form, may change its point of attachment, or may dissipate; and several loyalties may be in conflict at any given time. In Mazzini's Italy and in Germany, loyalty to the present nation began to supersede other loyalties in the nineteenth century. Some decades after Fichte's addresses, his fellow-nationalists Hegel and Ranke saw not in Germany but in the Prussian state the highest embodiment of the national spirit.[24] In the present day, as Renan foresaw, common European loyalties are beginning to compete with French, German, Italian, and other national allegiances of the past, and to that extent the European countries are beginning to lose their characteristics of nationhood. Perhaps some day in the future, the historic nations of Europe will become fully submerged in a more inclusive sense of loyalty, and then we (or rather our descendants) will be able to speak of a European nation.[25]

The fluidity of allegiances is illustrated even more sharply in some of the "new nations" outside Europe. The Arab-speaking peoples of the Middle East and North Africa offer an extreme example. At the Paris Peace conference of 1919, the Egyptian nationalist Sa'd Zaghlul refused to support a delegation of Syrians. "Our problem," he informed them curtly, "is an Egyptian prob-

[24] The point is made by Otto Vossler, Der Nationalgedanke von Rousseau bis Ranke (München: Oldenbourg, 1937), p. 15.

[25] For a similar view see Carl Joachim Friedrich, "Nation-Building?" in Karl W. Deutsch and William J. Foltz, eds., Nation-Building (Atherton, 1963), p. 32; and a work by Count R. N. Coudenhove-Kalergi, single-minded advocate of European political unification since the nineteen-twenties, Die europäische Nation (Stuttgart: Deutsche Verlags-Anstalt, 1953).

lem and not an Arab problem."[26] But to Nasser's generation, the Egyptian problem itself has become an Arab problem. Meanwhile, contemporary Syrian nationalists are caught in an intense, and as it were concentric, conflict of political loyalties: to Syria in its present borders; to a Greater Syria including Lebanon, Jordan, and, hopefully, Palestine; to a Fertile Crescent community including Iraq; and to an Arab linguistic nationality from Morocco to Oman. It is not uncommon, as a specialist on Africa has noted, "that during a period of struggle for independence from foreign rule the shape of the nations-to-be should remain somewhat cloudy and undefined, and that various competing nationalisms, appealing to narrower or wider loyalties, should be thrown up in the process."[27]

NATIONS, TRADITIONAL AND MODERN

It follows logically from the definition given earlier that nations can exist during any historical period, modern or traditional; it is clear empirically that modernization began in Europe, in Russia, in Ottoman Turkey, and in many of the colonial realms long before the emergence of any national feeling; but it also is evident that in Asia, Africa, and Latin America today, modernization and nationhood are intimately linked. The nature of the relationship therefore must be more precisely stated.

In France, in June 1789, a *National* Assembly was brought into being by the revolutionary merger of the three estates; in August, it resolved on its Declaration of the Rights of Man and the Citizen which included the principle that "all sovereignty rests essentially in the nation" and abolished all status privileges; in November, it replaced the established regional and provincial institutions of the Bourbon monarchy with a set of uniform de-

[26] Quoted by Anwar G. Chejne, "Egyptian Attitudes Toward Pan-Arabism," *Middle East Journal*, Vol. 11 (Summer 1957), p. 253.

[27] Thomas Hodgkin, *Nationalism in Colonial Africa* (London: Muller, 1956), p. 29.

partments that were to be the arbitrary creation of a central legislature. "The substance of the ideas of 1789," said Acton, "is not the limitation of the sovereign power but the abrogation of intermediate powers."[28]

Whatever the word "nation" meant to earlier generations, its future meaning was profoundly affected by the egalitarian and centralizing pronouncements of the French Revolution. National allegiance, as the term must be understood today, is therefore not merely the highest in an ascending series of loyalties; within the political sphere, it claims to be the exclusive one.

In deciding which of the myriad of pre-modern human communities may properly be classified as nations, the relevant question is whether there was any single group on which overriding loyalties in fact were focused, and whether every individual was conceived as having a direct relationship to that group. Most of the pre-Columbian Indians, many of the precolonial social-linguistic groups of Africa, and the Arabian bedouin clans (both before and immediately after their unification through Muhammad) probably had all the essential characteristics of nations. Certainly, it is a semantic accident, reflecting changing usage and changing prejudices, that in English the term nation has been applied to some North American Indians whereas the corresponding African groups have commonly been called tribes. It is also clear that in a number of European and Asian countries, notably in Poland, Hungary, Ireland, Iran, Thailand, and Japan, the present consciousness of national identity goes back to pre-modern times, though the traditional sense of nationality in such countries lacked the egalitarian overtones of 1789. But which of all these groups at which periods were indeed nations is a question that may safely be left to any anthropologists and historians who find the term nation useful for their researches.

A great many pre-modern societies, on the other hand, proba-

[28] John Emerich Edward Dalberg-Acton first Baron Acton, "Nationality" (1862) in his Essays on Freedom and Power (Beacon, 1948), p. 176.

bly a majority, clearly were not nations. No common loyalty bound slaves to citizens in the Greek city states of antiquity. In medieval Europe, popes and emperors, kings, dukes, and counts, cities and villages offered competing foci of loyalty, and the chain of feudal obligation only partially reconciled the resulting conflicts. The typical structure of empires has been that of a small group of conquerors (whether Romans at the beginning of the Christian era, or Ottomans or Incas in the fifteenth century, or Fulanis in West Africa, or British in East India in the nineteenth) spread over a congeries of distinct local communities. In contemporary Africa, loyalty to ethnic groups (and in Asia to religious groups and castes as well) conflicts with that to the postcolonial state with its single party or "charismatic" leader. No nations therefore existed in classical antiquity, in the traditional empires, or in the feudal periods of Europe and other regions; and few nations have as yet begun to reemerge after the colonial interlude in Asia and Africa.

The first political effect of modernization in Europe between the fifteenth and nineteenth centuries typically was not a direct transition from feudalism to national consciousness, but rather a growth of central authority under so-called "absolute" governments. A similar development occurred in most secondary settings of modernization, including Russia, Turkey, Japan, and the European colonial empires. Only at a later stage, most spectacularly in the French Revolution, was this centralized power transferred from an absolute ruler to the representatives of the entire people, and only at that stage can modernizing societies be said to have become modern nations.

Proclaimed as the symbol of revolutionary France, the ideal of the nation-state was realized in Italy and Germany by 1871, applied to a broad belt of Eastern European peoples after World War I, and espoused in Asia and Africa mostly after World War II. The close link between modernization and the nation-state is strikingly demonstrated in all those nonnational states that have

survived intact and are today the most advanced in modernization. The United Kingdom of the Stuarts and their successors, the
Japan of the Tokugawas and of Meiji, the Russia of the Roma-
novs and the Bolsheviks—all have in fact been transformed into
nation-states. Elsewhere, where modernization resulted from the
impact of a European civilization already committed to nationalism, the two have been linked as closely as they were in Europe.

In line with a distinction drawn earlier, it may be suggested
that nationalism, as it was transplanted from Europe to other
continents, came to include three cultural ingredients—some that
are essential to a relatively advanced form of modernization,
some that reflect traditional European history, and some that are
traditional and indigenous to the new nationalist settings. The
first of these elements—the essential link between modernization
and nationhood—consists of course in the need for an intensive
division of labor. A modernizing society attains its growing understanding and control of the forces of nature through the cooperation of ever wider groups and at length of the entire population, and such cooperation requires an increasing degree of equality of opportunity, of merit promotion, of achieved status rather
than traditional privilege. The modern nation-state has been the
only political framework within which these principles of equality
and of achievement can be maintained in the long run.

The same connection may be demonstrated conversely if it is
recalled that a nation exists by virtue of a network of mutual loyalties and that the factors promoting such loyalty will tend to
vary with the cultural setting. A traditional nation of bedouin no-
mads or African villagers can maintain such a feeling on the basis
of common descent, unquestioned custom, and effective isolation
from the rest of humanity. Once contact with a wider world has
been made and modernization has set in, however, overriding
loyalty will be given only to a group capable of a wider division
of labor and, where necessary, of defense against attacks from
other modernizing societies. Loyalty presupposes trust; and in the

modern world only a modernizing nation is likely to retain the loyalties of its people in the long run.

To sum up the relationship, there can be nations in traditional settings in the absence of modernization; there was incipient modernization in Europe and elsewhere in the absence of national sentiment or national organization; but only societies transformed into nations have shown themselves capable of attaining the more advanced forms of modernity, and only modernizing nations are likely to retain their identity in the present era of modernization. Whereas nationalities were rather an exception in traditional eras, they have become the ideal of the present modern age. It is conceivable that in some future period the connection between modernization and nationality will disappear, that modernization will find expression in political institutions that transcend and transform the nation-state. For the present, throughout Asia, Africa, and Latin America, nationalism and the drive for modernity are parts of the same dual revolution.

PART ONE

THE ESSENTIALS
OF THE MODERN NATION-STATE

CHAPTER TWO

NATIONAL IDENTITY

*To forget and . . . to get one's history wrong, are essential factors
in the making of a nation. . . .*
RENAN

. . . the criterion of Nationality in the shibboleth of Language.
TOYNBEE

. . . the people cannot decide until somebody decides who are the people.
JENNINGS

MODERNIZATION TRANSFORMS MANY ASPECTS of human society and culture, including psychology, economics, and politics; its favored political vehicle today is the nation-state—that is, a group of individuals who rule themselves on the basis of a sense of ultimate mutual loyalty. A modern nation-state is such a group embarked upon the grand venture of modernization and large enough to undertake that task with some prospect of success. Whatever their economic level, their social customs, or their psychological inclinations, such a people must fulfill three specifically political requirements. To succeed in their experiment in modern self-government, they must know what territory and what persons are included in their national community; they must be willing to accept a large measure of authority for the performance of public services; and they must participate in their common affairs on a basis of approximate equality.

These requirements are not arbitrary or fortuitous. The need for authority, common to all government,[1] sharply rises as mod-

[1] See Carl J. Friedrich, *Man and His Government* (McGraw, 1963), Chap. 12.

35

ern man becomes more dependent on his fellow man and as his demands for public services multiply. Identity of territory and citizenry must be clearly enough defined to allow behavior to be predictable, interests to be complementary, and mutual trust to grow—that is, to lay the foundation for a secure sense of nationality. Participation and equality are necessary to channel the community's full human resources into its modern division of labor. In short, identity is essential to the nation, authority to the state, equality to modernity; the three together form the political basis of the modern nation-state.

There is no need to specify these three requirements with precision. The extent of public authority and services will vary with the demands of individuals and the pressure of circumstances. "The greater the difficulties," as General de Gaulle has said, "the greater the need for government."[2] Authority, moreover, may be accepted in part because it is considered legitimate and in part because it seems inescapable. Immigration and emigration or minor boundary changes may blur the definition of community membership without destroying the basic sense of group identity. Death and birth, in any case, continually change the group's composition, and hence each succeeding generation must be brought anew into the continuing community. The elaborate division of labor in modern society accentuates individual differences of ability and interest; hence political equality will at best be an equality of opportunity, and in practice opportunities will also be unequal. In sum, there may be greater or lesser acceptance of authority and more or less clearly defined group identity among people participating more or less equally in their common affairs. The political requisites of the modern nation-state, like modernization and nationhood themselves, can show many gradations. Nation-states therefore will more or less closely approximate to a common ideal type.

The notion of a scale of nation-statehood implies the possibility of movement along that scale. Recent writers, therefore, have

[2] Charles de Gaulle, *Mémoires de guerre, Vol. 3, Le salut (1944-1946)* (Paris: Plon, 1959), p. 45.

given much thought to the problem of political development, which often is taken to mean development of modern nation-statehood. Some have given currency to the term "nation-building." Others have sought to identify a series of "crises" of political development or of modernization.[3] Both terms may mislead us.

There are indeed times when the founders of states are highly conscious of their architectonic task; and the present era, when so many newly proclaimed states are eager to ascend to the foremost ranks of modernity, is one of those periods. But even a Washington, a Bismarck, an Atatürk, or a Nehru must build on foundations laid long before; nor is the structure likely to settle within their lifetime. The founder of a commonwealth, Rousseau suggested, must work in one century to reap his reward in another.[4] The history of some of the most durable nations, moreover, such as Great Britain, France, Sweden, and Japan, records the name of no single architect and of no specific time when the total blueprint was drawn.

True crises are as rare as master-builders. The problems of identity, of authority, and of equality are indeed critical in the sense that their solution is essential to full nation-statehood. Some countries confront these problems in times of rapid change, resolving each in a single cathartic crisis; but even then, much additional effort is required to make the solutions endure. More commonly, the struggle brings many advances and reversals. If the development of Western Europe and its overseas off-shoots—that is, of the early modernizers—can serve as a guide, a modern nation-state may be expected to become fully established only after

[3] On "nation-building" see Lucian W. Pye, *Politics, Personality, and Nation Building* (Yale University Press, 1962); Reinhard Bendix, *Nation-Building and Citizenship: Studies of Our Changing Social Order* (Wiley, 1964); and Deutsch's discussion of the merits of the terms "growth" and "building" with regard to nations, Karl W. Deutsch and William J. Foltz, eds., *Nation-Building* (Atherton, 1963), p. 3.

For "crises" see Robert E. Ward and D. A. Rustow, eds., *Political Modernization in Japan and Turkey* (Princeton University Press, 1964), p. 446; Seymour Martin Lipset, *The First New Nation* (Basic Books, 1963), p. 16; and Leonard Binder et al., *Crises in Political Development* (Princeton University Press), forthcoming.

[4] Jean Jacques Rousseau, *Contract Social* (1762), Book 2, Ch. 7; cf. below, p. 156.

a tortuous process of several generations or centuries. Hence this study has more to say about growth than about building and more about quests, searches, and demands than about crises.

There is an obvious analogy between the triad of identity, authority, and equality and the triple battle cry of the French Revolution. The substitution of identity for fraternity is of no import; but that of authority for liberty may be thought to represent an about-face from the principles of 1789. Yet it should be kept in mind that the stormers of the Bastille launched their battle after many centuries during which royal authority had been imposed with mounting severity on the French kingdom; and that they soon gave way to the Committee of Public Safety, the Directoire, and Napoleon who established sterner systems of authority than France had known under its kings. Most of the developing countries of today have had no Philip the Fair, no Henry IV, and no Louis XIV to look back to; and not all of them will be able to avoid their versions of a Terreur, a Thermidor, and a Brumaire in the future.

Reserving authority and equality for later, the discussion will turn first to the search for national unity and identity. The ideal of national self-government suggests two fundamental problems; of these, Chapter Three will take up the problem of government, and the present chapter that of the national self. It is at this point that the various factors commonly invoked by nationalists as warrants of nationality or by scholars as objective characteristics of a nation may properly be examined. Geography, history, language, and popular will—all these are important in the formation of national identity, although not always in the way in which nationalists and students of nationalism have assumed.

The Myths of Geography and History

The division of labor within a modern society and the sense of common loyalty within a nation rest on a pattern of interdependence. In this pattern, men as individuals remain anonymous and for many purposes interchangeable, but men as members of the same group are known, behave predictably, and can be trusted. To allow for such predictability and interchange, the nation-state must claim exclusive authority over a precisely defined portion of the globe so that its rules can apply indiscriminately to all residents of that country. Any arrangement such as medieval feudalism or the Ottoman *millet* system, whereby each individual or member of a subgroup carries his distinctive rights and obligations from place to place is incompatible with modern nationality. Not all territorial states, of course, are nation-states, but all nation-states must be territorial.

Nor can just any territory furnish the necessary base. A modern nation-state must reconcile the imperatives of unity, which impose maximum limits of membership, with the imperatives of an effective division of labor, which impose minimum limits. Modernization and the growth of nationality therefore have commonly involved a wholesale reorganization of states, a redefinition of the geographic units within which the political process takes place. Few countries—such as Russia, China, Japan, Iran, and Morocco—have retained their geographic identities from traditional to modern times; almost everywhere else, realignments have been extensive. The Holy Roman, Habsburg, and Ottoman Empires and the European colonial realms proved too disparate and unwieldy to permit effective modernization. At the opposite end of the scale, the petty principalities of Germany and Italy, the nomadic tribes of the Middle East, and the village communities of Monsoon Asia and Tropical Africa proved too small. In all these areas, large empires and small parochial communities have yielded to nations or would-be nations of intermediate size.[5]

Within such approximate upper and lower limits of size, there are innumerable ways of drawing the boundaries among territori-

[5] The diminutive European states of Monaco, Liechtenstein, San Marino, and Andorra are the sort of exception that confirms the rule. Each of them is an independent state with a common language and a long history of self-government, but they are too small to engage the full loyalties of modern men. Hence even at a time when usage tends to equate state and nation, they lay claim to statehood but not to nationality.

al states. The "natural frontier" has been frequently adduced as an argument in border disputes, but it is not an objective concept. Neither mountains, nor rivers, nor seas divide nations naturally or unequivocally from each other. The Pyrenees have long separated Frenchmen from Spaniards, but the Alps have helped to make the Swiss into a single nation. Portions of the Rhine Valley have at times marked off Frenchmen from Germans, but the Nile has united the Egyptians into a single community. Insular location has helped the Japanese preserve their distinctiveness, but it did not protect Britons from invasion by Anglosaxons, Danes, and Normans, each of whom made their contribution to British nationality. It is not mountains, valleys, or islands that constitute nations; it is their human inhabitants.

To say that a nation's frontiers are defined by the birthplace of the nationals brings us no closer to a geographic delimitation; indeed, it sends us off on a circular argument. As Karl Deutsch has rightly insisted, "No person can be born at more than one spot on the map. The actual place of birth has the size of a bed or a room, not the size of a country. If he finds himself in a 'country' or within a set of borders, then no numbers of births can have created these borders or any unity of the country within it."[6] The cultural and political conventions prevailing at the time of the birth locate the bed or the house within a particular national territory.

History is no less equivocal than geography. There are few border areas in Europe that have not changed political control several times in a single century and to which three or four alternate "historic claims" could not be readily contrived. Even the "historic existence" of an entire nation is often a tenuous reconstruction of later times. In any case, the attitude of nationalists to history should not be taken at face value.

The early nationalist like the religious reformer (it was already noted) professes to be rediscovering when indeed he is innovating.[7] History serves him as a grab-bag from which he instinctively

---

[6] *Nationalism and Social Communication* (Wiley, 1953), pp. 4-5.
[7] See Chap. 1, p. 26.

selects past themes that suit his present purpose; and national mythologies, like national loyalties, can change their point of reference.

The Arab countries in the twentieth century illustrate the variations in that process. About the time when Zaghlul in Paris rebuffed his Syrian colleagues, Egyptian historical writers such as Taha Hussein glorified the Pharaohs and stressed Egypt's historic connections with the Mediterranean and with Europe. Lebanese of this same period looked back with pride to the Phoenicians, and Iraqis to the Babylonians and Assyrians. But as they became converted to Arab nationalism, Egyptians, Iraqis, and even Christian Lebanese[8] found fresh meaning in the history of the early Caliphate. But why should the seventh-century Caliphs be capable of making Arabia into a nation in the mid-twentieth century, when demonstrably they lacked such force in the intervening thirteen hundred years?

For all his preoccupation with history, the early nationalist, like other historical romanticists, is straining for a break with his living past, with his immediate social and cultural context.[9] The historical themes he invokes are significant not as hypotheses of historic causation but as part of a psychological search for symbols of confidence in the present. The conditions that give rise to a feeling of national loyalty or a desire for nation-statehood must therefore be distinguished from the historical myths that are themselves the symptom of such a national evolution.

Modernization and the creation of nation-states are departures into uncharted terrain that entail great risks. Old cultural values and social patterns decay faster than their modern counterparts emerge. The rival aspirations of neighboring nations or empires, moreover, introduce additional hazards. Hence there are among

---

[8] The latter included George Antonius, author of the leading nationalist history, *The Arab Awakening* (Lippincott, 1939).

[9] The point is made with regard to German and European romanticism by Alexander Rüstow, *Ortsbestimmung der Gegenwart*, 3 vols. (Zürich: Rentsch, 1950-57), Vol. 2, p. 451.

would-be nations many cases of still-birth and infant mortality that serve as a warning to others. The Baltic countries, after only two decades of national self-assertion between 1918 and 1939, once again became provinces of a Russian Empire. Somewhat earlier, the Armenians were decimated and dispersed in a vain bid for nation-statehood. Nkrumah has warned of the danger of "Balkanization" in Africa; many Israelis have feared the "Levantinization" of their country; and other postcolonial countries have shrunk from the prospect of becoming "banana republics."

Modernization changes man's time perspective and conveys a new sense of purposeful social action. The intellectual and political leaders in that process must mediate as best they can among present realities, visions of the future, and memories of the past. In the midst of rapid changes, a feeling of continuity must be projected backward as well as forward. In the face of towering uncertainties, a new historical consciousness is needed. Everywhere the spokesmen of nascent nationalism must fight against the humiliations of the recent past—invasion by older nations, colonial or dynastic imperialism, princely or tribal fragmentation. Everywhere they must seek to enlist energies for a difficult and hazardous task. Their most persuasive argument is that what once was can surely be again. The glories of a remote past—real or mythical—become the allies against the immediate past in the struggle for a better future.[10]

The more desperate the present, the greater the need for such historic comforts. The Germans, beaten by Napoleon at Austerlitz and at Jena, revel in the victory of Arminius over other Latin troops eighteen hundred years before. The British Gold Coast

[10] "We are accustomed to say that 'the present is the product of all the past' . . . It is equally true . . . to say that the past (our imagined picture of it) is the product of all the present. We build our conception of history partly out of our present needs and purposes. The past is a kind of screen upon which we project our vision of the future; and it is indeed a moving picture, borrowing much of its form and color from our fears and aspirations." Carl Lotus Becker, "What are Historical Facts?" [1926], Western Political Quarterly, Vol. 7 (September 1955), pp. 327-40, reprinted in Hans Meyerhoff, ed., The Philosophy of History of Our Time (Doubleday, 1959), p. 133.

and the French Soudan on reaching independence adopt the names of the half-legendary kingdoms of Ghana and Mali, the boundaries of which have only a remote and uncertain relation to these latter-day colonies. And the Mexicans, after escaping the threats of French and American conquest, erect statues to the last Aztec king Cuauhtémoc—even though the inscription on the pedestal is unmistakably in the language of Hernan Cortés.

Modernization and nationalism are accompanied by profound changes in the value placed on the collective self and on others. Modernization emerged spontaneously only in Western Europe. As the leaders in a world-wide process, the Europeans were spared any sense of backwardness. But from Europe, moderniza-tion spread by colonial conquest to the Americas, to South and Southeast Asia, and to Africa, and by threat of conquest to Rus-sia, Turkey, Iran, Thailand, Japan, and China. Both in colonial and noncolonial countries, it gave rise to a keenly felt gap be-tween aspiration and reality, to ambivalent feelings toward the West—and conversely toward one's own tradition. Late modern-izing societies combine admiration of the foreigner with strenu-ous opposition to his domination, consciousness of inferiority of the indigenous tradition with a determination to reassert its strength and individuality.

Some peoples, such as the Japanese, have a long tradition of cultural borrowing and take pride in successful imitation. But most others feel humiliated by the need to borrow from a superi-or antagonist. One means of relieving this psychological pressure is the belief that elements taken over from the more advanced, modern culture are in fact pre-formed in one's own tradition, that the new acquisitions are restorations of a rightful heritage. While Islamic theologians for 1200 years had sanctioned polygamy and autocracy, the Islamic modernists of the last century have read into the Koran an injunction of monogamy and have seen in the early assemblies of the Muslim faithful a first forum of democra-cy. Every new edition of the *Great Soviet Encyclopaedia* has claimed for Russian scientists technological discoveries previously credited to Westerners. By an analogous rationalization, African nationalists today blame their economic backwardness on willful exploitation by their colonial rulers. Industry and higher standards of living, they imply, would have naturally developed if only their peoples had been left to themselves.

Some of this mythology may sound quaint or extravagant; yet all of it reflects the search for symbols of confidence that is an integral part of early modernization and insecure nationalism. "History," in the words of the most perceptive Western student of Middle Eastern thought, "has to be consulted . . . closely to yield the glories of the . . . past which may be taken as a warranty for a glorious future."[11] Or, to quote from Renan: "To forget and—I will venture to say—to get one's history wrong, are essential factors in the making of a nation." Indeed Renan, overrating perhaps the influence of scholarship on human affairs, concluded that "the advance of historical studies is often a danger to nationality."[12]

It is possible, furthermore, to make explicit the considerations that underlie the choice of a suitable past—that, consciously or more often unconsciously, guide the nationalist in selecting this or that item from the historical grab-bag. Where these principles come into conflict, some synthesis or compromise must be attempted.

1. The historical period, personage, or motif ideally suited for inclusion in the national myth should enjoy wide respect in the world at large and particularly among more "advanced" nations. The praise bestowed by Tacitus made Arminius all the more attractive to the Germans. The tendency of nineteenth-century European scholars to derive all Western culture from Egypt or Babylon strongly recommended the Pharaohs and Hammurabi as ancestors for latter-day Middle Easterners.

2. These motifs should be equally acceptable to all groups which the nationalist leadership seeks to enlist in its movement

[11] Gustave E. von Grunebaum, *Modern Islam* (Vintage Books, 1964), p. 35.
[12] Ernest Renan, "What is a Nation?" in Alfred Zimmern, ed., *Modern Political Doctrines* (London: Oxford University Press, 1939), p. 190.

rather than accentuate divisive tendencies. For de Gaulle in 1940, Joan of Arc was a better symbol than Louis XIV or Napoleon, who would have set the French Right against the French Left.

3. The motifs chosen should have a clearer connection with the nation and its leaders than with their rivals at home or abroad. The Muslim Mughal dynasty has a stronger appeal for Pakistanis than for Indians. Muhammad Ali, an Albanian-Ottoman soldier who spoke no Arabic but ruled Egypt from 1805 to 1849 and extended his power into other Arab countries, once was proclaimed as a precursor of pan-Arabism. But after King Farouk had been deposed in 1952, his ancestor could not remain in the nationalist pantheon; instead, Colonel Urabi, who in 1881-82 had revolted against Farouk's uncle, became a favorite hero of the regime set up by Nasser and other colonels.[13]

The application of these rules to changing circumstances is illustrated in the transition, between about 1895 and 1925, from an Ottoman imperial to a Turkish national consciousness.

The Ottomans had long been proud to be the chief defenders of Islam, and their heroes had been Muhammad, the early Caliphs, and the victorious sultans from Mehmed the Conqueror (1451-81) to Süleyman the Magnificent (1520-66).[14] As the Ottomans went from defeat to defeat and embarked on a difficult program of Europeanizing reform, this traditional Ottoman-Islamic pride suffered. By the 1890's, some of them were reading the writings of European Turcologists which extolled the deeds of Jengiz and Timur. When Kemal (the later Atatürk) abolished sultanate and caliphate (1922-24), further glorification of the

[13] The three principles are implicit in the suggestive essay by McKim Marriott, "Cultural Policy in New States," in Clifford Geertz, ed., *Old Societies and New States* (Free Press, 1963), pp. 27-56, where India, Pakistan, Ceylon, Indonesia, and Tropical Africa are compared. For the contrasting views of Muhammad Ali, cf. Antonius, *op. cit.*, pp. 21ff., and Anwar El Sadat, *Revolt on the Nile* (John Day, 1957), p. 15.

[14] That Muhammad and the early Caliphs were "Arabs" did not trouble them. Like Jefferson's generation which considered itself the true heir of Roman republicanism, they were innocent of the genetic fallacy—the notion that a man must not boast of his precursors unless they are also his ancestors.

Islamic and Ottoman past became impossible. The pre-Ottoman non-Muslim Byzantines, whose influence is visible enough in the Ottoman architecture of Istanbul and in early Ottoman administration, had been preempted by the Greeks, who had launched the Greek-Turkish War of 1919-22 with the idea of restoring the old Byzantine empire. The pre-Islamic Turkic-speaking horsebreeders of the Central Asian steppes had the twofold disadvantage that their cultural level was low and that their territory was part of the Soviet Union.

Kemal blended several of these motifs in the theory "that the Turks were a white, Aryan people, originating in Central Asia, the cradle of all human civilization. Owing to the progressive desiccation of this area, the Turks had migrated in waves to various parts of Asia and Africa, carrying the arts of civilization with them. Chinese, Indian, and Middle Eastern civilization had all been founded in this way, the pioneers in the last named being the Sumerians and Hittites, who were both Turkic peoples. Anatolia had thus been a Turkish land since antiquity. This mixture of truth, half-truth, and error was proclaimed as official doctrine, and teams of researchers set to work to 'prove' its various propositions."[15]

The Turkish experience indicates that the tendency to resort to myth varies in inverse proportion to the availability of historic symbols that meet the three criteria mentioned above, and in direct proportion to the psychological needs and pressures confronted by the nationalists. One of Kemal Atatürk's mottoes, inscribed on the pedestal of a monument in Ankara, lists these needs in an admonition in characteristic sequence: "Turk, be proud, work, be confident!" There must be self-respect to motivate hard work, and hard work to justify confidence. Once the confidence-inspiring results of hard work have been achieved, the extravagant mythology may be discarded. In Turkey, Atatürk's "National History Thesis" enjoyed its greatest vogue from ten to

[15] Bernard Lewis, *The Emergence of Modern Turkey* (London: Oxford University Press, 1961), p. 353.

twenty years after the founding of a Turkish national state on the ruins of the Ottoman Empire. Since that time, with the growth of industrialism and democracy, little has been heard of it.

Whatever courage nascent nationalism may derive from its tendentious image of history, its real tasks—and its tests of achievement—lie in the present and the future.

The Common Coin of Language

No less a scholar than Arnold Toynbee has roundly condemned those who seek "the criterion of Nationality in the shibboleth of Language."[16] Yet in the heyday of European nationalism from 1848 to 1919, language was more frequently invoked than any other criterion. Unlike geography, language is a human phenomenon. Unlike history, which is continuous and can mean many things to many men, language divides human beings into distinct groups. There is also a close connection between language and modernization. Traditional communities survive best in isolation; but the principle of modernity is interdependence. More people in modern society talk and write to more others than ever before. Language therefore is to a modern society what money is to its economy: a universal currency of exchange. Far from being a shibboleth, linguistic unity can be a modern nation's most precious possession.

POLITICS AND LANGUAGE

Still, Toynbee is right that language supplies no adequate criterion of nationality, and for several reasons. First, it is sometimes overlooked that language is not a fixed datum and that politics shapes language as much as language shapes politics. The new literary idioms fashioned by Dante and Luther established Italian and German cultural unity through centuries of political fragmentation and thus facilitated the rise, many centuries later, of

[16] *A Study of History* (London: Oxford University Press, 1934-54), Vol. 8, p. 536.

modern nationalism. But the opposite connection is at least as frequent. The linguistic divisions on the Iberian peninsula—between Portuguese, Castilian, and Catalan—still reflect the dynastic boundaries that evolved from the eleventh to the fifteenth centuries. As French kings at Paris extended their rule over Gascony, Provence, Brittany, Burgundy, and other outlying regions, they made the dialect of the Ile de France the common language of the realm. The revival of Latin as against Slavic elements in Romanian, the development of *Katareousa* (the neo-classic Greek literary language as distinct from the vernacular *Dhimotiki*), the literary evolution of *Landsmaal* in Norway (the popular language in contrast to the quasi-Danish *Rigsmaal*) were both consequence and cause of an awakening sense of nationality. In Ireland, the flow of causality is unmistakable: twentieth century nationalists did not rebel against Great Britain because of differences of language; rather they attempted to revive Gaelic to express their dissatisfaction with British rule.

Second, in most parts of the world, linguistic communities are not of a size suitable for modern nation-states. Only in Europe and in South and Southeast Asia is there a prevalence of languages with about five to fifty million speakers. In most underdeveloped regions, the language areas are either too large (as in Spanish America or in the Arab Middle East) or too small. In Tropical Africa, most language communities number fewer than one million speakers. There is only one language with 13 million (Hausa), three others with about six million (Yoruba, Rwanda, Fulani), and about half a dozen with two to three million speakers. Ironically, the postcolonial boundaries have merged more than a dozen major language groups in India (each with tens of millions of speakers) in a single state. In Africa, linguistic difficulties have been compounded by splitting up some of the larger groups or submerging them with a multitude of others. The Hausas, for example, live in Nigeria, Niger, Cameroun, Dahomey, and Togo; the Yorubas constitute only 18 percent of Nigeria's population and the three million Luba Lulua make up 17 percent of Congo-Kinshasa.

Third, the transition from empire to nation often has brought a complete reversal of attitudes toward linguistic diversity. Where the older nation-states of Europe were to find in ethnic loyalty and linguistic unity their stablest foundation, dynastic and colonial empires sought their security in diversity and mixture. What empires built up, nations had to undo; what empires suppressed, nations revived.

Often the imperial rulers preserved or accentuated ethnic distinctions or even created them where none existed. At times, they might be following the cynical precept of divide and rule, and at other times an unconscious instinct of self-preservation or some positive concept of imperial mission. The Habsburg and Ottoman emperors, locked for three centuries in mortal combat, settled loyal populations in enclaves along either side of the shifting frontier: Germans in the Banat and Transylvania, Muslims in Bosnia and the Dobrudja. When the British announced their support of the Zionist policy of Jewish settlement, they promised "that nothing shall be done which may prejudice the civil and religious rights of existing non-Jewish communities in Palestine" —disregarding the fact that 87 percent of all Palestinians at the time were Arabs and 77 percent belonged to a single Sunni-Muslim community.[17] To the north, the French in 1920 doubled the size of Lebanon so as to transform a Christian-Arab territory into one almost evenly split between Christians and Muslims. In predominantly Sunni-Muslim Syria, they gave autonomy to Druzes and Shiis. French officials in combating Arab nationalism in Algeria in the 1950's spoke invariably of the "peoples" of Algeria and refrained from calling any of them Arabs.

In staffing their military and civil services, moreover, the imperial rulers relied by preference on immigrants from outside the realm or small minority groups within. The rolls of the Habsburg public service were replete with Italian, Spanish, Belgian, and Irish names. The early Ottomans recruited their ruling class from

[17] Quote from the Balfour Declaration of 1917; see J. C. Hurewitz, *Diplomacy in the Near and Middle East* (Van Nostrand, 1956), Vol. 2, p. 26. Statistics (for 1914) from Hurewitz, *Middle East Dilemmas* (Harper, 1953), p. 152.

Balkan Christians converted to Islam and from Caucasian immigrants. The British built up their Indian army from among Sikhs, Gurkhas, and Muslims, and their Iraqi levies from the tiny Assyrian-Christian minority.

Fourth, in many parts of the globe an ethnic division of labor grew up in traditional times, and this often accentuated the divisiveness of imperial rule. The cultural patterns of subsistence agriculture are not easily reconciled with the requirements of commerce. Hence long-distance trade (and later banking and industry) became the monopoly of geographically more mobile groups distinct in language, religion, and customs from their agricultural customers: Chinese in Southeast Asia; Indians and Arab Muslims in East Africa; Syrian Christians in West Africa; Parsis in Bombay; Greeks, Armenians, Jews, and Levantines in the Near East.

A slightly different economic-political pattern led to the wholesale importation of Africans as plantation workers in the tropical and subtropical parts of America. In British Guiana, when emancipated Negroes flocked to the towns, East Indians were imported to take their place on the plantations; a century later, Guyana, bitterly divided between Africans and East Indians, became the scene of smoldering communal tensions verging on civil war. In Malaya, Chinese workers were brought to work in the rubber plantations and tin mines, and their descendants today constitute an even half of the population.

The minority groups of warriors, administrators, traders, or agricultural workers that lent stability to the imperial tapestry disrupt the warp and woof of emerging nationality. The Germans in the Danubian basin, once a mainstay of Habsburg rule, became potential irredentists or subversives in the successor states. In Turkey, early in this century, the Armenians were massacred and the Greeks transferred in a forced population exchange. Newly independent Iraq in 1933 wreaked a terrible vengeance on its Assyrian minority. More recently, Nasser has expropriated Greeks and Copts, and Sukarno has tried to wrest local trade from the

Chinese. Everywhere the loyal instruments of empire and the prosperous practitioners of trade face the perils of expulsion, expropriation, or extermination. Where empires found their strength in checkerboard diversity, new nation-states dread the prospect of Balkanization.

In short, the dream of Herder, Mazzini, and other romantic nationalists of humanity composed of national states each including a solid and distinct community of language is far from realization, and nowhere farther than in the postcolonial states of Asia, Africa, and Latin America.[18]

PATTERNS OF LANGUAGE AND STATEHOOD

To obtain some perspective on the importance of language problems in these successor states, it is useful to identify six different linguistic constellations, keeping in mind not only the number and size of language groups in a given country but also the degree of relatedness and distinction among them, and, above all, whether one or more of them have a substantial literary tradition.

A distinct language predominant throughout the country. This is the situation in most European countries; in Japan, Korea, Mongolia, Vietnam, Turkey, and Madagascar; and in the countries settled by European overseas immigration.[19] Here linguistic unity provides a secure foundation for nationality. The problems that remain are likely to be of manageable scope. For many languages, a modern technical vocabulary has to be devised—as in Europe since the days of Dante, Luther, Shakespeare, and Rabelais. For some others, there has been the task of eliminating vocabulary elements felt to be alien and to be reflecting a pre-na-

[18] Appendix Table 3 lists the 31 linguistically homogeneous and distinct countries of the world—that is, all those peoples speaking a single language who constitute two-thirds or more of a country's population as well as two-thirds or more of the speakers of that language. Note that 17 of these are in Europe, 10 in East and Southeast Asia, and one each in Tropical Africa and South America.

[19] Three of these linguistically homogeneous states, however, have been politically divided by the East-West conflict: Germany, Korea, and Vietnam.

tional imperial past—such as Japanese words from Korean, Arabic ones from Turkish, or Dutch ones from Indonesian.[20] In the immigrant countries, educational and social policies must be geared to the task of rapid cultural assimilation of newcomers. In some countries, the political status of the small remaining linguistic minorities must be clarified—the major choices being assimilation, emigration, or boundary revisions for irredentas.

A *single language predominant in several neighboring countries*. This is the situation among the Spanish-speaking countries of Latin America and the Arab countries of the Middle East and North Africa. The movements for wider unity or federation at the time of independence have encountered major difficulties. Yet there has been a freer interchange of political leadership personnel and greater hospitality for political exiles within each of these groups of countries than anywhere else. To cite a few examples, Che Guevara, who was instrumental in establishing a Communist regime in Cuba was a native of Argentina; Cecil Hourani, long a political adviser to President Bourguiba of Tunisia, is of Lebanese origin; and Abdul Rahman Azzam Pasha, Egyptian ex-secretary of the Arab League, later became an adviser to the royal Saudi government. Latin American countries have regularly given asylum in their embassies to political leaders on the losing side in any given internal upheaval. A school in San José, the capital of Costa Rica, is dedicated to the training of party organizers for liberal and democratic parties throughout Spanish America. And Nasser at one time or another has supported political exile movements from almost every other Arab country.

Clearly, despite the existing political divisions, there is an underlying feeling of political community within each of these groups of states that blurs the dividing line between internal and external politics and allows ideological conflicts to be fought across territorial boundaries. If in Latin America the present hesitant efforts at economic coordination should in the future pro-

[20] The elimination of Latin and French elements from German offers a close parallel.

duce a full-blown movement of functional integration on the European model, the ease of communication in a single language may lead to a more rapid growth of sentiments of common loyalty. Perhaps among the Arab states, too, functional integration will be found to provide a safer path to unity than the recent practice of *faits accomplis* by subversion, coup, or military intervention.

A variety of closely related languages, one of which serves as official language. This is the situation in Indonesia, where a variety of languages of the Western Malayo-Polynesian family are spoken. One of these, Bahasa Indonesia, traditionally has been the language of commerce and now has been adopted and developed as the official language of government and education.[21] In the Philippines, the situation is somewhat similar, although Tágalog (the official language) faces serious competition as a literary language from English and even Spanish. In Tanganyika, the majority speak a great variety of Bantu languages, none of them including as many as one-fifth of the population. But roughly half of all Tanganyikans speak Swahili—a language with a Bantu base and strong Arabic influences which has long been the lingua franca of trade and was promoted for official uses by the German colonial regime before World War I. Swahili is the only African language that was written before the European conquest, and its connection with Arabic gives it access to a far richer vocabulary than is available to other Bantu tongues. Swahili among all African languages is therefore the likeliest to offer a serious competition to the former colonial language as a national medium of communication in the future.

The countries just named—Indonesia, the Philippines, and Tanganyika—all face a similar problem of linguistic unification and development of a modern vocabulary. There is some prospect here that linguistic identity will follow on political identity, somewhat as it did in Western Europe.

[21] Except for differences in spelling, reflecting the Dutch and English colonial heritages, Bahasa Indonesia is almost identical with Malay, the majority language of Malaya and Malaysia.

A variety of unrelated languages of which only one has a substantial literary tradition. In these situations, there is a strong possibility that the literary language will win out as the national language, even if it is spoken only by a bare majority or a mere minority. The most striking examples are Morocco, where the majority speak Arabic and the minority a variety of Berber tongues; Peru, where Spanish faces Quechua, the ancestral language of the Incas which spread as a second official language in the South American Andes under Spanish rule; Bolivia, where the majority speak Quechua or Aymará, the indigenous language of the high plateau; Burma, where the Burmese of the Irrawaddy valley confronts Karen and other languages of the "hill tribes." Other examples are Mexico, Guatemala, and Ecuador among the Spanish-American and Algeria and the Sudan among the Arabic countries. As the Berber tribesmen or the Quechua-speaking villagers move from the mountains to the city, acquire an education, or rise on the social ladder, they become Arabized or Hispanized.

There are several further variants of this basic situation. In Paraguay, the majority language, Guaraní, has been elevated to the status of second official language, but, if the official statistics can be trusted, a majority of the population are bilingual in Spanish and Guaraní, and eventual assimilation to Spanish therefore seems likely. Yet the experience of the Kurds in Iraq since 1958 and of southern groups in the Sudan since 1961 shows that weakness of the central government and heavy-handed attempts at repression can delay the process—perhaps indefinitely.

A variety of distinct languages without literary tradition. This is the typical situation in Tropical Africa. The multiplicity of indigenous languages and their lack of literary evolution have so far prevented any serious challenge to French or English as the dominant language of higher education and of politics. In former French West Africa, a substantial body of poetry in French has grown up. Some of the indigenous African languages are used in the primary schools and as a second official language. But since in most countries linguistic unity can only be established if a majority take up a foreign tongue, it seems more advantageous to place increasing reliance on English and French in the future. For a Tiv of Northern Nigeria, Hausa is as difficult to learn as English, but English provides far wider access to the modern world. Hence the pressure in favor of English or French can be expected to come especially from the smaller language groups in each country.

A variety of distinct languages each with its own literary tradition. This is the situation in India, Pakistan, Ceylon, Malaysia, and Cyprus. In India, the situation is attenuated by the multiplicity of languages, by the unifying factor of Hindu religion, and by the continued use of English as the language of government and higher education. Although the Indian constitution accepted English as the official language only for a ten-year transition period, this delay has been extended. Understandably, the shift to Hindi is opposed with particular tenacity by the Dravidian language groups (Telugu, Tamil) in the South. They fear that it would further accentuate the preponderance of candidates from Uttar Pradesh in the civil service.

In Ceylon, Malaya, and on Cyprus, linguistic and religious divisions coincide, and the contrast is mainly between two solid groups. This clearly is the most explosive situation. In Malaysia, Prime Minister Abdul Rahman attempted to preserve a Malay-speaking plurality by including not only Singapore but also the three former British territories on Borneo in his federation. Yet the secession of Singapore in 1965 at Abdul Rahman's insistence put the success of the experiment in grave doubt. In Ceylon, by contrast, the Tamil Hindus have been in danger of being reduced to second-class citizenship ever since the "Sinhalese Only" campaign and the upsurge of militant Buddhist sentiment after 1956. On Cyprus, ethnic conflict between Greeks and Turks broke out into the open late in 1963 after only two years of operation of a precariously balanced constitution.

DYNAMIC FACTORS

In concluding this survey, it is well to reemphasize that the language situation is rarely static, and that current conditions in Asia and Africa are not unique but offer some analogy to the problems confronted earlier in Europe. Linguistic developments, moreover, are closely related to other social, political, and economic changes. What language will become established as the common medium in any Asian and African state in the future will depend on patterns of geographic and social mobility, on economic opportunities, and on access by various ethnic groups to government employment. Among the most fateful decisions that newly independent states in Asia and Africa must make, therefore, is the choice of a written language for their schools, universities, and government offices. As India's recurrent attempt to replace English by Hindi indicate, these decisions can also be among the most painful and explosive. In a country where only a small elite can read and write, it makes little difference in what language the vast majority are illiterate. Concerted drives for literacy and mass education, by contrast, emphasize the importance of the linguistic alternatives.

The situations in India and in Tropical Africa today resemble that in Europe during the Renaissance. In all three settings, literacy was at first concentrated in a small upper class which read, wrote, and even spoke an international language alien to the lower classes—Latin in one case, English and French in the others. Once a person had been recruited into this elite, he lost contact with the social environment of his origin, and communication proceeded mainly horizontally within the elite. With the advent of modernization, however, this traditional pattern was severely strained. Social mobility increased, economic opportunities expanded, and contacts between rulers and subjects became more intensive. In sum, vertical channels of communication between the elite and mass in any given region became more important than horizontal ones across the regions.

In bridging the linguistic gap between elite and mass, there were two basic possibilities. The priests, scholars, and rulers of Renaissance Europe could have taught Latin to the merchants and craftsmen of the towns and ultimately to the peasants of the countryside. Or some members of the intellectual elite could take the initiative in developing the primitive vernacular of the countryside into a more sophisticated language suitable for literature, science, and government in an era of modernization. One by one, the leading intellectual figures of modern Europe opted for the second alternative: vernacular literatures developed from the thirteenth century onward, and by the eighteenth century Latin was abandoned even by scientists and philosophers. Clearly, the second alternative recommended itself because the intellectual pursuits of the elite gave it more mental flexibility than had the lower classes. In Luther's Germany, for example, following the development of printing, it was easier for the leaders to write political pamphlets in German than for their growing audiences to read them in Latin.

The major difference between this European experience and the current Asian and African situation is the more active and deliberate role of government and the greater pressure for solutions that can be accomplished in decades, not centuries. Yet the basic alternatives are similar. In India, where Hindi, Tamil, Bengali, and a dozen other languages already have their developed literary traditions (richer perhaps and far older than that of English), the pressures in favor of the Renaissance solution—in favor of developing the vernaculars—would seem to be even greater than they once were in Europe.

In Africa, the outcome still is uncertain. With a variety of languages and the absence of literary traditions, the situation is transitional: it will change significantly if and as literacy increases. Deutsch has shown from the history of Bohemia, Finland, and other countries, that the crucial question is what language the modernized (or "mobilized") population of the growing cities will use in writing and in economic life.[22] If in countries like Senegal or Ghana, for example, rural migrants to the towns adopt French or English, these will become established as indigenous tongues. Such countries would then have a variety of languages but with one that has a literary tradition. If, by contrast, the future urban

---

[22] *Nationalism and Social Communication*, pp. 104-08.

populations of Senegal or Ghana retain their African languages, the situation will become like that in India, Pakistan, Malaysia, and Cyprus, where there are many languages, each with its own literary tradition.

Even within the latter category there is a wide range of political possibilities—as illustrated both from Western and non-Western experience. Switzerland is the model multilingual country where the language question has become thoroughly depoliticized. In Belgium, on the other hand, hostility between Flemings and Walloons—reinforced by religious, economic, and political issues—flares up periodically. In Finland, a Swedish-speaking former ruling class adjusted itself to the rise of a Finnish urban elite. In Bohemia, a corresponding adjustment of Germans to Czechs was prevented mainly by the aggressive policy of neighboring Germany in the 1930's. In Asia today, Malaya, Ceylon, Iraq, and Cyprus suggest a wide spectrum of possibilities.

Popular Will and "Social Communication"

If neither geography, nor history, nor language can supply clear-cut criteria of national identity, what then of the fourth factor commonly invoked, that of the "will of the people"? If nationality is indeed a matter of loyalty—an "everyday plebiscite"—why not let an actual plebiscite set the boundaries of nations?

Let us state the problem accurately. It is not a process, as political thinkers from Hobbes to Rousseau presented it, of men abandoning some nonpolitical condition of nature, deliberating freely the terms of a social compact, and thus contriving a first political community. Society is man's natural state, and men have always lived in political communities. Hence the empirical question is how nonnational states may be converted into national ones. Renan's phrase is valid enough as a literary metaphor, which is all he intended; but as a practical expedient, plebiscites can determine boundaries at most in marginal situations.

Of all political problems, those relating to geographic identity are perhaps least amenable to decision by popular vote. As Sir Ivor Jennings has remarked with some acerbity of the Wilsonian doctrine of self-determination: "On the surface it seemed reasonable: let the people decide. It was in fact ridiculous because the people cannot decide until somebody decides who are the people."[23] It is inconceivable that Jefferson Davis and Abraham Lincoln should have taken turns at four-year intervals pursuing alternate policies of union and secession; that Germans in the mid-nineteenth century should periodically have chosen between a "greater German" and "little German" solution; or that Syrians today should ballot at regular intervals the merits of Little Syria, Greater Syria, Fertile Crescent, and Pan-Arab unity schemes. Such issues of necessity will be settled by other means—by diplomacy, by war, by coup d'état—as in fact they were in all three countries.[24] The plebiscites held in Europe after World War I and more recently in some of the African trust territories (British Togoland and British Cameroons) are only apparent contradictions of this argument. If nations were to be constituted by plebiscite alone, the possible solutions would be so numerous and indeterminate as to make a clear formulation of alternatives and any rational choice among them impossible.

All these difficulties arise if a popular vote is to draw boundaries even once; if the process were to be repeated from time to time—let alone from day to day—they would multiply astronomically. Before even a single plebiscite can take effect, there is need, first, for an authority constituted previously and by means other than plebiscite, which must delimit the area that is to vote as one unit, must narrow down the alternatives, and must enforce the voters' verdict. Second, the government under which the voters have decided to live must offer some assurance that their decision will remain valid for an indefinite period. Such authority

[23] *The Approach to Self-Government* (Cambridge: University Press, 1956), p. 56.
[24] For a similar critique of plebiscites as an instrument of self-determination see Elie Kedourie, *Nationalism,* 2d ed. (Praeger, 1961), pp. 125ff.

and assurance were provided in the 1920's by the concert of victorious powers at the Paris Peace Conference and in the League of Nations, and more recently by agreement between the trustee and the adjacent country or countries. The Congo crisis of 1960-62 and the campaign for linguistic member states in the Indian Union confirm that the principle of self-determination cannot define geographic identities except as it is applied within a political order preestablished on some other basis.

The conventional discussion of the allegedly "objective" factors in the formation of nationality leaves a significant gap by its failure to differentiate between nations and other types of political community. Defensible frontiers are a major asset to empires as well; historic continuity of institutions can strengthen a feudal system or a city state; and city states and imperial elites have need of a common language. Even popular will is, in a sense, of universal importance under any form of government; if the citizens or subjects do not actively support a given regime, at least they must acquiesce in its continuation.

Thus the literature does not usually specify what precise aspects of geography, history, or language contribute to national identity rather than to feudalism, city states, or imperialism. Writers "have suggested that nationality somehow involves common relationships to parts of men's physical environment—their 'country'—and to some events in the past, transmitted to the present as 'common' history—although they could not tell what made a country or a history 'common'."[25] The Germans, Hungarians, Czechs, and other inhabitants of the Danubian basin; the Greeks, Albanians, Bulgarians, Serbs, and Turks on the Balkans—each of these populations participated in the same historical events for many centuries. Why did politically conscious men in each region feel a sense of common purpose in the heyday of the Habsburg and Ottoman empires but a growing sense of mutual antagonism in the nineteenth century? What circumstances turned acquiescent subjects of empire into restless nationalists? What social

[25] Deutsch, *Nationalism and Social Communication*, p. 13.

forces eroded one sense of community and allowed the emergence of another?

Once the haze generated by the conventional discussion of geography and history, language, and popular will is lifted, the most suggestive contributions toward an empirical theory of the growth of modern nations derive from the work of Karl Deutsch. In his earlier book on *Nationalism and Social Communication,* Deutsch adopts mostly a sociological point of view. In a subsequent collective work on *Political Community and the North Atlantic Area,*[26] he examines the political process of national integration in Western Europe and North America. Deutsch's major premise would be obvious if it had not been so consistently disregarded by the classic nationalist writers and by earlier scholars. Nationality is not an inborn characteristic but the result of a process of social learning and habit forming. Such learning typically resulted from a marked increase of social communication (that is, of trade, travel, correspondence and the like) within a network linking a number of cities and each of these with its rural hinterland. "In the political and social struggles of the modern age," Deutsch has written, "*nationality* . . . means an alignment of large numbers of individuals from the middle and lower classes linked to regional centers and leading social groups by channels of communication and economic intercourse both indirectly from link to link and directly with the center."[27] In sum, a new style of life emerged from a process of "social communication"—which is nothing but the social aspects of modernization. An outside challenge to that new way of life and the advent of a new generation then acted as catalysts in shaping a political consciousness of nationality.

The political integration of nation-states, according to Deutsch, usually began in the prenationalist or the nationalist era with the rise of a core area—a region where administrative and economic

[26] By Karl W. Deutsch et al. (Princeton University Press, 1957), especially pp. 22-116.
[27] *Nationalism and Social Communication,* p. 75.

capabilities exceeded the load of political demands. If a durable nation-state is to form around a core area (such as the Ile de France, or Prussia, or Piedmont), there must be a compensating flow of advantages and sacrifices linking the outside regions to the core, and rival plans for integration must be eliminated, often by force. The formation of political coalitions cutting across both classes and regions and the prospect of mutual economic advantages are helpful in consolidating each step toward integration. Throughout, Deutsch stresses the importance not of identity of views and interests, but of their complementarity and mutuality.

The political part of Deutsch's analysis converges with the findings of Hans Kohn and other earlier writers on nationalism. The sense of nationality in Western and Northern Europe that arose in the eighteenth century was securely based on a continuity of political rule going back to the Middle Ages. Where this political tradition was absent, as in most of Central and Eastern Europe and in the Middle East, nationality came to be based on cultural factors.[28] Nationalism was more precarious and hence, by a familiar dialectic, more aggressive. The distinction applies outside of Europe as well. Indeed, in the postcolonial states of the Americas, of Asia, and of Africa, the imperial contribution to national identity has been greater than Kohn perhaps appreciated.

Identity and Authority

Four patterns of state formation may be distinguished: (1) the post-dynastic states of Western Europe and certain other regions; (2) the linguistic states of Central and Eastern Europe and the Middle East; (3) the countries of overseas immigration; and (4) the postcolonial countries of Asia, Africa, and Latin America. Each category involves some simplification; some few countries

[28] The distinction is summed up by Louis L. Snyder, *The Meaning of Nationalism* (Rutgers University Press, 1954), pp. 117-20, who terms it "the Kohn dichotomy." Among Kohn's own works, see especially *The Idea of Nationalism* (Macmillan, 1948), Chaps. 4-5.

do not neatly fit into the classification; and others combine features of several categories.

POST-DYNASTIC STATES

In Western Europe, most of the nation-states that emerged in the nineteenth century coincided with linguistic communities, but these communities had themselves been shaped earlier by warfare and inheritance among dynastic rulers. Great Britain emerged as a "United Kingdom" after Welsh Tudors and Scottish Stuarts in turn claimed the inheritance of Norman England. The French kings at Paris over many centuries extended their rule to the outlying provinces in a process that one historian has likened to the painstaking composition of a mosaic.[29] On the Iberian peninsula, the same process occurred in seven centuries of Christian conquest from Arab-Berber (or "Moorish") rulers. In Scandinavia, the division among Norway, Sweden, and Denmark follows the natural configuration of mountains and seas: here, geographic, political, and linguistic identity over the centuries came to reinforce each other.

The pattern of state-formation has been similar in a number of countries outside of Western and Northern Europe that escaped subjugation by European imperialism. Russia, located at the outer edge of European civilization, from the sixteenth to the nineteenth centuries expanded toward the Black Sea, the Caspian, the Arctic Ocean, and the Pacific—much as the rulers at Paris expanded toward the Atlantic, the Channel, and the Mediterranean. The chief difference was that Russian language and culture displayed an even stronger assimilative force as they encountered peoples of different origin. In China, the boundaries fashioned by successive dynasties, most recently by the Manchus, have survived with minor variations into the present age. In Iran, too, territorial and cultural identity was periodically reasserted from the

[29] Joseph R. Strayer in Deutsch and Foltz, eds., *Nation-Building*, pp. 23ff.

Achaemenids in the fourth century B.C. to the Safavids in the sixteenth century A.D., although the later escapes from European imperial domination were if anything closer than in China.

In Japan, as in Scandinavia, geography came to the aid of dynastic and cultural integration. Except for the diminutive group of Ainu aborigines in the North, the Japanese archipelago has been inhabited since prehistoric times by a people with a distinct language and a culture which (despite borrowings from China and more recently from the West) has remained equally distinct.

Turkey presents a further variation on this pattern. Here a form of linguistic nationalism has grown up since the turn of the nineteenth century. The national boundaries of the Republic of 1923 resulted essentially from the creative adaptation by Mustafa Kemal and his followers to the defeat of 1918. Yet within these boundaries, an organic connection with the political tradition of the late Ottoman Empire was preserved.

There are well-known exceptions in Western and Northern Europe to the rule of linguistic nationality based on old dynastic frontiers: Belgium, Finland, and Switzerland. The latter in particular has confounded those theorists who have mistakenly included a common language in their definition of nationhood. Its remote location athwart the strategic Alpine passes, a strong tradition of cantonal self-rule, and a political evolution (by no means free from conflict and turbulence) of nearly seven centuries all contributed to shaping and preserving a sense of Swiss national identity. Hence Switzerland has become a model of that rare political accomplishment: a viable multilingual nation-state.

LINGUISTIC STATES

Further to the East, the Western European sequence of political and linguistic evolution toward nationhood was reversed. The poetry of Dante and Petrarch and Luther's bible translation shaped an Italian and a German cultural identity that transcended the kaleidoscopic array of petty states. In the Danubian and Balkan countries, there was an upsurge of vernacular literatures in the late eighteenth and nineteenth centuries; in the Middle East, modern Arabic and Turkish literature began to flourish toward the turn of the twentieth. It was this literary-national resurgence that heralded the ultimate doom of the Habsburg and Ottoman empires and contributed to the downfall of the Tsars.

In all these countries, from Finland to Greece and from Germany to Syria, poets, writers, and artists played the role of early shapers of national identity that kings and ministers had played in France and Great Britain: the political careers of the poet Namik Kemal who helped to write the Turkish constitution of 1876, and of the pianist Paderewski and the philosopher Masaryk who became presidents of Poland and Czechoslovakia in 1918, furnish vivid illustrations. For some of these awakening nations, notably Poland and Hungary, memories of political independence provided a source of inspiration.

Still, when it came to translating the romantic yearnings of poets, writers, and artists into practical policies of state formation, rival factions often fought for sharply divergent territorial solutions. In the nineteenth century partisans of Prussia's "Little Germany" clashed with advocates of a "Greater Germany" including Austria, and with bitter-end supporters of the existing principalities in "duodecimo size." In the Muslim parts of the Ottoman Empire, the principle of linguistic nationality was slow to win out over dynastic and religious loyalties. In the Balkan, Danubian, and Baltic areas, border conflicts after World Wars I and II, plebiscites, precarious minority guarantees, and tenuous federal experiments all testified to the difficulty of defining nationality by language alone without the added cement of political tradition.

COUNTRIES OF OVERSEAS IMMIGRATION

An important variant of the Western European pattern occurs in countries that began as overseas colonies of European powers and were subsequently populated by immigrant settlers—the United States, Australia, New Zealand, Argentina, Brazil, and (with some additional variations on the common theme) Canada and Israel. Here, too, linguistic identity grew up later within boundaries politically drawn—in this case by colonial conquest. In most of these countries, the small indigenous population died out or severely diminished during the colonial period; the earliest settlers imposed their language and culture; and successive waves of immigrants were assimilated, even though a majority of them might come from other countries.[30]

Canada, large portions of which changed hands between France and Great Britain in the colonial period, faces in Quebec a problem of linguistic conflict not unlike that between Flemings and Walloons in Belgium; but in its Western provinces, the process of assimilation to English has proceeded with the same dynamic force as in the United States.

In Israel, the dominant social and cultural structure was created during the Palestine mandate period by Zionist immigrants from Eastern Europe who decided to revive Hebrew as a unifying national language. To this Hebrew-speaking culture, successive waves of Jewish immigrants from Europe and the Middle East have been rapidly assimilated after independence. The resident Arab majority of the Israeli parts of Palestine fled or were expelled in the war of 1948. Today less than 10 percent of the population form an unassimilable Arab-Muslim and Arab-Christian minority. "Assimilation in language or culture," Deutsch has pointed out, "involves the learning of many new habits, and the unlearning of many old ones—habits, in both cases, which often interlock and reinforce each other. Such learning as a rule is slow; its changes are counted in decades and generations."[31] In immigrant countries, one might add, the new settlers who flee

---

[30] In the United States, immigrants from Great Britain and Ireland have constituted only 20.7 percent of the total since 1820; in Argentina, Italian immigrants over the last century have vastly outnumbered those of Spanish descent.

[31] *Nationalism and Social Communication,* p. 99.

from oppression and come in search of new opportunity can compress this rehabituation into a few years or at most a single generation.[32]

POSTCOLONIAL STATES

In most of Asia, Africa, and Latin America, language has been a negligible criterion in state formation. As observed in an earlier context, Spanish-speaking America and the Arabic-speaking Middle East have each been divided into well over a dozen separate territories. In Tropical Africa, some of the few medium-sized language groups, such as Hausas and Mandingos, have been split among as many as four or five countries; and everywhere a multitude of diminutive groups have been thrown together.

The colonial experience in the vast majority of instances determined the geographic identity of the successor states. Colonial conquest drew the lines among French, British, and other imperial zones. Later, during the period of colonial devolution, the imperial rulers had an even more decisive influence in delimiting the territories on which they conferred self-government and eventually independence. Only in a few cases did the imperial government prove unable to enforce schemes of federation or resist demands for partition. Thus, in contrast to East-Central Europe, political rather than linguistic factors were paramount; yet in contrast to Western Europe, the earlier political structures were erected by alien rather than indigenous rulers.

The British in the 1930's separated Burma from India and in 1947 yielded to demands for partition between Muslim and Hindu areas. Yet they did not give effective support to any separatist claims by the Indian princely states, and they managed to construct a federal government for Nigeria. The boundaries among Arab countries, except in Palestine, still follow the lines of imperial partition of the Ottoman Empire between 1830 and 1920. In Spanish America, a large colonial empire was fragment-

[32] On countries of overseas immigration, see the suggestive discussion by Louis Hartz et al., *The Founding of New Societies* (Harcourt, 1965).

ed as a result mainly of the decentralization of the independence movement. Nevertheless most of the boundaries that emerged in the early nineteenth century coincided with those of the presidencies, audiencies, and captaincies of the colonial period.

In Africa, France in 1958 was eager to keep its colonies within a French overseas community. Hence it conferred separate autonomy on the twelve territories of French West and Equatorial Africa as well as the adjoining trusteeships of Togo and Cameroun. The French government had little choice but to confirm that decision when, in an abrupt reversal, it gave them complete independence in 1960.[33] The administrative cadres left behind by the French and other rulers in Africa were in any case diminutive; and the Réassemblement Démocratique Africain, which once had extended throughout French West Africa, quickly broke apart into separate territorial parties.

In the Congo, the departing Belgians bequeathed a precarious unity to the succeeding regime, though some of them subsequently supported the abortive secession movement in Katanga under Moise Tshombe. In their neighboring trust territory, they conferred separate independence on Rwanda and Burundi—although the separation of hostile ethnic groups was by no means clear enough to prevent a major wave of post-independence genocide.

The experience of Latin America since the early nineteenth century, of the Arab countries since the two world wars, and of Tropical Africa more recently all suggest that territorial identities established in the generation after independence tend to endure into an indefinite future. Any boundary, no matter how arbitrarily drawn, tends to engender its own vested interests that henceforth perpetuate it. An extreme case is Transjordan, a barren desert which the British in 1922 carved out of the Palestine mandate to offer it as a consolation prize to Sharif Abdullah, who in turn promised to abandon his plans of restoring Sharifian rule in Syria. A generation later, Abdullah's grandson Hussein and a small

---

[33] Cf. Michael Crowder, "Colonial Rule in West Africa—Factor for Division or Unity," *Civilisations*, Vol. 14, No. 3 (1964), pp. 167-78.

group of military and civilian officials were fighting against great odds, but so far with remarkable success, to preserve the separate identity of a slightly enlarged Jordanian kingdom.

On the mainland of Spanish America, there have been a number of long-standing border disputes; but the total number of states has remained the same since the breakup of the federations of Gran Colombia in 1829 and of Central America in 1839—except for various attempts to revive the latter between 1842 and 1898 and for the secession of Panama from Colombia enforced by the United States in 1903.

In the more recently emancipated areas, hopes for political integration of areas administered separately in colonial and mandate days have almost everywhere been disappointed. The federal structure of Nigeria was worked out before independence and in any case embraces a region that had already been jointly administered in the imperial days; it was severely strained by the coups of 1966. Elsewhere, only the smallest of the Asian and African colonial or mandate territories have been joined to their larger neighbors: Spanish to French Morocco; British Togoland to Ghana; British to Italian Somalia; the Northern and Southern British Cameroons to Nigeria and Cameroun respectively; Goa to India; Dutch New Guinea to Indonesia; the British territories on Borneo to Malaysia; and Zanzibar to Tanganyika.

The many attempts to merge or federate larger, more populous, or more distant countries have uniformly ended in failure—whether in British West India, in West Africa (the short-lived and largely nominal Mali-Senegal and Ghana-Guinea-Mali schemes), in the Rhodesias and Nyasaland, between Malaya and Singapore, or among the various Arab countries (where the Egyptian-Syrian United Arab Republic of 1958 broke up by 1961). In East Africa, too, economic cooperation among Kenya, Tanganyika, and Uganda rapidly disintegrated after independence. Only in Central America —after more than a century of separate independence—have concrete steps been taken toward a functional-economic integration that may pave the way for further steps to unity in the future.

In Tropical Africa or elsewhere, it obviously is not any love of the former colonial rulers that has perpetuated the boundaries drawn by them. Rather, in regions poor in political tradition, these boundaries represent what little tradition there is. Federation or integration of independent states has proved difficult in the absence of Deutsch's "core areas"—where administrative capabilities exceed political loads: in most postcolonial states, the loads rather than the capabilities have seemed excessive. Revision of boundaries on plebiscitary principles would open Pandora's box. To quote Immanuel Wallerstein, "every African nation . . . has its Katanga. Once the logic of secession is admitted, there is no end except in anarchy."[34] It seems safe to predict that boundaries that have become fixed in the generation after independence will be difficult or impossible to remove by political negotiation or agreement alone.

The ideal of national self-government, it was suggested at the outset of this chapter, poses the question of the national self and the question of government. The exploration of the first question has taken us some distance into the second. The following chapter will continue this discussion of authority.

Meanwhile, it may be noted that identity can be understood not only in the strict and somewhat formal sense implied throughout this discussion, but also in a broader sense that is partly political and partly cultural and psychological.[35] The main concern here has been with the criteria of membership in a modern nation. But even after it is known who is a member of the nation, the more diffuse question persists: what does it mean to be a German, a Turk, a Burmese, a Mexican, a Ghanaian, or an American? A nation is a community of purpose; it can preserve its iden-

[34] *Africa: The Politics of Independence* (Random House, 1961), p. 88.
[35] This is the meaning of "identity" in Erik H. Erikson, *Young Man Luther: A Study in Psychoanalysis and History* (Norton, 1958), and in the subtitle of Lucian W. Pye's book, *Politics, Personality, and Nation Building: Burma's Search for Identity* (Yale University Press, 1962).

tity of membership only if the joint purposes of the nationals are periodically redefined, if Renan's plebiscite is held, as it were, every day. While the more purely psychological aspects are beyond the scope of this study, later chapters will touch on related themes, including the blending of tradition and modernity in a modernizing nation's policies, and the circumstances in which a leader's individual qualities become identified with the collective purposes of an entire nation.

CHAPTER THREE

AUTHORITY AND EQUALITY

The greater the difficulties, the greater the need for government.
DE GAULLE

Organization is the weapon of the weak in their struggle with the strong.
MICHELS

AUTHORITY IS OF THE ESSENCE of all government. One of the most striking political features of modernization is the immense broadening of the scope of public functions undertaken by governmental authority. Traditional rulers were wont to invoke heavenly sanction for their claims of omnipotence. Yet their earthly authority, their ability to influence or control the daily lives of their subjects, was narrowly circumscribed. Villages and tribes, subsisting on primitive forms of agriculture or animal husbandry, could get along with a modicum of public authority defined by unquestioned custom and age-old ritual. Traditional empires, whether dynastic or colonial, often were nothing but networks of military organization cast loosely over vast congeries of such self-contained agrarian communities. Hence the emperors needed only to institute a system of military recruitment and requisition for the imperial service and to forestall the emergence of local armies that might challenge the imperial peace. Their recruiting agents and tax collectors provided at best tenuous and intermittent links between the common people throughout the country and central authority in the distant capital.

The Growing Scope of Public Functions

In the modern nation-state, both the need and the potential for authority rise sharply as modernity tightens social organization and economic interdependence, and as an awakening sense of nationality launches the popular masses on the political stage. The expansion of governmental power ever since the period of so-called "absolutism" in Europe may be illustrated by the example of land taxes. According to a leading historiographer of the period: "In France in the eighteenth century, as in the United States today, assessments tended to become frozen or stereotyped, the difference being that the mighty Bourbon monarchy lacked the flexibility in raising the rate that the smallest American municipality enjoys."[1]

In the early modernizing countries of Europe, a distinct sequence of the growth of authority may be discerned. Throughout the Middle Ages, warfare was the most prominent function of government. The feudal system linked this function into a continuous chain of mutual obligation whereby each vassal provided military service and goods in kind in return for the military protection afforded by his lord. As barter gave way to monetary exchange, the rulers began to collect taxes to keep up their courts and to hire troops of mercenaries. During the era of absolutism, the king's retainers, joined by nobles turned courtiers, grew into an elaborate bureaucracy for the maintenance of internal law and order. Mercantilism added the regulation of trade and the stimulation of production to the functions of the state. During the nineteenth century, governmental activity came to embrace universal education, conscription, and the construction of public works. In the twentieth century, economic planning, social welfare, and propaganda have been added to the list.

The manner in which these various functions are performed

[1] Robert Roswell Palmer, *The Age of the Democratic Revolution*, 2 vols. (Princeton University Press, 1959-64), Vol. 1, p. 90.

differs sharply in democratic and totalitarian states, but their total scope varies much less. Although communist governments claim ownership, in the name of the people, of most of the economy, their planning mechanisms seem clumsy when compared with the more accurate instruments of regulation of private enterprise in liberal-democratic countries. With respect to the plenitude of functions undertaken by public authority, there is today less difference between the United States and the Soviet Union than between either of them and Yemen, or Afganistan, or Paraguay: the true dividing line runs not between East and West but between North and South.

Yet it is the "advanced" countries, democratic or totalitarian, that are setting the standards to which leaders in newly modernizing countries aspire. The result is a widespread confusion in the organic sequence of public functions as they evolved in Europe. Time was when a flag, a newly composed anthem, and a fresh issue of postage stamps fully symbolized a country's certified independence. But today's founding fathers are inspired by loftier visions: a capital city with glittering boulevards and towering hotels, hydroelectric dams and steel mills, an international airline, a university or two, a nuclear reactor—and frequent "summit meetings" to show off these accoutrements to the envious leaders of less fortunate "new nations."

Governments feel impelled to proclaim ambitious schemes of economic planning and social welfare before they have ensured an orderly flow of tax revenues, instituted effective systems of judicature, or tabulated a reliable census. Everywhere governments pour forth vociferous streams of domestic and foreign propaganda before they have opened schools for a majority of the country's children. Indeed, radio and television can be relied upon to inculcate the rulers' message in the illiterate masses.

LIMITED AUTHORITY IN UNDERDEVELOPED COUNTRIES

Despite such efforts and ambitions, a low degree of governmental authority remains one of the prime characteristics of the so-called underdeveloped countries. The symptoms are manifold and ubiquitous. In Bolivia, tin miners, resentful of the government's attempts to reduce employment in the state mines, take a foreign diplomat hostage. Kenyan officials discover a quantity of Chinese arms shipped from Tanzania to Uganda not when it first crosses into Kenya but when it is about to leave again. University students in Dacca, the capital of East Pakistan, spend more days in political strikes and demonstrations than at their studies. In Peru and Colombia, peasant squatters appropriate land on large estates while oligarchic legislatures are deadlocked in futile oratory about land reform.

In few countries of Asia, Africa, and Latin America are universal schooling and conscription enforced more than sporadically. Public revenues derive primarily from customs and excises (or, in a few fortunate countries, from mineral revenues shared with foreign companies) rather than from income taxes. Control of inflation proves impossible even in countries with lavish natural resources such as Brazil or Indonesia. It is a rare government that can fully cope with the supposedly minimal functions of the nineteenth century "night watchman state" in Europe: law and order, security of travel, enforcement of private contracts, and collection of customs at the frontiers. And the line that separates public remuneration from private enrichment is thoroughly blurred.

It is difficult to apply exact measures to the scope of governmental authority. The most pertinent figures are those for government revenues in proportion to national product and of government employment in proportion to population. Such data are available for many industrial countries and for a few of the nonindustrial countries of Asia, Africa, and Latin America. Their comparability and accuracy are doubtful, since they are based on widely differing methods of public accounting and on estimates of production or even of population that are often quite tenuous. Also, there are no such figures for the communist countries.

Still, the contrast revealed by the available figures is so great as to exceed the combined sources of error. In nearly all the noncommunist industrial countries, public revenues amount to between 22 and 51 percent of the gross national product whereas the governments employ from 6 to 13 percent of the potential labor force. The United States is at the lower end of both these ranges. In the nonindustrial countries, on the other hand, the governments collect in revenues only between 7 and 37 percent of the gross product (with a clustering in the 11 to 20 percent range) and employ only from 1 to 9 percent of the working-age population. It may be assumed, moreover, that countries for which no data are available rank in the lower part of this twofold spectrum.[2]

The pressures for wider authority include the desire of newly mobilized masses for economic improvement and expanded education and the search by governments with a precarious base of internal support for stronger administrative systems. To some extent, these pressures are stimulated and accommodated from the outside through programs of economic and technical aid. Of the three requisites of political modernization, new and would-be nations are generally left to struggle as best they can in their quests for identity and for participation, whereas the growth of authority receives ample encouragement from the outside.

STIMULI TO THE GROWTH OF AUTHORITY

The internal structures of political authority in countries outside of Europe are predominantly a legacy of colonial rule, or of a pe-

[2] Appendix Table 4 lists the detailed figures that support these generalizations. It will be noted that some of the highest revenues in preindustrial countries derive from petroleum or other minerals—for example, Iraq, Venezuela, and the Congo.

For Great Britain the historic growth of government expenditure has been studied in some detail. War and peace, not surprisingly, prove to be the major variable, but the overall trend is upward. The pattern is "two steps forward, one step back." During the French Revolutionary wars, the government spent from 11 to 29 percent of the Gross National Product; during the next century (1815-1914) only from 9 to 19 percent. New peaks were reached in 1918 (52 percent) and 1943 (74 percent); but in each case the postwar lows (24 percent in 1929 and 37 percent in 1955) were higher than any year of the previous period of peace. See Alan T. Peacock and Jack Wiseman, *The Growth of Public Expenditure in the United Kingdom*, National Bureau of Economic Research, General Series, No. 72 (Princeton University Press, 1961), pp. 37, 165f.

riod of autocratic-defensive modernization. Yet the specific content of this legacy varies from country to country. Some areas were populated by immigrants who had taken part in the earlier European evolution and proceeded to replicate it, with some variations, overseas—as in the United States, Canada, Australia, and Israel.

In the North American colonies, although some of the early settlers had been eager to escape certain forms of governmental authority, they brought with them a complete system of common law. They rebelled against the arbitrary regimen of bishops and presbyteries, but submitted willingly to the sterner commands of the congregation. While the open frontier encouraged individual initiative in the struggle against nature, it also brought forth new demands for public services—at an earlier period for protection from Indian raids or cattle thieves, and later for land grants to homesteaders, to railroads, and to public institutions of higher education. Government-sponsored programs of social welfare in Australia and New Zealand developed earlier, and in Israel more comprehensively, than in almost any European country.

A second group of countries outside of Europe—Japan, Russia, and Turkey—were the fortunate heirs of ancient and elaborate administrative services that could be adapted to the performance of modern functions. A third group experienced alien colonial government for a long enough period to develop an indigenous administrative machinery that could effectively serve the postcolonial successor state. India here provides the outstanding example; significantly the principle of civil service recruitment by examination was first applied in British India in 1854 and transferred to the British Isles only in 1870.

To most countries of Asia, Africa, and Latin America, however, political modernization came late and by way of imitation of more advanced countries or of defensive reactions against their aggressive designs. Colonial rule in many countries lasted long enough to disrupt traditional patterns of authority but too briefly to erect any equivalent new structures. Such ambiguous practices as "indirect rule" in British Africa and mandate government in the Arab Fertile Crescent further weakened authority by blurring the lines of ultimate responsibility.

The development of military establishments outside of Europe was as uneven as that of civilian administration. Japan and Turkey inherited large fighting forces from their imperial past, and one of the first concrete steps toward modernization was the replacement of the traditional Samurai class or Janissary corps with forces trained according to the latest European principles. A few of the former colonies—notably British India and French Senegal were used as manpower reservoirs for overseas wars of the imperial power. In a few other colonies or mandates—Palestine, Algeria, Cyprus, Indonesia—independence was won as a result of extensive military or guerrilla operations. In both these types of former colonies, the newly independent regimes started out with military cadres of some size and complexity. In Latin America, where the creole military forces led the fight for independence in the early nineteenth century, these became quickly fragmented into private armies of local caudillos, and it was only in the late nineteenth and early twentieth centuries that countries such as Chile, Argentina, and Brazil established modern professional forces.

In most Asian and African colonies, however, the technological disparity between foreign rulers and indigenous population had been so great as to require only a minimum of imperial military force for the initial conquest and for the later maintenance of order. Even in India in the nineteenth century, the British Empire as a rule kept fewer troops than it did in Ireland. Most of the Asian and African colonies, too, gained their independence by negotiation and as a result, ultimately, of the weariness of the former colonial rulers. Hence most new states of the mid-twentieth century have begun their careers with military forces even less adequate for the support of authority than were their administrative and educational systems.

The breakup of colonial or dynastic empires often led to an unequal division of the instruments of authority, and the result has been a marked difference among neighboring states in respect to their later political evolution. Turkish and Arab nationalism, for example, emerged in the second decade of this century; but the Turkish sense of nationality has been more secure—partly because it preserved a direct link with six centuries of Ottoman political tradition. The difference was most vivid at the time of the breakup of the Ottoman Empire after 1918, when 85 percent of its trained civil servants and 93 percent of its military staff officers continued service in Turkey and only the remaining small fractions in the Arab successor states.[3] Whereas the Turkish Republic of 1923 was founded by Ottoman generals and colonels, the nationalist Syrian and Iraqi regimes of 1920-21 were installed by Ottoman captains and lieutenants. Because of the ethnic-religious division of labor that had come to prevail in India under Mughal and British rule, the partition of 1947 resulted in the transfer of most indigenous military officers to Pakistan and of most higher civil servants to India. Generally, it may be said that the degree of political integration in postcolonial states has been roughly proportionate to the number of indigenous administrators, military officers, and politicians trained under the colonial regime.

The Demand for Political Equality
and Participation

The quest for equality and participation differs from the quests for the two other ingredients of modern nation-statehood. The growth of authority, once well launched, can advance almost indefinitely: the modern leviathan often seems to feed on its own sprawling powers. The search for national identity comes to rest at its goal: once the citizens have drawn the boundaries that define membership in the nation, they expect them not to shift again in generations to come. Only a new secular development, such as the loss of world power by the nations of Europe, can reopen the issue of identity on a different scale, as in the current

[3] Cf. Robert E. Ward and D. A. Rustow, eds., *Political Modernization in Japan and Turkey* (Princeton University Press, 1964), p. 388.

movement of colonial independence and toward European unification.

The development of equality is impelled by no such automatic momentum and drawn to no such stable destination. Equality is the most widely proclaimed political ideal of the modern age; but it is the one most imperfectly achieved. Modern life creates strong pressures for equalization along with pressures of organization just as strong that threaten and thwart equality. The ever-present gap between aspiration and reality causes uneasiness and sharpens polemics. Any attempt to assess the degree of political equality in a given society is hazardous, any comparison among different societies becomes invidious. Amid the egalitarian pressures and the organizational counterpressures, the quest for equality and participation turns into a precarious and never-ending contest. Amid the swirls of prejudiced argument, its assessment remains a matter of intense controversy.

Even the most modern countries have not attained the egalitarian ideal, and in some of the late-modernizing countries egalitarianism has hardly got launched to any kind of start.[4] Nor is it merely a matter of modern pressures for equality battering away at the traditional hierarchy. Modernity itself engenders important counterpressures against equality that like modern egalitarianism have their origins in the large-scale human division of labor for control of the environment. The social situation in every contemporary society thus reflects to varying degrees the modern pressure for equality, the traditional pressure for inequality, and the modern pressure for inequality. Although these three are blended in reality, they may be distinguished in theoretical analysis.

PRESSURES AND COUNTERPRESSURES

The egalitarian pressures of modernity are closely related to the empiricism of modern thought and the pragmatism of modern ac-

[4] Cf. David E. Apter, *The Politics of Modernization* (University of California Press, 1965), p. 133.

tion. As men take part in an ever more intensive pattern of orderly interaction, they tend to be judged not by their antecedents but by their ability and performance. Modern transport and communication introduce new habits and ideas; modern industry pours forth a flood of new goods and sucks in a growing stream of workers; modern government extends its control into every home and working place and responds to a myriad of demands from articulate individuals and groups. Modernity in these and other ways spreads to the traditional localities of a country and to the traditional countries of all continents, threatening ancient status and privilege.

The nation, which exacts the same loyalty from all citizens, considers all as equals. Each of the prevalent political ideologies of the modern age—liberalism, nationalism, democracy, socialism, communism—proceeds from a similar egalitarian premise. Even dictators and totalitarian parties honor this premise by staging ceremonial plebiscites and mock elections. The modern revolution is a revolution of mobility and interaction, of participation, and of equality.

The counterpressures are just as powerful. While modern science and philosophy supply no overt justification for human inequality, there is an endless variety of rationalizations and subterfuges that will suggest themselves to the traditional holders of privilege. Wealth can be converted into power and power into wealth, so that each upholds and perpetuates the other. The growth of government and of social organization confronts the individual with a force more solid and more irresistible than that of tradition and custom. Manipulation, apathy, and frustration are among the great enemies of universal participation and of effective equality in modern public life.

In the early phases of modernization, the pressures of equality assault the positions of privilege embedded in tradition. This early progress of political and social equality is well-known from the history of Europe in the eighteenth and nineteenth centuries and of Asia, Africa, and Latin America in the twentieth. A composite, generalized picture may therefore be attempted.

All larger pre-modern societies are based on an uneven distribution of political power, of economic wealth, and of social status. Political consciousness and participation are limited to a small social stratum. The central factor may be the monopoly of land ownership in the hands of a small upper class, the control of government by a hereditary caste of conquering warriors, or the privileged position of colonial administrators from overseas.

Modernization challenges these various forms of inequality in different ways. Because of the expansion of governmental functions, larger numbers of people must be recruited into the public service. Universal military training brings conscripts from the diverse parts of the country into close contact and opens for them visions beyond their village horizons. Universal education enhances the aspirations of the school graduates. The government's greater need for funds and the consequent spread of taxation suggests the possibility of fiscal policy as an instrument of distributive justice. Intensified contact with foreign countries spreads knowledge among the lower classes of the more egalitarian ways of advanced societies. Industrialization creates a demand for skilled workers and enhances the power, through collective bargaining or strikes, of those who possess rare skills.

All these developments create opportunities for an equalization of power. Within this setting, the initiative for changes toward greater political equality and more widespread participation come from within the society (more specifically, from the ruling class itself or from the lower classes) or from outside. The initiative may be taken by the ruling class in a variety of ways.

UPPER-CLASS INITIATIVES

First, the ruling class is rarely completely homogeneous. It may be tightly organized with a single apex, a monarchy ruling with the help of an aristocratic class. The aristocracy rarely will be a blind, pliant instrument in the monarch's hand. It has some political interests of its own. If the status of the aristocracy is fairly close to that of the monarch, some of its upper members may be his rivals for top power. If the gap between monarch and aristocracy is wide, the aristocracy will be closer to the lower classes, and may make common cause with them. In either situation, the monarch may attempt to strengthen his position by an alliance with aspiring elements in the lower aristocracy or among the commoners.

If there is no single monarchical apex, political power is shared by an oligarchic class. The social pyramid is flat rather than pointed at the top. In that situation, there are sure to be dissensions and rivalries within the oligarchy, and these will in various ways benefit the lower classes. The mere fact of competition within the upper class is likely to loosen its grip on the lower. Furthermore, the weaker of two factions in the oligarchy may be actively seeking support among lower class elements, thus further loosening the structure.

Second, the upper class may be committed to certain egalitarian tenets of ideology. Religious doctrines of universal brotherhood undermine rigid divisions between ruler and ruled—whether between whites and Negroes in the South of the United States or between colonial administrators and their subjects in Asia and Africa. Missionary efforts by nationals of the colonial power may accelerate this development. The legal fiction of universal suffrage —no matter how much hollowed out by property or literacy qualifications, by an organizational monopoly of a government party, or by apathy or intimidation of lower-class voters—creates a standard of aspiration, a rationale for lower-class protests that insist on taking seriously the legal proclamation of universality. The ideology of colonial rulers may undergo subtle but profound changes due to factors outside the colonial system. As a result, the conquerors who once sallied forth for God, mammon, and Good Queen Bess may succumb to wistful Victorian thoughts about "the white man's burden."

The transformation of a strongly hierarchical into a thoroughly egalitarian society is likely to be a long, tortuous process of decades or centuries. In England, the first serious challenge to the oligarchic order came from the Levellers of the 1640's; yet it was not until the Chartists and the Birmingham Caucus in the nineteenth century that political mass organizations prepared the way for a thoroughly egalitarian political system with full participation of all social groups; and not until 1918 that such a system was fully achieved.

A long-range historical transformation, moreover, is likely to include many false starts and partial reversals. The advent to power of any new social class is likely to lead to an at least temporary deterioration of political manners, a release of crude and ruthless appetites. Yet, in the successful cases, the broad evolutionary process continues. Any newly established ruling class is likely to retain from its opposition days certain egalitarian and universalistic convictions which provide a ready-made ideological weapon in the upward struggle of the next social stratum. Even the false starts thus may contribute to a fuller success next time.

Third, the task of ruling may become too complex to remain a monopoly of the upper class. Colonial penetration, because of the enormous differences in technology between the conquering and subject societies, required little manpower. But administration of the conquered territory required a new and changing *modus vivendi* between colonial invaders and subjects, such as indirect rule through tribal chiefs, establishment of an indigenous civil service, and inauguration of a modern system of education.

Outside of colonial situations, increasing specialization may create distinct, and potentially competitive, interests (for example, bureaucracies and armies) in a once homogeneous upper class. The spread of education seems a particularly effective means by which earlier class divisions can be eroded. A history curriculum including the egalitarian slogans of the North American, French, or Spanish-American revolutions will sooner or later encourage challenges to established systems of colonial rule or of tight indigenous oligarchy. The re-education programs in occupied Germany and Japan presented a different version of this combination of foreign rule and education of the subject population. Here the egalitarian impact of the schooling was intended by the rulers; but its effectiveness was somewhat weakened by the knowledge on both sides that occupation would be temporary.

Finally, an existing balance may be changed by attempts of the upper class to enlarge its power or wealth at the expense of the lower class. Thus R. R. Palmer has argued that the "democratic revolution" of the late eighteenth century came in response to a threatening "aristocratic resurgence."[5]

None of these forms of change initiated by the upper class will produce important or lasting results unless there is a reinforcing response from among the lower classes.

LOWER-CLASS INITIATIVES

Just as increasing complexity and specialization of social organization or economic activity are likely to bring about conflicts of interests in the upper class, they are likely to put some lower-class elements in a position to challenge the power monopoly of the rulers. For example, industrialization calls forth trade unions which possess a political drive and purposefulness that the peasantry lacks. The political rise of elements of the lower classes is likely, then, to be the result of gradual economic and social developments. A sudden, revolutionary explosion is likely to occur when such a gradual rise has been temporarily checked or challenged.

Before political control shifts from the old upper class to a rising lower class, a number of accommodating changes are likely to occur within the upper class. Tory reformers, becoming convinced that maintenance of the status quo is hopeless, will advocate partial or gradual reform to prevent total and sudden upheaval. Individual dissidents from the upper class will join the rising elements of the lower classes, where their greater education and experience is likely to secure them prominent positions of

[5] See Palmer, *op. cit.*, Vol. 1, p. 22 and *passim.*

leadership. Numerous examples from the history of the democratic and socialist movements in Europe and of the anticolonialist movement in Asia can be cited. Among the most eloquent advocates of the interests of the Third Estate in 1789 were individual members of the other two like Sieyès and Condorcet. The most effective protagonists of the socialist movement were members of the middle or upper-middle class—Marx, Engels, Kautsky, Branting, Shaw, Kropotkin, Lenin—compared to whom early socialists of working class origin—Proudhon, Weitling, August Palm—remained insignificant. Robert Michels, with his slightly bombastic tendency, saw in such examples a "historical law that class movements are led by members of the classes against which they are aimed . . . the bourgeoisie becomes the fencing master of the proletariat. . . . "[6]

But non-Western nationalism and Western agrarian movements illustrate the same connection. In the early history of the Indian National Congress, Motilal Nehru, a high-class Brahmin, and Annie Besant, a dissident Englishwoman, played prominent roles. The "Sinhalese Only" election campaign in Ceylon in 1956, which swept the Buddhist farmers of the backlands into power positions once held by rich coastal planters, was led by Solomon W.R.D. Bandaranaike, himself a wealthy planter who had been brought up in the English language and the Christian faith and had adopted Sinhalese and Buddhism only after he returned from his studies at Oxford.[7] In Sweden, the Ruralist party of 1867, the first effective champion of peasant power, was led by Count Arvid Posse, an aristocrat disgruntled by the replacement of the traditional estates with an elected parliament. A generation later, the combination of universal suffrage and proportional representation that won out in 1907 was first proposed by Swedish upper-class conservatives, notably Bishop Gottfrid Billing, who were eager to institute "guarantees" that would "forestall or mitigate the dangers of an extension" of the franchise.[8] Effective reform thus is likely to come about through the interaction of aspiring lower-class groups with dissident or reform-minded members of the upper class.

INFLUENCE OF OTHER SOCIETIES

The processes of internal change are complicated—but also generally accelerated—through contacts with other societies. The most extreme forms of such contact, that is, colonial conquest and temporary occupation, have already been mentioned. Warfare, whether or not it results in conquest, has always been one of the effective stimuli for social change. Lenin called war the midwife of revolution, and Bertrand de Jouvenel has cited an impressive array of evidence from European history that prolonged warfare, through conscription and taxation, has both increased the scope of government and promoted the rise of lower classes.[9] The parliaments called by medieval kings of England to help finance their wars in France and the Prussian reforms after the disastrous defeat of 1806-07 are classic examples.[10]

Hardpressed belligerent governments try to enhance their support by promising better treatment to their own subjects and, in case of victory, to those of the enemy. The two world wars thus were a major factor in promoting political equality in the Western countries and greater independence for their colonies.

Universal suffrage won its final victories in Europe and North America after 1918—often on the plea that men who had served in the forces and women who had worked in munitions factories could no longer be denied a voice in the affairs of government.

[8] Dankwart A. Rustow, *The Politics of Compromise* (Princeton University Press, 1955), pp. 28, 59 (quote from Billing). In 1902, another Tory reformer warned, "If we wish to get universal suffrage with guarantees, we must get it now. If we tarry, make no mistake about it, we shall assuredly get it without guarantees." (*Ibid.*, p. 64.)

[9] Bertrand de Jouvenel, *On Power* (Viking, 1949), especially Chap. 8.

[10] The programs of "defensive modernization" in Russia, Turkey, Egypt, and Japan will be discussed in more detail in the next chapter.

The reliance that Great Britain placed in 1914-18 on support from the settlers' colonies led to the formation of an Imperial War Cabinet and at length to the recognition of dominion status in 1931.[11] Both the Bolshevik propaganda of self-determination and Wilson's Fourteen Points represented the psychological aspect of the final desperate efforts of the great war.

In World War II, the precarious British and French situation prompted such measures as the de Gaulle-Lyttleton promise of postwar independence for Syria and Lebanon (1941), Eden's Mansion House speech offering British support for Arab unity (1941), the Cripps mission to negotiate postwar independence for India (1942), and de Gaulle's Brazzaville declaration (1944) regarding a future French overseas community.

The foreign impact may take subtler and less direct forms than foreign military threats. There may be growing commercial contact. Migration may have important social consequences both for the country of emigration and the country of immigration. In a world of intensified communications, the awareness among the lower classes of a good life and greater social equality abroad will be enhanced. Formal enactments such as the Universal Declaration of Human Rights and the charter of the International Labor Organization reinforce this trend. The same factors may contribute to a sense of futility, of the inevitability of retreat among the upper class. Thus, the French defeat in Indochina in 1954 had progressive repercussions, intensifying demands for independence, and inclinations toward colonial withdrawal, in French North Africa, then in West and Equatorial Africa, and at last in the Belgian Congo. In today's interdependent world, one of the greatest powers in world politics is the power of example.

The foregoing discussion of stimuli and patterns in the quest

[11] In 1917, the Canadian Prime Minister, Sir Robert Borden, trenchantly informed his diplomatic representative in London that "it can hardly be expected that we shall put 400,000 or 500,000 men in the field and willingly accept the position of having no more voice and receiving no more consideration than if we were toy automata." Quoted by Alexander Brady, *Democracy in the Dominions*, 2d ed. (University of Toronto Press, 1952), p. 107.

for equality and participation may be summed up in a single more general formula. Political control by a narrow social group may be widened either (1) because of ideological commitments of the rulers, (2) through competition within the ruling group, or (3) through domestic or foreign pressures on that ruling group. Ideology will be of special importance where the ruling group has come to power recently and retains some of the universalist appeals of its earlier opposition days. In a competitive situation, the weaker contestant (and in one of mounting burdens the ruling group as a whole) is likely to seek reinforcements from among the lower classes. The increases in burdens may come about through defeat, threats, or pressure from abroad. Growing complexity of social and economic structure, including pressure from rising elements of the lower classes, may also constitute such an increased burden; it also may lead to divisions and competition within a formerly unified ruling class. Although the various stimuli to reform can be distinguished in theory, several or all of them are likely to converge in empirical situations.

NEW FORMS OF PRIVILEGE

Along with mounting pressure for greater equality and participation, the growing complexity of modern life affords many opportunities for the growth of new forms of privilege, discrimination, and manipulation. The rationalizations by which minority power can be justified in an egalitarian era have already been mentioned. Lack of ability is charged against those who were given no opportunity to develop it. In nineteenth century England, welfare legislation was rejected on the grounds that the poor were indolent and likely to spend any extra pay on drink and on raising more children. Liberal and socialist theory—Malthus' population hypothesis and Lassalle's "iron law of wages"—concurred that material gains for the workers within the existing economic order were illusory.

In Latin American countries in recent years, the seemingly reasonable requirement of literacy for the franchise has given oligarchic legislatures a powerful motive to perpetuate their power by halting the spread of education. The needs of economic development, phrased in a variety of homely metaphors, are adduced against egalitarian land reform and progressive taxes: the best way to spread wealth is to make it trickle from the top; the economic pie must be enlarged before it is sliced; and the goose that lays the golden egg must not be killed. Advocates of white supremacy in South Africa have asserted that Negroes are happier when kept apart and in the American South that crowded schools and dingy public rooms are "separate but equal."

The mere passage of time, too, may convert equality into privilege and discrimination. The depopulation of American farms since the early days of the republic has created a pattern of rural overrepresentation comparable to the "rotten boroughs" of England before 1832—a trend only recently halted by the Supreme Court. The influx of rural masses to the cities strains urban housing, transport, and utilities and creates the festering misery of shantytowns and slums. Tax assessments throughout the world rarely keep pace with rising real estate values and falling currencies, so landowners time and again escape their allotted share.

Conversely, taxes may be levied on land alone, giving a de facto exemption to intangible wealth. The infant industry argument for tariff protection is overworked by businesses that may in fact be suffering the decrepitude of old age. The needs of defense are invoked to restrict the peacetime import of watches and petroleum. Farmers, once rescued by the public treasury from the ruinous effect of a world depression, develop subsidies and price supports into a fine art of exploitation of the taxpayer and consumer. In a free-enterprise system, economic privilege has a constant tendency to entrench itself; for the rich can afford a better upbringing for their children, can offer better rewards for skilled lawyers and propagandists, and can maintain far closer relations with the rulers of a country. In a government-managed economy, the rulers are under constant temptation to secure additional perquisites for themselves and their associates. Social position and wealth tend to grow imperceptibly, whereas egalitarian laws must be deliberately framed; hence the holders of privilege have the force of inertia on their side. Unequal apportionment is particularly difficult to remedy by legislation since the new scheme of representation would have to be voted by the beneficiaries of the old.

Subterfuge and inertia, nonetheless, are on balance among the minor obstacles to political equality and participation. The most formidable ones are inherent in the nature of complex, large-scale organization whether in government or in nongovernmental associations. Scientific specialization, it has been remarked, causes each scientist to know more and more about less and less. Similarly, modern political organization allows more and more citizens to participate, but each of them with a smaller and smaller effective radius. Organization is an ambiguous instrument, moreover, both for the dispersion of power and for its renewed concentration. "Organization," in the words of Robert Michels, echoing Lenin, "is the weapon of the weak in their struggle with the strong."[12] But organization as Michels well knew, also is the weapon whereby political leadership can perpetuate itself with scant regard to the wishes and interest of those who propelled it into power.

The "underdeveloped" countries are underdeveloped notably with regard to political and social organization. The cadre of capable government employees is small. There are few private associations, and their membership is limited. Collective action and mutual trust are based on the family or other traditional and ascriptive relations rather than on associations for abstract, impersonal objectives. In economics, family enterprises predominate over anonymously owned joined stock companies. In politics, nepotism, ethnic loyalty, and personal allegiance to a leader are more effective than party machines or ideological programs. Political participation is largely restricted to the urban population

[12] *Political Parties*, translated by E. and C. Paul (Dover, 1959), p. 21. For Lenin's statement, see below, p. 100.

and to the educated. Sharp inequalities therefore remain between this political class and the lower-class members of parochial rural communities.

The Dilemma of Organization

The effects of modern organization on political participation and equality can best be observed in the constitutional democracies and in the communist totalitarian regimes of the present day. There is no doubt that democracy and communism represent the two most comprehensive and deliberate attempts in mankind's history to establish political equality and universal participation on a grand scale. For this reason, both of them must be considered characteristically modern political movements. Both of them confront the ambiguous effects of modern organization, but each confronts them in very different ways. The differences are sharpest in the organization of political power.

CHANGING THEORIES OF DEMOCRACY

In the liberal-democratic systems that have grown up since the late eighteenth century in Western and Northern Europe, in North America, in Australia and New Zealand, there has been a steady elaboration of the major instrumentalities of constitutional government. There has also been a corresponding shift in the emphasis of political theorists. Rousseau, the most radical democratic spokesman of the eighteenth century, was convinced that popular rule was possible only in small communities where all citizens can assemble to deliberate their laws and elect their rulers. He rejected all political representation and pitied the British people who lost their liberty each time they elected a parliament.[13]

Popular government, nonetheless, developed in large national states, and everywhere elected assemblies became its instruments.

[13] Jean Jacques Rosseau, *Contrat Social* (1762), Book 3, Chap. 15.

Suffrage at first remained restricted by property qualifications. Against the propertied interests in the early legislatures, popular organizations arose such as the Chartists, the Jacksonians, the Birmingham caucus, and the European socialist movements. These in time consolidated into nationwide parties linking constituency and parliament. Liberal thinkers of the eighteenth and nineteenth centuries who had specifically endorsed representation remained skeptical or apprehensive about the growing power of parties. Burke denied the right of his Bristol constituents to instruct their member of parliament; Madison condemned factions as sharply as had Rousseau; and Mill at some length argued on both sides of the question, "Ought Pledges To Be Required From Members of Parliament?"[14]

Theorists of the early twentieth century, by contrast, discovered in parties an essential instrument of democracy which, through competition for votes, subjected parliament and cabinet to popular control. Yet many of them eloquently warned of the danger to democracy from pressure groups and organized interests.[15] More recently, political scientists in the United States and in Europe have accepted organized groups, too, as a major asset to democracy and liberalism.[16]

Parliaments, parties, pressure groups: each organizational instrument that one generation had rejected as a threat to free and popular government was embraced by the next as one of its mainstays. In truth, every one of these views was valid in part. Each of the three institutions helped break the older power monopolies of

[14] See Burke's Bristol address (1774); but cf. his earlier defense of party in Edmund Burke, *Thoughts on the Cause of the Present Discontents* (1770); James Madison, *Federalist Papers*, No. 10 (1787); John Stuart Mill, *Considerations on Representative Government* (1861), Chap. 12.

[15] Abbot Lawrence Lowell, *Governments and Parties in Continental Europe*, 2 vols. (Houghton Mifflin, 1896); M. I. Ostrogorski, *Democracy and the Organization of Political Parties* (Macmillan, 1902); Michels, *Political Parties*; André Siegfried, *Tableau Politique de la France de l'Ouest* (Paris: A. Colin, 1913); Karl Staaff, *Det demokratiska statsskicket* (Stockholm: Wahlström & Widstrand, 1917); James Bryce, *Modern Democracies* (2 vols. (Macmillan, 1921).

[16] Harold J. Laski, *A Grammar of Politics* (London: Allen and Unwin, 1925); E. Pendleton Herring, *Group Representation Before Congress* (Johns Hopkins Press, 1929); David B. Truman, *The Governmental Process* (Knopf, 1951).

kings, of landed aristocracies, and of industrial bourgeoisies. Yet each has erected new hierarchical structures far beyond the control of the common citizen.

Current democratic theory tends to rely on a combination of these institutions as they have historically evolved. In a democracy, it is held, political groups freely express a variety of opinions and interests and disseminate the relevant facts. Parties, by assembling lists of candidates and platform planks, devise formulas for the partial integration of these opinions and interests and submit them to the electorate's verdict. Elected legislatures approve the broad lines of policy. Executives (directly elected or responsible to the legislature) elaborate details of policy and direct the administrative machinery of government that carries policy into effect. In this way, the will of the majority is periodically enforced throughout the government. Since majority control changes from time to time and every voter has an equal chance of becoming part of the winning combination, political equality is ensured as far as is possible in a modern state.

In sum, the key elements of the contemporary theory of democratic equality are: (1) the free flow of information and the free expression of opinion; (2) the competition of party programs and candidates for electoral approval; (3) the control of the government by elected representatives; and (4) either (a) periodic changes in the composition of the ruling majority or (b) representation of all major electoral trends within it.[17]

It is readily conceded that political reality does not always fully correspond to these postulates. Certain classes of citizens may in fact be excluded from the franchise (for example, Negroes in the South of the United States) or may habitually abstain from voting. Occasional fraud or intimidation may falsify and malap-

---

[17] For somewhat different lists see Robert A. Dahl, *A Preface to Democratic Theory* (University of Chicago Press, 1956), pp. 67-71, 84; and Robert A. Dahl, ed., *Political Oppositions in Western Democracies* (Yale University Press, 1966), pp. 387f., 393. The last passage includes a discussion of point (4) (a), above, which is often neglected. Cf. Nils Herlitz, *Svenska statsrättens grunder* (Stockholm: Norstedt, 1940), p. 90, and Rustow, *Politics of Compromise*, pp. 223f.

portionment or gerrymandering may distort the outcome of the vote. Nepotism or corruption may thwart the electoral control of the administration. These are common defects of democratic practice, and reform movements have periodically sprung up to remedy them.

In view of the experience particularly of the Weimar Republic, it is also generally accepted that democratic freedoms of opinion and of association may have to be curtailed for militant minorities that are bent on undermining and subverting the liberal-democratic order itself. Such occasional lapses or deliberate restrictions do not seriously detract from the validity of the theory. The real difficulties of democratic egalitarianism are more deep seated, and touch more closely on the four basic assumptions themselves.

DIFFICULTIES OF DEMOCRACY

1. Political information and opinions can effectively be circulated only by large organizations that control or gain access to the media of press and broadcasting. It is well-known that determined minorities with specific demands can often defeat the more diffuse interests of a large majority. The mounting cost of publicity in large societies makes for a further concentration of power. Few Americans would lightly dismiss a Yale professor's complaint about the head of the *Time* and *Life* publishing empire—that "Mr. Henry Luce has a thousand or ten thousand times greater control over the alternatives scheduled for debate and tentative decision at a national election than I do"—except perhaps to wonder how many real issues, however proposed, get debated or decided in an election.[18]

The most powerful organization—the most compact and determined minority that "manages the news"—tends to be the incumbent government itself: in many countries, it controls broadcasting, and in all countries, it must determine the timing, form, and content of its news releases and press conferences. The cost and

[18] Dahl, *A Preface to Democratic Theory*, pp. 72-73.

far-flung organization of propaganda make it easier for rulers to influence the minds of subjects than for subjects effectively to control the action of rulers. In countries that follow the British practice of dissolution, the government also selects the time, and hence often the issues, of a national election of parliament. The free market place of ideas in practice resembles a forum of oligopolistic competition with the government itself having the largest corner on the market.

2. If there is to be an effective popular choice of rulers or programs, parties must narrow down the alternatives to only two. A larger number of serious contenders removes the choice from the voters—whether by parliamentary selection of a coalition premier or by the election of a president in the United States House of Representatives. United States experience also suggests that procedures for popular control of nominations, such as mandatory primaries, may enhance rather than reduce the need for party organization. The larger the electorate and the costlier the campaign, the more surely control of the parties devolves on their organizers and financial backers. The citizen's free choice of government commonly is reduced to a choice of the lesser of two evils.

3. Once elected, presidents or responsible ministers can only within limits control and direct the administrative establishment of a modern state. "Poor Ike," Harry Truman would compassionately sigh when contemplating his successor's task; "he'll say, 'Do this! Do that!' And nothing will happen."[19] For every device by which a responsible politician can impose his will, or that of his constituents, there are several by which the bureaucracy can collectively narrow down, deflect, or resist his choices. The difficulties increase with the growing size of government, with the mounting complexity of its economic and military functions, and with the proliferation of secret and technical information.

Conversely, the ability of ministers to shape policy is reduced

---

[19] For a brilliant demonstration of the difficulties of the American president's task see Richard E. Neustadt, *Presidential Power* (Signet Books, 1964). The quote from Truman is on p. 22.

by insecure tenure and unstable parliamentary support—as in Weimar Germany and in France and Italy after World War II. In a shrinking world liable to wholesale destruction, democratic powers of the first and second rank have to make fateful decisions in response to swift developments—as on the invasion in Korea, war at Suez, and missiles on Cuba. There is no time to submit these decisions to the full legislature, let alone to the electorate. Both the bureaucracy within modern states and the foreign relations among them proceed largely on their own momentum and to that extent are not easily amenable to political and popular control.

4. A regular alternation of parties in the government is in fact much rarer than may be supposed. Many states of the United States have been controlled by a single party for several generations—not only in the "solid South" but also in New England and the West—and urban party machines often have been even more thoroughly entrenched. In the federal government itself, the voters between 1860 and 1932 only four times chose a Democratic president, and since 1932 only twice a Republican. In Scandinavia, the Social Democrats have been predominant since the 1930's. In the Commonwealth countries, too, prolonged periods of one-party control have been common.

In the continental multiparty countries, cabinets have fallen frequently, but have been formed and reformed among the same pivotal group of parties and "ministrables" at the center. In France and Italy, the long-time exclusion of working class representatives from the government has contributed to the alienation of their supporters from the political system, and their estrangement has reinforced the original evil of exclusion.[20] The danger of exclusion and alienation is particularly acute in situations of rigid ethnic alignment such as in the French-speaking parts of Canada and in Belgium. In a comparative perspective, the regular alternation between two inclusive parties at four- to seven-

[20] See Gabriel A. Almond et al., *The Appeals of Communism* (Princeton University Press, 1954).

year intervals that has been characteristic of Great Britain since 1832 would seem to be the exception rather than the rule.[21] There is no need to belabor the significance for political equality. A citizen whose grandfather once voted for a winning candidate and whose grandson may do so again can hardly be considered the political equal of a supporter of the majority.

One possible alternative to the model of two parties taking frequent turns in office is that of a multiparty system with coalition governments. Under such a system, the party or parties at the center tend to be in office perpetually, joined now by groups on the center-right and now on the center-left. The voters have some influence on shifting the coalition in this or that direction, but the detailed conditions of the shift are somewhat unpredictable and depend not on the election itself but on back-stage negotiations among members of parliament during each cabinet crisis.

This system, which prevailed in the German Weimar and French Fourth Republics and today persists in Italy and Israel, tends to combine a number of drawbacks. One party, such as the German Zentrum, the French MRP, the Christian Democratic Party in Italy, and the Mapai in Israel is permanently in the government, or nearly so. Other sizable parties are permanently ex-

[21] In Britain since 1832, there have been only two periods when the same party won three general elections in a row (the Liberals in 1906, 1910, and 1911; the Conservatives in 1951, 1955, and 1959). The suspension of electoral processes during the two world wars also prolonged the duration of governments, but their composition each time was enlarged to include the opposition. Even so, the longest periods that the Prime Minister has been of the same party have been 17 years (1905-22), 13 years (1951-64), and twice 10 years (1895-1905, 1935-45). On the "pendulum theory" and its antecedents in Bryce and Lowell, cf. Bernard Crick, *In Defense of Politics*, rev. ed. (Harmondsworth: Penguin, 1964), p. 193 and literature cited. Samuel Lubell, in view of American experience since the Civil War, has instead proposed a "sun and moon theory." A major party predominates in the government for a generation or more. "It is within the major party that the issues of any particular period are fought out; while the minority party shines in reflected radiance of the heat thus generated." Lubell, *The Future of American Politics*, 3d ed. (Harper, 1965), p. 192. See also Donald V. Smiley, "The Two-Party System and One-Party Dominance in the Liberal-Democratic State," *Canadian Journal of Economics and Political Science*, Vol. 24 (1958), pp. 312-32. For various empirical data on democracies, see Appendix Table 5.

cluded. The parties of the center-left and center-right are now in and now out and hence (together with disaffected elements in the pivotal party) have a strong incentive for periodically overturning cabinets by parliamentary votes of nonconfidence.

Under another variant of the coalition system, as long practiced in Austria, the major parties are permanently allied. Here all major electoral trends are represented in parliament, in the government, and (through the system of proportional patronage known to Austrians as the *Proporz*) in the administration. But major political decisions, as under any other coalition system are removed from the electoral hustings to the smoke-filled lobbies of parliament.[22]

The tensions just surveyed between democratic theory and the organizational realities of modern political life have time and again enhanced the popular appeal of critiques—from Michels' "iron law of oligarchy" to C. Wright Mills' *Power Elite*—that depict democracy as a mere façade for minority rule. This type of reasoning ignores the manifest complexity and confusion of modern organizational life. Instead, it proceeds from a simple and false major premise—often unstated but always tenaciously embraced. Somebody, it is assumed, does control the government; since the popular majority does not, then it must be a minority; if no such minority is visible, it must be hidden—and hence all the more pernicious.[23]

But the effect of modern organization in a pluralist liberal soci-

[22] Party alignments in governments, parliaments, and electorates of the United States, Great Britain, and continental Europe are analyzed in Dahl, ed., *Political Oppositions in Western Democracies.*

[23] Michels, *Political Parties*, pp. 377ff.; C. Wright Mills, *The Power Elite* (New York: Oxford University Press, 1956). For pertinent rebuttals see Robert A. Dahl, "Critique of the Ruling Elite Model," *American Political Science Review*, Vol. 52 (June 1958), pp. 463-69; and especially Carl Joachim Friedrich, *Man and His Government* (McGraw, 1963), pp. 324-26, who rightly stresses that the theorem of the "ruling elite" can be valid "only if it can be shown that such a group is a cohesive one with a sense of group identity, and that it has grip on the governmental power in that community approaching a monopoly. . . ." (p. 326). See also D. A. Rustow, "The Study of Elites: Who's Who, When, and How," *World Politics*, Vol. 18, No. 4 (July 1966), especially pp. 708-14.

ety is to remove, to a considerable extent, the possibility of control over government by any one determinate or cohesive group. Democracy is a political market place for organizational giants rather than for atomic individuals freely grouping and regrouping into majorities. The plurality of competing organizations, their overlapping membership, in short their "countervailing" force, provides the most effective restraint on the tyranny of modern governmental power. The organizations which prevent the individual from "governing himself" also prevent any single group from governing him. Pluralism thus turns against the rulers themselves their old maxim of divide and conquer. The voter's choice, even where it is only one between several evils, is still a very real choice. Oligopolistic competition turns out to be the best available guarantee against monopoly, "polyarchy" (to use Dahl's term) the closest real approach to democracy.[24]

COMMUNISM AND ORGANIZATION

The power of organization, which is a major embarrassment for most classic statements of democratic theory, is the principal support of communist-totalitarian political systems. Organization, which to many democrats is a necessary evil, to the communists becomes a prime virtue.[25] Marx tended to stress the spontaneous and inevitable aspects of the proletarian revolution he predicted. Lenin, by contrast, expected it to come about as the result only of systematic organization. "The proletariat," he wrote in 1904, "has no weapon in the struggle for power except organization . . . the proletariat can and will inevitably become an unconquerable force only as a result of this. . . ."[26] And the Comintern in 1920

[24] Cf. John Kenneth Galbraith, *American Capitalism: The Concept of Countervailing Power* (Houghton Mifflin, 1940); Dahl, *A Preface to Democratic Theory*, pp. 63-89.
[25] For a cogent and concise analysis of the relationship between traditional, democratic, and communist systems in somewhat similar terms see T. H. Rigby, "Traditional, Market, and Organizational Societies and the USSR," *World Politics*, Vol. 16 (July 1964), pp. 539-57.
[26] Lenin, "One Step Forward, Two Steps Backward," translated in Robert V.

proclaimed: "The Communist Party is the lever of political organization, with the help of which the more progressive part of the
working class directs on the right path the whole mass of the
proletariat and the semi-proletariat."

It is significant, in this connection, that Marx and Engels were
minor participants in the unsuccessful revolution of 1848, and
that Marx wrote a moving but tendentious epitaph for the spontaneous proletarian uprising of the Paris Commune of 1871.[27]
Lenin's organization, on the other hand, through an audacious
coup d'état, propelled him and his minority following into a position of power in a vast country.

In the first decade after the communists' seizure of power in
Petrograd in 1917, their system of minority rule was extended and
tightened throughout the entire former Tsarist empire, except for
the loss of the Western provinces. For a quarter century after
that, the system was converted into an even tighter, personal tyranny under Stalin. Under Lenin and during the succession struggle of 1924-29, there was a certain amount of plural, collegial
leadership in the higher echelons of the party elite. Under Stalin,
organizational competition among party, bureaucracy, army, and
secret police often was systematically encouraged—but this pluralism only served to consolidate Stalin's personal power. The
mass murder of the Tsarist intelligentsia, of the kulaks, and of
most of the old Bolsheviks themselves, and the forcible transfer or
elimination of entire nationalities during World War II created a
regime of terror unparalleled in history. Manifestly, no regime
has more crudely and more sweepingly denied equality and even
life itself to its subjects.

Yet communism in its ideology retained, under Lenin, and even
Stalin, its radical egalitarian appeal, insisting on its image of an
ideal society based on the complete abolition of all privileges of
social class, of unequal wealth, of nationality, of parentage. In
this respect, it differs sharply from other dictatorships in modern

---

Daniels, ed., *A Documentary History of Communism* (Vintage Books, 1960), Vol.
1, pp. 26f.
[27] See Karl Marx, *The Civil War in France* (1871).

Europe, notably that of Napoleon, who recreated a nobility and courtly pomp only a decade after the revolution of 1789, and that of Hitler whose mysticism was biological rather than egalitarian and whose appeal was narrowly restricted to supposedly "Nordic" or "Aryan" elements in the German people.

The communist appeal has been explicitly to all "toilers"— workers and peasants anywhere in the world, and implicitly to radical intellectuals eager to participate in the systematic organization of power and the systematic transformation of society. In the eyes of both the personnel of the Soviet regime and of their supporters and sympathizers abroad, the egalitarian appeal and the utopian final vision of a classless society have justified the enormous human cost even of the Stalinist period. The real explosive force of the Marxian dialectic has manifested itself in the moral sphere by harnessing the highest moral motives to the naked pursuit of power.[28]

Although power under communism has been most unevenly distributed, political participation within the framework of the official ideology and of the regime has been consistently stimulated and encouraged. Elections and party organization, which in democracies are instruments for the dispersion and control of power, have been developed within communist regimes for the purpose of maximizing participation and commitment to the regime by the masses. Under Malenkov, Khrushchev, and Kosygin a far greater amount of public discussion and criticism on details of policy and administration has been possible than was thinkable under Stalin. The unified hierarchic power structure of the regime has been preserved, but the penalty for dissidents was more likely to be reassignment to a remote tractor station than physical liquidation.

Democracy rests its claims for political equality on the myths of equal participation of all citizens in the formation of opinion

[28] Cf. Michael Polanyi, *Personal Knowledge* (University of Chicago Press, 1958), pp. 236ff.

and of their equal influence on the selection of rulers. It prevents any full concentration of power through the pluralism of political groups and the dispersion of power within the government. Communism concentrates organizational and governmental power within a single, tightly hierarchical structure, and rests its claim for political equality on the even more precarious myth that these concentrated powers are exercised in the interest of the entire population. It is perhaps regrettable that so much of recent theory and polemics have concentrated on the single aspect of political power—where the need for organization limits the range of practical possibilities to one from oligopolistic competition of large groups to complete concentration in a single monopolistic structure.

There are other respects in which political equality can be more nearly approximated—notably equal treatment of all citizens by the laws, the courts, and the police; equalization of incomes through progressive taxation; and equal access to the benefits of education and to political careers. In these aspects of political equality, there are significant variations from country to country and from period to period. But insofar as data can be gathered and precise criteria formulated for valid comparisons, it will probably be found that the variations over time within the same country tend to be greater than differences between countries in any given period.

For the survivors of the Stalin regime, equality before the law in the Soviet Union today is more nearly like that in the United States than like that in Russia in the 1930's. In respect to equality of income after taxes, the Soviet Union today ranges somewhere between the United States in 1900 and the United States in 1960. In equality of political recruitment, it is a significant landmark when a Georgian or Ukrainian attains positions of high power in the Soviet regime, or a Catholic or Jew in the United States. Parentage clearly plays less of a role in political success in Russia than in the United States. On the other hand, the Soviet organizational structure precludes any horizontal mobility from nonpolitical to a political career as typified, for example, by Wendell Willkie. In short, the democratic and communist performances with regard to the nonpower aspects of equality differ according to time and place but can be measured along a common scale.

The choice of modern forms of government for the developing countries is often said to be a choice between democracy and totalitarianism, or, more specifically, communism. In fact, neither of these forms can readily and immediately be reproduced by most of the countries of Asia, Africa, and Latin America before they have resolved a number of problems of transition from tradition to modernity and of fuller development into nation-states. When they have undergone these further stages of development, it may well turn out that the choice of forms of modern government for them is by no means limited to just two.

CHAPTER FOUR

THE RHYTHM OF POLITICAL MODERNIZATION

. . . in the game of cultural intercourse . . . one thing lead(s) to another . . .
TOYNBEE

Si cambia il maëstro di cappella, mà la musica è sempre quella.
ITALIAN PROVERB

POLITICAL MODERNIZATION, like other aspects of the modern revolution, is never smooth in its course, uniform in speed and direction, or certain of success. The intellectual, psychological, economic, social, and political aspects of the modern transformation, to be sure, all reinforce each other. Over the short run, however, there are likely to be many imbalances and reversals—and the longer run offers scant comfort to those societies that may not survive intact to witness it. Disparities and setbacks of this sort are known to everyone from the sphere of material culture. Modern hygiene often aggravates poverty by cutting death rates while fertility remains high and economic production lags. Industrialization, despite its long-run egalitarian tendency, may at first sharpen the contrast between rich and poor. The technology of war wantonly destroys what peaceful industry has laboriously built.

The political disparities are no less striking. Societies that experience a modern impact from the outside find that traditional institutions generally are disrupted more quickly than modern

105

equivalents are built up and hence suffer much disarray in the interval. This was the common experience under such modernizers as Peter I of Russia, Mahmud II of Turkey, and Muhammad Ali of Egypt. The initial impact of the West on Asia often has widened the gap among the traditional classes: the young Brahmin who completes his studies at Oxford adds a cultural dimension to what would have been a mere social distinction within a homogeneous Hindu culture.

Modern means of communication can serve to strengthen traditional autocracy or may enhance the propaganda appeal of traditionalist or fundamentalist ideologies. Centralized administration and universal schooling, which can be among the most effective instruments of national unification, also may exacerbate divisive tendencies in a polyglot population.

For all peoples who come into extended contact with it, the pressures of modernization are so formidable as to prove in practice irresistible. Yet there is nothing uniform about the details of that process nor anything foreordained about its outcome. Societies in contact with the modern world cannot ignore these pressures; but there is a variety of ways in which they can attempt to divert, accommodate, or absorb them. There are many junctures, then, at which a modernizing society must make, by resolution or default, a number of basic choices. One choice concerns the speed of the modernization process, its reformist or revolutionary nature. Another concerns the scope of the process, the particular spheres of social life that are first to be modernized while tradition continues or is reinforced in other spheres. A third, of particular interest in the present context, concerns the timing of the three political quests for authority, identity, and equality.

Reform Versus Revolution

In Europe, modern intellectual attitudes emerged in the thirteenth to sixteenth centuries. Three hundred years later, the discoveries of modern science were finding wide application in the industrial economy. But it was not until the turn of the twentieth century that in most countries the egalitarian tendencies of modernity had appeared in full force—that the popular masses had secured a controlling voice on the political stage. During six or seven centuries, that is to say, substantial elements of tradition survived while modernity was making its unhurried progress from philosophy to science, from technology to industrial production, and from dynastic absolutism to democratic politics in modern nation-states.

In the countries of Asia, Africa, and Latin America, the pressure of this European example, transmitted through the forces of industrial technology, of world-wide communications, and of international power politics, has lent far greater urgency to modernization. But even in these newer settings and even in an impatient century, that wholesale effort of collective habit-breaking and relearning cannot be accomplished instantaneously, nor can the effort proceed at equal pace on all fronts.

Modernization in Europe at first proceeded largely unconsciously and by means of unintended results. The men of the Renaissance and of the Enlightenment had no consciousness of having to "keep pace" or to "catch up" with other societies. The scholars of the fifteenth century were more concerned to recapture the wisdom of the ancients than to prepare that of the moderns. Luther, preoccupied with questions of individual faith, had little notion of launching a development that would replace a universal political order of Christendom with so many secular nation-states. Calvin did not intend to found a school of dissent that would make its contribution to political liberalism and to capitalism. The cosmopolitan philosophers of eighteenth century France might have welcomed the egalitarian and libertarian effects of the Great Revolution but would have been surprised at the impetus it gave to modern nationalism. Even Columbus, in search of a shorter trade route to the Far East, did not intend to discover the Americas.

But once the over-all structure of modernizing society and culture had taken shape in Europe and its expansive dynamics been carried overseas, no other society was free to engage in modernization with equal disregard of consequence. For the latecomers, the quality of freedom and of innocence that attached to early modernization in the West has been irretrievably lost. Societies that have come into external contact with ready-made patterns of modernization have had to take a conscious stand, to choose a deliberate course. Many political and cultural leaders in these newer settings have been inclined to pick and choose—to adopt specific items of modern technology while keeping intact the traditional social and political structure, or to transform government and society while preserving the spiritual and religious heritage of their country's past. Other modernizers, by contrast, have been eager to effect a forcible revolution that would transform traditional society so as to inaugurate some vision of the modern millennium.

Whether the policy was one of cautious adaptation or of wholesale transformation, social reality often made a different selection and set a different pace, with scant regard for the intentions of the cultural and social planners. Technology cannot be neatly separated from social structure, and social structure cannot long be insulated from intellectual culture. Once the alien, modernizing impact has set in, as Arnold Toynbee put it with disarming simplicity, "one thing leads to another."[1]

Even before cautious statesmen have succeeded in their first measures of selective reform, they are likely to have unloosed forces that will erode the position of social power that they had meant to strengthen and preserve. Nor are the utopian revolutionaries likely to conjure up results of greater reliability. One thoughtful historian has suggested that, whatever the long-range intellectual repercussions of the French Revolution, its most tangible results in France by 1815 were two: after a quarter century

[1] Arnold J. Toynbee, The World and the West (New York: Oxford University Press, 1953), p. 75.

of riot, terror, coups d'état, and convulsive wars, the country re-tained a more orderly system of law and of administration, and the welter of traditional weights and measures had been replaced by a uniform decimal system.[2]

Such a purely pragmatic and short-run assessment may indi-cate sufficiently that major revolutions are not the fulfillment of a preconceived plan, that their immediate results are likely to differ vastly from the expectation of the revolutionaries. The more im-portant results of a revolution such as that of 1789 can only be evaluated over a longer period. By transferring power and prop-erty to a new class, it put in question all prescriptive titles of so-cial inequality. By attempting a rational transformation of all of society and government, it set new standards for deliberate and collective human action. And a comparison of the writings of eighteenth- and nineteenth-century conservatives—say Fénelon, de Maistre, and Carlyle—shows that even where its opponents carried the day, they did so on the basis of arguments adapted from the vocabulary of the revolution itself.

COLONIAL RULE

Two of the most potent stimuli for rapid modernization outside of Europe have been colonial conquest and the effort at resistance by societies warding off such conquest. Both the aggressive mod-ernization of European imperialism and the defensive moderniza-tion of such traditional societies as Ottoman Turkey and Japan began as limited, selective programs; yet both were sooner or later carried far beyond original intentions.

The European colonial conquest of most of the other continents may best be understood as a phenomenon intermediate between tradition and modernity. The practice of conquest had been com-mon to all ages of recorded history and most traditional states had been founded on it. In the further course of modernization,

[2] Crane Brinton, *The Anatomy of Revolution*, rev. ed. (Random House, 1960), p. 253.

as shown earlier, colonial empires like dynastic realms and post-feudal principalities have had to make way for a new national form of political organization. But though conquest itself was traditional, the methods of the European colonialists of the sixteenth to nineteenth centuries were modern. Unlike their predecessors, they used modern arts of navigation that carried them to the far corners of the globe and a modern military technology that for more than three centuries rendered them invincible to other, pre-modern societies. Furthermore, European colonialism generated a self-propelling dynamism which, for the first time in history, made all parts of the human race known to each other; and this incipient unification of mankind further added to the world-wide momentum of modernization.

The colonial conquerors were impelled by a mixture of motives: desire for adventure, for riches, for power; protection of traders or of missionaries; and preemptive conquest to forestall the expansion of rival colonial powers. Whatever the purposes, a certain number of changes in the conquered society were essential to the establishment and maintenance of colonial rule. Internal peace must be secured, some amount of revenue collected, lucrative natural resources exploited, and, for those ends, a more effective network of transport developed. In politics, colonial modernization concentrated heavily on the strengthening of authority: there obviously was no initial desire to transplant ideas of national identity or of political equality to the subject societies.

Except for areas where conquest was followed by settlement—where colonialism implied colonization—the impact on the indigenous social structure was kept to a minimum. This restraint was imposed not so much by regard for the allegedly happier ways of primitive life as by a shortage of personnel by which to administer any broader impact. Yet the very shortage of colonial personnel forced a search for local auxiliaries, and the most convenient auxiliaries often turned out to be traditional potentates who already enjoyed local authority. Hence, under the British system of "indirect rule," indigenous chiefs were transformed into extensions of the colonial administration.

But the concept of indirect rule involved a basic self-contradiction. An Indian maharaja or a Fulani emir in Northern Nigeria who owed his tenure to traditional claims plus loyal cooperation with resident British officers did not retain the same position that his forebears had held. The foreign rulers at one and the same time enhanced his power by putting more effective instruments of transport and administration at his disposal and made his title to that power conditional. Nor did British administrators always come upon the indigenous tribal chiefs that their stereotyped view of traditional social structure led them to look for. In an assessment of the British impact on indigenous political systems in Africa, a group of British anthropologists found that colonial rule had weakened the chiefs in the traditionally more authoritarian and centralized systems, and enhanced or newly created the political position of chiefs in more egalitarian and diffuse systems.[3] In India, an indigenous civil service, institutions of higher education, and local representative bodies were introduced so as to strengthen British rule after the severe blow of the 1857 mutiny: all three eventually supplied personnel for the independence movement organized in the Indian National Congress a generation later.

Throughout Asia and Africa, colonial systems of education, however limited in scope or intent, supplied one of the most forceful stimuli for later demands for independence. A young African who learned in primary school about liberty, equality, and fraternity in France in 1789 might well dream of applying these lofty ideals to Africa in the 1950's. Institutions of self-government in the British colonies or participation in metropolitan elections by the so-called évolués of French Africa did more, over the long run, to reinforce than to satisfy demands for political rights. Indian and Senegalese soldiers recruited into the British or French forces in 1914-18 had the heady experience of winning military battles against Europeans. The colonial rulers' attempt to limit their modern impact on the subject society thus was doomed to

[3] Meyer Fortes and E. E. Evans-Pritchard, eds., *African Political Systems* (London: Oxford University Press, 1940), pp. 15-16.

eventual failure. Independence granted to some colonies reverberated in demands for self-government in others. At length the
modern demands for political equality and participation swept
away the entire semimodern colonial system.

REFORMING MONARCHS

Defensive modernizers, such as Peter I of Russia (1689-1725),
Selim III (1789-1807) and Mahmud II (1808-1839) of Turkey, Muhammad Ali of Egypt (1805-1849), and the statesmen of the Meiji
reign in Japan (1868-1912) had even more limited and clear-cut
objectives than the early colonialists—an even better rationale for
making haste slowly. Their most ardent desire was to muster such
military strength as would enable them to resist the threat by
modern powers to the integrity and independence of their realms.
Defensive modernization in Russia began in response to the military campaigns of Charles XII, in Turkey to those of Prince
Eugene and the generals of Catherine II, in Egypt to those of
Bonaparte, and in Japan to the threat of Western navies. Military
reorganization, prompted by defeat abroad, in most instances en-
tailed a showdown with the traditional military caste at home. In
a series of surprisingly similar moves, Peter destroyed the Streltsi,
Muhammad Ali the Mamluks, and Mahmud the Janissaries. The
purpose of these early reforms was not the transformation of the
entire society in any modern image, but, on the contrary, resistance to modern conquest and the strengthening of the ruler's
own position; not deliberate modernization but the forcible reassertion of tradition against the modern challenge; not revolution
but conservation. Yet this is precisely where "one thing led to another." The Ottoman case is particularly instructive.

Ottoman modernization at first took the form of a piecemeal program of which the conscious aim was not acceptance but rejection
of modern Europe. Yet by a compelling logic the program slowly
spread. The army could not be reformed in isolation from the rest
of the body politic. The new soldiery needed officers schooled in
mathematics, French, and geography, and army surgeons with *alla*

franca medical training. Military conscription required a tightening of administration in the provinces, where powerful vassals ruled in increasing defiance of the sultan. The costs of the new army and administration had to be borne by systematic taxation. An entire new school system was instituted to prepare the future officers, administrators, and tax collectors for their tasks. The schools required more money—and yet more schools for the training of teachers.

. . . By the end of the nineteenth century these higher schools had produced a new elite of officers and officials to whom Europeanizing reform was no longer an occasional expedient for preserving tradition but an instrument for transforming tradition itself. Modernization, starting out as the command of an autocrat, had become the project of ministers and at last the fervent mission of a new social class. In laying the foundation for military reform, the sultans, like the sorcerer's apprentice, had released a process which became increasingly autonomous and which they eventually became unable to control. In 1922 the heirs of Selim III's new army deposed his cousin's grandson and brought in a coroner's verdict on the Ottoman state and sultanate.[4]

The reforming monarchs of the eighteenth and nineteenth centuries responded to the threat or the reality of foreign attack. They had to overcome resistance from the domestic forces of tradition, but only in the further course of political modernization did internal pressures and internal disagreements about the direction of the reform program arise.

The reforming monarchs of the mid-twentieth century are more likely from the start to be confronting domestic pressures and discontents. For reasons which will be touched upon later, the danger of outright military attack on smaller states appears to have greatly diminished in the years since World War II. Meanwhile, however, intensified world trade and communications, competitive programs of foreign aid, and the varied activities of international organizations have vastly magnified what has come to be called the "demonstration effect." Even predominantly traditional regimes, such as those in Iraq (until 1958), Jordan, Iran,

[4] D. A. Rustow, "The Military: Turkey," in Robert E. Ward and Dankwart A. Rustow, eds., *Political Modernization in Japan and Turkey* (Princeton University Press, 1964), pp. 353, 359.

Morocco, Libya, Ethiopia, Nepal, Saudi Arabia, Yemen (until 1962), and Afghanistan therefore face growing demands for modernization, specifically for economic development, for social equality, and for popular participation in the government.

Rulers who resist such pressures outright risk the revolutionary overthrow of their regimes—such as took place in Iraq and in Yemen and was narrowly avoided in Iran and Jordan in the 1950's. The only other alternative is piecemeal concessions to the forces of reform: agricultural development in Jordan, the tighter budgeting of oil revenues enforced by King Faysal in Saudi Arabia, the introduction of cabinet government in Nepal, the Shah's ambitious land-reform program in Iran, and the neutralist foreign policy of King Hasan II of Morocco. Many of these programs have gone hand in hand with a systematic strengthening of military forces to suppress any violent challenge to the ruler's position.

These twentieth century programs, like those of Peter, Mahmud, and Meiji, represent so many attempts to regulate the pace of modernization, to combine modern administrative, social, or economic politics with traditional political features. They stand in sharp competition with the more impatient formulas of modernization offered by rising groups of intellectuals, bureaucrats, and military officers—all of them called into being or strengthened by the monarchs' reform efforts. The Moroccan and Iranian programs are of particular interest, for they reveal the ruler's intention to form an alliance with the popular masses, to establish what amounts to a plebiscitary monarchy.

The risks that these programs involve, the questions that they pose, are obvious. If even the monarch acknowledges the need for sweeping reform, will he not lend cogency to the arguments of those who would begin reform at the top by sweeping away the monarch himself? Will a modernized and strengthened army in a country like Iran prove a reliable instrument against popular unrest, or will it ultimately turn against the Shah and assume leadership in a future violent revolution? The fateful test for these combinations of opposites will come as soon as a future plebiscite goes against a monarch claiming title by heredity—and in Morocco by descent from the Prophet.[5]

Colonial rule and defensive modernization in the past, and monarchic reform in the present furnish a range of examples where the modern transformation is likely to exceed the cautious speed and the narrow scope envisaged by conservative rulers. There are opposite examples where attempts at wholesale and instantaneous change have correspondingly miscarried.

REVOLUTIONARY CHANGE

Violent revolutions usually promise far greater changes than they in fact accomplish—for men are rarely motivated to take arms against their compatriots unless they expect vast and beneficial social changes to result. The Russian Revolution was meant to sweep away autocracy and class privilege and to serve as the spearhead of an international proletarian revolution at the culmination of which the state itself would "wither away." By the 1930's, however, Stalin had arrogated to himself far greater personal power than Lenin had ever wielded, and he applied it as capriciously as the most psychopathic of Tsars. From the inception of the Comintern in 1921, foreign Communist parties were systematically subordinated to the goals of Russian foreign policy; and in World War II (known to Soviet historians as the Great Patriotic War), nationalist propaganda themes of defense of the homeland became paramount. The social distance among the classes may have diminished, but the scale of economic rewards shows a far wider spread than in any Western country, and parentage continues as a major determinant of access to education. It took several decades of Soviet planning to regain, let alone surpass, the levels of economic production of 1913.[6]

[5] For a thoughtful and more detailed assessment of the problems and prospects of these regimes see Samuel P. Huntington, "The Political Modernization of Traditional Monarchies," *Daedalus*, Vol. 95, No. 3 (Summer 1966), pp. 763-88.

[6] Cf. Cyril E. Black, *The Dynamics of Modernization* (Harper, 1966), p. 80.

Lenin and Stalin have died, but, needless to say, the far-flung state bureaucracy and party apparatus show no sign whatever of "withering away." Only a shallow interpretation would assert that the Soviet system is a direct continuation of Tsardom; yet the two resemble each other far more than even the most skeptical revolutionaries of 1917 would have expected.

It may be objected—and rightly—that the Russian Revolution was more than a revolution of modernization, and that the Marxist promise of a classless society without government corresponds to vague chiliastic yearnings rather than to any realistic vision—whether modern or traditional—of human society on this earth. But the gap between promise and performance seems typical of all ideologically motivated revolutions.

Revolutions which aim at a rapid egalitarian revision of a traditional class structure are particularly prone to such disappointment. In any steeply hierarchical social structure, the upper class may be tightly homogeneous, but the lower classes almost certainly are not. Hence a program of sudden reform or a revolution will bring to power not the lower classes in their entirety but at best a portion of them. The temptation is for the victorious leadership of a lower-class revolt to create a regime equally hierarchical and equally oppressive as the system they have just overthrown. This temptation is especially strong after a violent uprising, since the mass of the population still remains accustomed to the old system of class domination. This is the situation that prompted Robert Michels to quote the cynical Italian proverb: "si cambia il maëstro di cappella, mà la musica è sempre quella."[7] ("The conductor changes, but the music remains always the same.") He might have added that it is possible for the music to grow more cacophonous: the new ruling class, unaccustomed to the responsibilities of power, may turn out to be more ruthless than its predecessors.

[7] Robert Michels, *Political Parties*, tr. E. and C. Paul (Dover, 1959), p. 391.

Blends of Tradition and Modernity

Modern political patterns may evolve too fast to allay the fears of monarchs and too slowly to fulfill the hopes of revolutionaries. But the rhythm of political modernization is a matter not only of speed and total scope; it also depends on a series of choices about particular items of reform and their timing, about the specific blend of traditional and modern elements to be included in a given program. In this respect, too, the control of political leaders and social planners is less than perfect: the course of development may furnish a recipe very different from their prescriptions.

A number of characteristic blends of tradition and modernity have already been indicated. The rise of nationalism is typically accompanied by a search for symbols of confidence within a people's history. Although the main concern of nationalism is with modernity and with the future, the search for symbols of the past adds a traditional element. As a leading student of Middle Eastern history has put it, the political actor on the modernizing stage finds "himself playing to two galleries at the same time."[8] The script, one might add, often calls for a modern plot to satisfy the one gallery, but for traditional costume to appeal to the other.

Aside from symbols, specific blends of tradition and modernity tend to vary with the social and political structure of modernizing countries. Both the colonial rulers and the defensive modernizers were eager to combine traditional domination and a traditional social structure with modern administration, a modern economy, and at times a modern system of education. Political modernization in these situations lagged behind the modernization of other spheres of social life; but, in a further phase of the transformation, politics caught up with administration and economy.

Anticolonial nationalist movements were directed at greater

[8] Gustave E. von Grunebaum, *Modern Islam* (Vintage Books, 1964), p. 34.

political equality or, as a minimum, at the replacement of an alien by an indigenous political elite. Domestic opponents of reforming autocrats championed new formulas of modernization. The New Ottomans in the mid-nineteenth century, for example, opposed the centralizing tendencies of the sultan and his ministers; instead they favored representative government, some measure of local autonomy, and a new civic spirit of patriotism. The Ottoman constitution of 1876 brought a remarkable, though short-lived, victory for this constitutionalist faction. After three more decades of autocracy under Abdülhamid, the Young Turk revolutionaries of 1908 adopted yet another, and this time a more purely modern, formula: centralized government based on partisan rather than dynastic control, and at length Turkish nationalism instead of Ottoman patriotism.

But political developments may also surge ahead of other aspects of modernization. The sudden advent of political mass participation in a modernizing country is likely to bring a renewed emphasis on traditional cultural values. Because democracy has been equated with modernity and political stability, the disruptive effects of its sudden introduction have often been underestimated. Yet the transfer of effective power from a small oligarchy to a mass electorate is nothing short of a political revolution. Turkey experienced such a revolution by ballot in 1950 and Ceylon in 1956. In both countries, the result was a new emphasis on religion and a shift from the liberal constitutional practices of the previous era to greater violence. In Turkey, the general upswing of the economy counteracted the conservative tendencies of the peasantry, who were interested in water wells, feeder roads, and wheat subsidies as much as in new mosques and Koran readings on the radio. In Ceylon, the situation was exacerbated by the outbreak of long-dormant Sinhalese-Tamil communal hostility. The Turkish military coup of 1960-61 and the election defeat of Mrs. Bandaranaike in Ceylon in 1965 reversed what in both cases seemed like an ominous drift away from democracy.

An even more explosive mixture of tradition and modernity is offered by a number of religious or communal protest movements, such as the Muslim Brethren in Egypt, Syria, and other Arab countries; the Fidaiyan-i Islam in Iran, the Jamaat-i Islami in Pakistan, the Nahdatul Ulama in Indonesia, the Agudath Israel, and the Jan Sangh and Hindu Mahasabha parties in India. These are often described as "traditionalist" parties, and indeed their avowed aim is the restoration of a traditional, religiously oriented way of life in sharp contrast to the prevailing trend of secularism in urban industrial life.

The bellicose restoration of tradition in a modern world, however, is a different matter from the continuation of an unbroken tradition. These groups typically appeal not to the traditional upper class, which has long since dissolved or become converted to modern, Western ways. Rather they appeal to artisans, small shop-keepers, residents of small towns or of the slum quarters of large cities—in short, to people who have been wrenched out of a traditional context without having found a satisfactory place in a modern one, who have experienced all the frustrations of modernity but none of its rewards.[9] And their organizational techniques usually are highly advanced and up-to-date, including streams of printed propaganda, a tight cell organization, and a strict organizational discipline.

A very different blend of tradition and modernity is represented by the Japanese leadership of the Meiji period. The political upheaval of 1868 is commonly known as the Meiji Restoration: the last of the Tokugawa shoguns was deposed and the Emperor Meiji "restored" to the traditional imperial powers that his ancestors were reputed to have forfeited a millenium before. This program has been called one of "reinforcing dualism"[10] because it used a traditional symbol of political unity and the traditional Shinto cult to enable a new oligarchic leadership to carry out one of the most far-reaching and effective programs of military, administrative, and economic modernization.

Manfred Halpern has rightly suggested that a policy of synthe-

---

[9] See, for example, Myron Weiner, *Party Politics in India* (Princeton University Press, 1957), pp. 170-71.
[10] Ward and Rustow, eds., *op. cit.*, pp. 445-47.

sis that would combine the best of tradition with the best of modernity is perhaps the least likely of all outcomes of the modernization process.[11] The Japanese experience stands out as an almost unique exception to this generalization. To a lesser extent, Turkey, too, from the reformers of the Tanzimat period to the Kemalists developed a constructive blend—a "reinforcing dualism"—of tradition and modernity. To the postcolonial countries, such a course is generally not open. Colonialism long ago destroyed both the traditional political structure at the top and much of traditional culture among the masses; African countries in particular have no precolonial political traditions embracing the entire territory of the postcolonial state. By the time an independent, postcolonial regime has taken over, both the best and the worst of tradition have disappeared beyond easy restoration, beyond any hope of using them to reinforce the modernization process. Noncolonial countries such as Japan and Turkey had the advantage of a continuing political structure that could be transformed from a traditional dynastic or oligarchic system into a modern national one. In the former colonial countries, and particularly in Africa, the political ingredients of a modern nation-state are largely yet to be assembled.

The Problem of Sequence

A further and most critical set of alternatives that confronts modernizing societies relates to the timing of the three quests for authority, for identity, and for participation and equality. Are all three to be undertaken at one and the same time, or are they to be pursued one by one? And if one by one, in what order are these political elements of the modern nation-state to be assembled? As with the alternatives examined earlier—those of speed and scope of modernization—the course of events is conditioned

[11] Manfred Halpern, "Notes on the Revolution of Modernization in National and International Society," *Nomos*, Vol. 8 (Atherton, 1965), p. 202.

by historical and contemporary circumstances. Within this setting of circumstance, however, there is a margin, now wider and now narrower, for deliberate choice. In an age of large-scale international economic and technical aid, moreover, the policy of the givers of foreign aid can be a factor of considerable influence. It is in the exercise of the available choices that the political leaders of a modernizing country can demonstrate their wisdom, the political followers their maturity, and the planners of foreign aid their foresight.

In traditional times, there was little if any direct relation between authority, identity, and equality. In all larger traditional societies, the social structure was steeply hierarchical, political participation narrowly limited, and equality therefore not a meaningful issue. Traditional authority often was quite independent of territorial identity. Large areas could easily be transferred among dynastic or colonial rulers by conquest, inheritance, or agreement. The Ottoman sultans, for example, founded their state in northwest Anatolia in the thirteenth century, later transferred the center of their operations to the Balkans while most of their Anatolian possessions were lost to Timur's invasion. They resumed their expansion into Anatolia and other parts of Asia in the late fifteenth and early sixteenth centuries.

In eighteenth century Europe, almost any peace treaty involved major reallocations of territory or thrones. The Duke of Savoy, for example, acquired Sicily in 1713 and exchanged it for Sardinia in 1720. In 1738, a Polish King became Duke of Lorraine while the Duke of Lorraine was transferred to Tuscany. During the same period, large portions of North America changed hands among the Dutch, British, French, and Spaniards. Clearly a traditional state, consisting of a court, an army, and a revenue service, could preserve its structure of authority regardless of such territorial changes and with disregard of the political attitudes of the subjects.

In an age of modernization, by contrast, authority and identity become closely interrelated. ". . . The greater the degree of common government, the greater must be the amount of effective mutual understanding and responsiveness."[12] The growth of authority and the acceptance of law and order by the subjects are greatly facilitated by cultural and linguistic unity. It is difficult to impose effective and acceptable authority on a checkerboard pattern of ethnic divisions or on isolated tribes and villages. The modern service state must have an identifiable and stable public to serve. Any change of territorial boundaries and any uncertainty of basic political identity undermines authority both by disrupting the continuity of administration and by throwing civic loyalties into confusion. For example, Syria merged with Egypt in 1958, seceded in 1961, and half-heartedly resumed negotiations for merger with Egypt and Iraq in 1963. Meanwhile, competition among rival schemes for Arab unity has tended to exacerbate political conflict and to undermine loyalties in almost every one of the separate states.

The connection between authority and equality is especially close. In eighteenth century France, for example, the strengthening of royal authority went hand in hand with a steady rise of the bourgeoisie at the expense of traditional aristocratic power, and this de facto alliance of monarchy and a rising lower class has been characteristic of many countries at similar stages of development.[13]

The fulfillment of the political demands of the lower social strata, and particularly any effective redistribution of wealth or social status, requires a strong government. Furthermore, the exclusion of any sizable social groups from political participation exposes a regime to challenge and potential overthrow. Conversely, general participation and equality greatly strengthen the acceptance of authority.

In view of these close connections, it might be concluded that

[12] Karl W. Deutsch, "Problems and Prospects of Federation," in Cyril E. Black, ed., *Challenge in Eastern Europe* (Rutgers University Press, 1954), p. 242.

[13] For a systematic exposition of this connection throughout history between "Power and the Common People" see, for example, Bertrand de Jouvenel, *On Power* (Viking, 1949), Chap. 10.

an ideal program of political development would launch into all three quests at once. The total vision of a strong state within securely defined boundaries and supported by wide mass participation in a unified population might help overcome the difficulties encountered in each separate quest. The triad of authority, unity, and equality, achieved all at once, might gratify the most ardent desire of modernizing countries, might propel them into marching proudly among the foremost nations of the world. But the case for such a synchronized rhythm of political development in regard to authority, identity, and participation is somewhat like the case for balanced economic growth in respect to such factors as capital formation, skills, consumption, production, and savings. Both are impeccable from some abstract points of view but reveal formidable difficulties on closer examination.[14]

If any attainment in authority, unity, or equality depended on a proportionate attainment in the two others, no progress in any of the three directions would be likely. The lack of unity and of equality would always defeat attempts at increasing authority, and the lack of authority would prevent any growth in either of the others. The result would indeed be balance, but instead of balanced growth there would be the balance of stagnation at a traditional level. Beyond such formal reasoning, several specific considerations may be adduced in favor of sequence rather than simultaneity of the three quests.

SEQUENCE RATHER THAN SIMULTANEITY

First, among the scarcest resources in any development process, economic or political, is the human capacity for innovation and for learning. Human attention has a variable but limited range in individuals and, even more, in any collective public debate. It is difficult for the participants in a political process to put their minds to too many basic issues at once. The ability of political

[14] For a trenchant critique of the model of balanced economic growth see Albert O. Hirschman, *The Strategy of Economic Development* (Yale University Press, 1959), especially Chaps. 3 and 4.

followers to develop new social habits is, if anything, even more limited than the leaders' attention span and capacity for innovation. It was noted that some of the more successful programs of modernization relied not only on blends of tradition and modernity but even on the device of "reinforcing dualism"—on strengthening tradition in some respects while forcefully pushing ahead with selected aspects of modernization. In his pioneering study of national integration in Europe, Karl W. Deutsch found that at a certain stage "the proponents of union had to make the union issue paramount in politics."[15] The failure of the German and Italian revolutions of 1848 was largely due to the fact that constitutional reform (that is, greater political equality) was hopelessly entangled with the issue of national unity: giving equal attention to both aims, the revolutionaries attained neither. Only when Cavour and Bismarck in the following decades assigned clear priority to national unification (with only minor concessions to constitutional reform) did the movement register solid success.

Second, each of the quests is likely to require different political skills, to be promoted by different myths and ideological symbols, and also to array different social groups in support and in opposition. While a skillfully combined program in some situations might maximize over-all support from a variety of groups, it is perhaps more likely that opposition rather than support will cumulate. For example, if proposed solutions to the problems of authority, identity, and equality each commanded the support of bare majorities of political participants, and if attitudes toward the three were related in random fashion, a combined program would command the support of just over one eighth of the total.

Third, there is a decisive difference in the speed appropriate to each of the three quests. Both authority and participation must grow fairly slowly and cumulatively over a period of several generations. The expansion of modern state services in communications, in education, in social welfare, and in economic planning

[15] Deutsch et al., *Political Community and the North Atlantic Area* (Princeton University Press, 1957), p. 113.

requires a steady growth of trained personnel; an over-ambitious pace is likely to lead to stagnation or to collapse of the governmental machinery. Similarly, a reliable expansion of the circle of political participants must proceed at a steady, gradual pace. A sudden revolution, whether by violence or by ballot, is likely to lead to the establishment of a new type of oligarchy or even to a temporary reversal of the modernization process.

By contrast, the establishment of a new political identity—such as the merger of smaller units into a new nation-state, or the secession of a country from a colonial or dynastic empire—must occur fairly rapidly and then be accepted as unchangeable for the future. Any prolongation of the process beyond a few years or decades is likely to lead to frustration and to kill off the original impetus; any lingering uncertainty will endanger the acceptance of the result.

Fourth, whereas authority, identity, and equality all tend to reinforce each other, the linkages are closer and more compelling in one direction than in others. Authority is reinforced, as just noted, by a sense of unity and of equality. But if identity and equality are to be newly established, a fairly strong system of authority must already be in existence so as to help secure the other two aims. The rise of the bourgeoisie and of monarchical power in France reinforced each other in the seventeenth and eighteenth centuries; but monarchical power had been growing from the time of Philip II (1180-1223) and Philip IV (1285-1314). By contrast, egalitarian lower-class movements without the support of state authority, such as the Albigeois (1209-29), the Jacquerie (1358), and the German Peasant Wars (1524-25), were doomed to failure.

Unless there is a fairly elaborate system of authority, there can be no large-scale division of labor, and the only equality possible will be on a primitive, pre-modern level of technology in small and isolated political and social units. Equality taken by itself can easily become an anarchic principle. Hobbes constructed his entire state of nature on the assumption that "Nature hath made

men so equall, in the faculties of body, and mind," in strength
and wisdom or rather in weakness and folly, that for all of them
equally life in the absence of authority becomes "solitary, poore,
nasty, brutish, and short."[16]

A successful quest for identity *pre*supposes authority just as
does any successful quest for equality. Deutsch found that a new
sense of national and territorial identity is most effectively built
around preexisting "core areas"—political units, that is to say, in
which there is an "excess of capability over loads," where the
trained administrative talent and the available economic
resources of the state exceed the demands placed on them by expressed popular needs.[17] Prussia in Germany and Piedmont in
Italy furnish classic examples of such core areas. It might be
added that the drive for Arab unity in recent years has been ham-
pered precisely by the absence of such a core area: Egypt has the
greatest pool of trained talent but the bleakest economic prospects among all the Arab countries, whereas countries like Kuwait, Libya, and Saudi Arabia have ample oil income but a shortage of administrative and political capability.

A fifth and final point is partly implied in the preceding discussion. Authority, and in many cases identity, can grow up in a
pre-modern, traditional context, whereas widespread political
participation and a closer approximation to political equality are
intimately bound up with other features of modernization in the
intellectual, social, and economic spheres.

SOME TYPICAL SEQUENCES

It seems clear, then, that the three political ingredients of the
modern nation-state are more effectively assembled one by one
than all at once, and that political participation and equality
should be the last, crowning achievement in the total process.

Among all possible sequences, there is little question that the

---

[16] *Leviathan* (1651), Book 1, Chap. 13.
[17] Deutsch et al., *op. cit.*, pp. 37-43, passim.

most effective one would be *unity–authority–equality*. This was the sequence in Japan which established national unity with the expulsion of the Ainus through the Japanese in prehistoric times and preserved its ethnic and cultural identity even at times when central authority dissolved into a welter of semifeudal principalities (1338-1573). Common authority was restored during the Tokugawa period (1603-1868) and buttressed by a highly developed educational system. Authority was further strengthened at the beginning of intensive and deliberate modernization during the Meiji period. Although there were some concessions to representative government, power remained in the hands of an imperial military and administrative bureaucracy. There was little clamor for broad political participation and equality until the 1920's and few effective moves toward it until after 1945.

But the Japanese sequence can hardly serve as a model for political modernization elsewhere. It emerged from a singular history which in turn was conditioned by a unique geographic situation. From the arrival of the Japanese themselves until 1945, the archipelago remained immune to invasion. In all these millennia, the only serious attempt at invasion, by Kublai Khan in 1275 and 1281, was beaten back by Japanese arms and by the stormy sea. The defensive modernization of the nineteenth century, in contrast to that in Russia and Turkey, was prompted by commercial penetration and an anticipated military threat rather than by any reality of attack. Although Japan between 1894 and 1941 repeatedly became involved in war, this was in each instance at its own option. It is clear that this record of cultural unity and geographic security is unmatched elsewhere in the world.

Even in Great Britain, which comes closest, Anglo-Saxons from the fifth century shared the archipelago with Celtic groups, and faced invasion by Danes and Normans, as well as serious threats from Philip II, Napoleon, and Hitler. For most countries, a century or even a generation of peace and freedom from external disturbance has been more than history would vouchsafe: the Japanese enjoyed these boons for well over a thousand years.

The second best sequence, and one more universally applicable, is *authority—identity—equality*. The earlier discussion showed that in most Western European nations linguistic frontiers came to follow the boundaries drawn over several centuries among dynastic realms. In Great Britain, France, Spain, Portugal, and the Scandinavian countries, both authority and identity were established in traditional times, before the advent of modernization and long before the rise of modern nationalism. Both evolved gradually, but authority generally took precedence.

There is another group of countries where authority grew gradually in a pre-modern or partly modern context and then served as the vehicle for the more rapid establishment of a modern national identity. The bureaucratic-military establishments of Prussia and Piedmont grew up in the seventeenth and eighteenth centuries and, as we have seen, served as the core areas for German and Italian national unification in the nineteenth century. In Turkey, conversely, the old imperial military and civil services presided over the formation of the nationalist republic. Significantly, in all three countries, concerted moves toward political equality came well after the establishment of authority and identity—in Germany first in 1918 and in all three countries after World War II. To expand Deutsch's theorem, it might be suggested that in Germany and Italy the "excess of capabilities over loads" was achieved by building up capability in one of a group of smaller states which then led the rest to unification. In the transition from Ottoman Empire to Turkish Republic, the "excess" was achieved by lightening the load. In each case, the build-up of a strong system of authority was essential to the successful accomplishment of the quest for national identity.

An opposite example may illustrate the difficulties of placing *equality* first in the sequence of political quests. The Mexican Revolution of 1910 originated in a revolt against the dictatorial regime of Porfirio Díaz and his narrow exploitive clique. Its slogan was "effective suffrage, no reelection" and its immediate aim to prevent Díaz, in rigged elections, from assuming an eighth presidential term. What had begun as an urban middle class movement broadened considerably during the following years. The constitution of 1917, drafted by an assembly for the first time elected by universal and equal suffrage, decreed far-reaching rights for farmers and workers. But the civil war that had broken out in 1910 still had barely subsided, and armed rivalry among the self-appointed revolutionary generals resulted in a number of coups and assassination of presidents. Order and continuity were not restored to Mexican political life until 1929, when Plutarco Elías Calles welded the various provincial political bosses into a single party machine which has been the country's effective ruler ever since. The first large-scale social reform program to implement some of the aims of 1917 came during the administration of Lázaro Cárdenas (1934-40). A social security code, envisaged by Article 123 of the constitution, was not enacted until 1943.

It may well be argued that the political chaos of Mexico was aggravated by this premature emphasis on equality at a time when governmental authority had collapsed and when national unity in a country part Mestizo and part Indian was still precarious; and that solid progress toward equality could be made only after the restoration of central authority by Calles and Cárdenas.

Having argued the advantages of a phased sequence of the three quests, it remains to point to an obvious danger—namely that the sequence will get stuck in one of the earlier phases, or even revert instead of progressing to the next phase. Because different personality types, ideologies, and alignments are suitable for the build-up of authority, unity, and equality, there is an inherent danger that a leadership that has successfully established authority will accentuate the divisive tendencies in the country or will use its power to perpetuate a narrow oligarchy and thwart rather than promote the search for equality.

The development of authority requires the expansion of the civilian and military bureaucracy. If this growing bureaucracy is recruited from increasingly wider social strata, trained for impersonal public service, promoted according to some objective system of merit, and dedicated to the rule of law, then it can at later stages promote integration. It can do this by responsiveness[18] to the demands of areas to be joined with the core and by facilitating redistribution of social power and the ascent of new classes. If, on the contrary, narrow patronage and corruption prevail within the bureaucracy, and exploitation, arbitrariness, and terror prevail in its dealings with the public, it will forfeit its opportunities for leadership in the quests for identity and equality; and it will ultimately risk the overthrow of the old system of authority itself.

The dangers could be illustrated from a number of contemporary programs of political modernization. But the development of authority in Mexico and in Ottoman Turkey before the revolutions of 1910 and of 1919 furnish examples within a more secure time perspective.

Porfirio Díaz had been widely hailed as a ruler who brought peace and prosperity to Mexico after the turbulence and anarchy of the first three-quarters of the nineteenth century. He also was, except for Benito Juárez (1867-72), the first Mexican president of lower-class, Indian descent. But the posts in the expanding government machinery of the "Pax Porfiriana" were concentrated in a narrower and narrower circle of personal followers. At one time, about two-thirds of the federal legislators were natives of his own province of Oaxaca. The benefits of economic development accrued either to foreign interests or to a narrow clique of Díaz's associates known as the Científicos. His rural police was notorious for shooting suspects while they were allegedly "trying to escape" instead of bringing them to trial. When the aging Díaz hinted in a press interview that he might allow opposition candidates in the next election but then rigged the result in his favor, the 1910 revolution broke out—with results, previously summarized, that swept away his entire structure of authority and, in a prolonged and bloody civil war, dissolved what unity Mexico had attained.[19]

[18] On responsiveness see Deutsch et al., *op. cit., passim.*

[19] On the Mexican Revolution and its aftermath see Howard Cline, *The United States and Mexico* (Harvard University Press, 1953), and Robert E. Scott, *Mexican Government in Transition* (University of Illinois Press, 1959), pp. 96-144.

The Ottoman Empire, during the decade before its collapse (1908-18), was governed mainly by the Committee of Union and Progress (also known to Westerners as the "Young Turks"). They were products of the European-type system of higher education instituted in the mid-nineteenth century and many of them had been further exposed to Western political and cultural influences during prolonged periods of political exile before 1908. Their aim was to transform the weak, divided, and semitraditional Empire into a strong modern state based on a common sense of civic loyalty. But the Union-and-Progress leadership was recruited almost entirely from the Turkish-speaking ruling minority of the Empire. When they proposed an expansion of the school system, it was Turkish-language schools they wished to open in Albania. When they applied a centralized system of administration to the Arab provinces, it was Turkish governors and army commanders whom they sent. When the Albanians rebelled in 1911-12 or some Armenians and some Arabs conspired with enemy powers in World War I, they applied sweeping programs of such ruthless repression that all these ethnic communities were hopelessly antagonized against the Empire.

In short, the Young Turks used their well-trained system of authority to disrupt rather than cement the precarious unity of their country. In these and other ways, they measurably hastened the collapse of the Empire which they had set out to save with such swashbuckling bravado.[20]

The argument just presented in favor of certain sequences among the three quests in preference to certain others should not be misconstrued into any unilinear theory of "stages of political growth." The attempt to interpret all of history as the repetition of a single pattern betrays a certain poverty and inflexibility of thought. The attempt to forecast future developments in all societies in terms of a single evolutionary "law" precludes any realistic insight into the diversity of human conditions and stultifies

[20] On the Young Turks see D. A. Rustow, "The Army and the Founding of the Turkish Republic," *World Politics*, Vol. 11 (July 1959), pp. 513-52, especially pp. 516-23 and 551-52.

the possibility of rational choice. Modernity, as suggested earlier, creates pressures which societies exposed to them cannot ignore; but they can respond to them in a number of different ways—each involving certain gains and losses. Among the three quests for authority, identity, and equality, thirteen different combinations of simultaneity and sequence are logically possible,[21] and (to the extent that the relevant phenomena can be clearly identified) historical examples could very likely be found for most of these.

Certain sequences may be foreclosed to a society at a given point in history: you can only start with what you have. Among the remaining patterns of sequence or simultaneity, there is nothing inevitable about a society adopting one rather than the other. Each pattern, however, has its peculiar advantages and disadvantages, its characteristic gains and costs; and the hypothesis has here been advanced in the light of certain historical examples that some sequences tend to maximize the overall gains and hence the chances for success.

A further and recurrent choice that societies have to make in the process of political modernization concerns the form of government, the pattern of political leadership under the aegis of which development toward nation-statehood will take place. This is a matter of supreme political importance which deserves separate discussion.

[21] Schematically, these patterns may be enumerated in the following list, where A(uthority), E(quality), and I(dentity) are represented by their initials, a hyphen denotes simultaneity, and a colon sequence: A-E-I A-E:I A-I:E E-I:A A:E-I E:A-I I:A-E A:E:I A:I:E E:A:I E:I:A I:A:E I:E:A

PART TWO

POLITICAL LEADERSHIP
IN NEW STATES

CHAPTER FIVE

THE NATURE OF POLITICAL LEADERSHIP

At the birth of societies, it is the leaders of the commonwealth who create the institutions; afterwards it is the institutions that shape the leaders.
MONTESQUIEU

Charisma is the one great revolutionary force in epochs bound to tradition.
WEBER

All leadership takes place through the communication of ideas to the minds of others.
CHARLES HORTON COOLEY

POLITICAL MODERNIZATION POSES with particular intensity the need for political leadership, and the more rapid the transition the more urgent the need. The first steps, as the earlier chapters have shown, are usually taken under traditional rulers. In Europe in the age of absolutism, and in Russia, Turkey, and Japan in efforts at self-defense against European expansion, hereditary monarchs undertook far-flung programs of reform. This incipient or defensive modernization generally concentrated on the instruments of state authority: on administration and the army, on public finance, and on education for public service. Elsewhere, colonial rule brought about a measure of similar modernizing innovations. But sooner or later, as modernization proceeded, the traditional leadership was radically and often violently transformed—in Great Britain in 1640, in France in 1789, in Japan in 1868, in Russia in 1917, in Turkey in 1919-22.

Americans pride themselves on living under a "government of laws and not of men." Communists look forward to a stateless society where "the government of persons is replaced by the administration of things."[1] Despite this touching motif of utopian anarchism in the rival political ideologies, the need for personal leadership has been recognized from Washington to Kennedy and from Lenin to Khrushchev. This need is even more obvious in countries that make the transition from colonial dependence to self-government. Many observers have suggested that in new states wise and firm leadership alone can make the difference between steady progress and early ruin. In short, in a world embarked on rapid technological change and involved in an unprecedented degree of global interdependence, the call for leadership has been continual and ubiquitous. Still, there has not yet developed an impressive or sophisticated theory of political leadership—whether in democracies or under dictatorship, whether in old nations or new.

The present chapter and those that follow will not attempt to fill this gap in theory. Rather, they will examine critically some of the current notions about forms of government in general and some of the typical patterns of leadership in modernizing societies in particular.

Forms of Political Rule

For centuries the problem of political leadership has been discussed under the heading of forms of government. The philosophers of ancient Greece opened the discussion with a plausible distinction: there can be government by one, government by some, or government by all. Aristotle and other thinkers varied the triad by distinguishing a healthy and a degenerate form of

---

[1] Friedrich Engels, *Anti-Dühring* (1877-78), Pt. 3, Ch. 2; also in *Socialism, Utopian and Scientific* (1880), see Lewis S. Feuer, ed., *Marx and Engels* (Doubleday, 1955), p. 106.

each type, or by advocating some mixture of the three. Aside from such refinements, however, the basic distinction survived through the ages. No government, clearly, could fall outside this trichotomy.

Yet if the logic of the distinction was impeccable, its application was dubious. That there can be no government by all, or even by a majority, at least outside of small and isolated communities, has been demonstrated by political theorists from Rousseau to Michels. That a single ruler cannot govern unassisted is no less obvious. As Harold Lasswell has put it, "Government is always government by the few, whether in the name of the few, the one, or the many."[2] But once all, or nearly all, empirical governments are conceded to be oligarchies, the utility of the triple scheme dissolves.

A generation or two ago, political scientists had arrived at a more elaborate and more empirical set of distinctions according to the manner in which a society's rulers were selected and in which the constitution, if any, allocated power among them. There were absolute and constitutional monarchies, presidential and parliamentary republics, unitary and federal states, unicameral and bicameral systems, and so forth. But these distinctions, too, seem today almost as outdated as the classic triad.

To appreciate how far the current concerns of political science have moved from these legal and constitutional categories, one need only glance at one of the earliest American textbooks in comparative government. In his book on *The State*, first published in 1889, Woodrow Wilson combined a treatment of Austria-Hungary and of Sweden-Norway in a single chapter on "dual monarchies" which he opened with the statement that these two were "Midway in character between unitary kingdoms like England and federal states like Germany."[3] It matters little that each of the dual monarchies broke up some years after Wilson

[2] "The Elite Concept," in H. D. Lasswell, D. Lerner, and C. E. Rothwell, *The Comparative Study of Elites*, Hoover Institute Studies, Series B, No. 1 (Stanford University Press, 1952), p. 7.

[3] Woodrow Wilson, *The State* (D. C. Heath, 1889), p. 336.

wrote; for no political scientist has it in his heart to blame a colleague for such a lack of foresight, nor do subsequent changes in the empirical facts invalidate the logic of their contemporary classification. Yet Wilson's chapter is today a curiosum because the very questions and assumptions about the nature of politics that underlay his presentation seem narrow, misleading, and quaint.

The transformation of the study of politics since Wilson's days came in several stages. From the time of World War I, political scientists began to carry their researches beyond laws and constitutions into parties and pressure groups, and later into public opinion and propaganda. By the nineteen-thirties, the European dictatorships had demonstrated what different political content could hide behind the same constitutional and legal forms. Hitler never took the trouble to abolish or formally amend the Weimar constitution, and Stalin's constitution of 1936, with its elaborate guarantees of rights and freedoms, hardly proved an accurate guide to the politics of the great purges.

In response to the rapid decolonization since World War II, students of politics have turned from their exclusive concern with Europe and North America to an extensive examination of Asia, of the Middle East, and of Africa; and the perspectives developed in these regions also have been applied to Latin America. In these non-Western settings, the older preoccupation with constitutional texts or even with formally organized groups proved altogether inadequate. In Iran, for example, the second chamber prescribed by the constitution of 1905-06 did not in fact convene until 1949; and even parties in much of Asia, Africa, and Latin America often are mere façades. The wider geographic horizons thus encouraged a keener interest in the social, economic, and cultural setting of politics and in political systems not just as they are at a given moment but as they evolve over longer periods of time.[4]

<hr>

[4] On these methodological developments see D. A. Rustow, "New Horizons for Comparative Politics," World Politics, Vol. 9 (1957), pp. 530-49, reprinted in Harry Eckstein and David Apter, eds., Comparative Politics: A Reader (Free Press, 1963), pp. 57-66.

CLASSIFICATION OF GOVERNMENTS

Even as scholars extended their researches in area, in subject, and in time, the number of sovereign states in the world doubled within less than two decades. Clearly, the task of classifying governments has today become more difficult and perhaps more urgent than it was in the days of Aristotle or of Wilson.

Such classification, once an evolutionary dimension is added to the scheme, constitutes far more than an academic exercise. It points to changes that may be expected in the real world, and hence provides guidelines, explicit or implicit, accurate or misleading, for the action of statesmen in influencing the future course of government in their own nations or in others.

Much of the foreign policy of major powers in the mid-twentieth century depends on the expectations formed by foreign offices of domestic political developments abroad. One evolutionary theory can lead Western policy makers to expect that parliamentary democracy in former colonies will result from the careful drafting of constitutional texts and other rules of procedure. Another theory may cause them to consider military coups and dictatorships in developing countries as normal and transitory occurrences or to expect the Soviet Union, given sufficient time, to evolve into a pluralist or even parliamentary system. A third theory may lead them to reject such notions of unilinear evolution and to think of the course of politics as a set of choices confronted by political men—choices differing from country to country according to its social setting and the outcome of political choices of the past.

Frequently, scholars as well as popular writers have arrayed governments along some sort of two-way spectrum. In the late nineteen-forties, journalists and orators began to divide the world into two zones, the democracies of the "free world" (which, ironically, was assumed to include their colonies) and the totalitarian regimes of communism. More recently a third, intermediate group has been added, labeled variously neutralist, nonaligned, or underdeveloped.

Some scholars have tried to correlate forms of government with levels of social or economic development and to fit these along a continuum of three, four, or five successive stages. The best known such effort is Walt Whitman Rostow's scheme of *The Stages of Economic Growth*, each of them said to be correlated with characteristic political patterns, and labeled (with generous mixture of metaphors) "traditional society," "pre-conditions for take-off," "take-off," namely into self-sustaining economic growth, "drive to maturity," and "age of high mass-consumption." Others have distinguished more broadly between traditional, transitional, and modern societies; among authoritarian, semicompetitive, and competitive political systems; or stable and unstable dictatorships from unstable and stable democracies.[5] Edward Shils has proposed five types of regime including traditional, totalitarian, and modernizing oligarchies and tutelary and political democracies.[6]

The propaganda phrase "free world" need not long detain us. It confuses internal form of government with external alignment in the American-Russian contest for world hegemony in the 1950's. A scheme that groups the United States and Norway with the regimes of a Trujillo, a Diem, or a Franco, that fails to distinguish between Czechoslovakia and Outer Mongolia, and that confuses

[5] See Rostow, *The Stages of Economic Growth: A Non-Communist Manifesto* (Cambridge, England: University Press, 1960), especially pp. 4-11; Max F. Millikan and Donald L. M. Blackmer, eds., *The Emerging Nations: Their Growth and United States Policy* (Little Brown, 1961); Lucian W. Pye, *Politics, Personality, and Nation Building: Burma's Search for Identity* (Yale University Press, 1962), pp. 15ff.; Gabriel Almond and James S. Coleman, eds., *The Politics of the Developing Areas* (Princeton University Press, 1960), pp. 538ff., 578ff.; Seymour Martin Lipset, "Some Social Requisites of Democracy: Economic Development and Political Legitimacy," *American Political Science Review*, Vol. 53 (1959), pp. 69-105, adapted in chapter 2 of his book *Political Man: The Social Bases of Politics* (Doubleday, 1960), pp. 45-76.

[6] *Political Development in the New States* (Mouton, 1962), previously published in *Comparative Studies in Society and History*, Vol. 2 (1959-60). An elaboration of the same scheme (with additional categories of "terminal colonial democracy," "colonial and racial oligarchy," and "conservative oligarchy") is used by Coleman in Almond and Coleman, eds., *op. cit.*, pp. 561ff.

Sweden with the Congo furnishes no effective clues for an understanding of domestic political processes.

The more scholarly efforts have the virtue of being concerned with the dynamics of political change, not just with the temporary condition of a political system; and Shils rightly stresses the possibility of "alternative courses of political development." But most of these schemes suffer from one or another of several defects which one would do well to avoid in constructing a classification for political systems in an age of modernization.

SOME COMMON FALLACIES

The first danger is the fallacy of unilinearism. Wherever quantitative indices are available, it is of course possible (and for some purposes useful) to arrange countries along a single spectrum. Nonetheless, the proposition that such a spectrum corresponds to a uniform evolutionary sequence should be empirically tested rather than axiomatically asserted. Since there has been no stage in the political history of the United States closely corresponding to present political conditions in the Soviet Union, in Yemen, or in Dahomey, there is no good reason to suppose that any of these will duplicate American conditions at any future time. At best the unilinear scheme becomes plausible only at a level of generality that abstracts from the crucial issues confronting statesmanship in the modern age. It is as if Darwin had expected the amoeba, in five successive stages of growth, to evolve into a fern, an elephant, a sequoia, and a dinosaur.

The assumption of unilinear evolution is, of course, one of several that many American writers share with communist theorists. Each school asserts that all societies move along a single path, though not at equal pace, toward some single, preordained goal. There is some disagreement about the exact sequence of stages. Communists from Marx to Mao have denounced "bourgeois democracy" as a case of arrested development en route to the proletarian millennium. American theorists have been tempted to change the sign at the finish line to "high mass consumption," while deploring totalitarianism as a childhood disease contracted in the transition to the "take-off stage" toward that ultimate condition.[7] Yet the notion of unilinear evolution hardly gains in cogency from this change in signposts.

The second danger is anachronism. Whereas Marx erected his grand evolutionary scheme on detailed historical researches, some contemporary unilinearists are basing their conclusion on a comparison only of current statistical data.[8] Specific levels of economic consumption or social skill should not be identified as contributing causes of the emergence of modern democracy without taking the precaution of inquiring whether such levels were reached in the days of Jefferson, of Gladstone, or of Clemenceau.

A third danger is that of ethnocentrism or other hidden biases. In a program of applied research, it is, of course, proper to inquire how the United States might go about propagating its system of government throughout the world. The value premise would not vitiate the findings as long as it is clearly stated. But in a scheme of pure analysis, the performance of political functions in developing countries should not be measured against a "model" based on Anglo-American democracy[9] without first demonstrating the relevance of the model. A different sort of hidden bias lurks in the distinction between "tutelary democracy" and "modernizing oligarchy" which conveys a value preference corresponding to no clear empirical difference—aside from the obvious self-contradiction in the phrase "tutelary democracy."

A fourth danger is the disregard of politics as a factor that can decisively shape social reality. Curiously, it is a danger to which non-Marxists or anti-Marxists in the United States seem to be much more prone than the Marxists themseves. For all their

---

[7] Rostow, op. cit., p. 162. The above paragraph is adapted from Robert E. Ward and Dankwart A. Rustow, eds., Political Modernization in Japan and Turkey (Princeton University Press, 1964), p. 5.

[8] Lipset, op. cit. For a cogent critique see Leslie Lipson, The Democratic Civilization (New York: Oxford University Press, 1964), p. 242.

[9] Coleman in Almond and Coleman, eds., op. cit., pp. 562ff.

professions of economic determinism, Marx and Engels held that the state had been founded in the political act of conquest, that relations among social classes were based on the legal ownership of land or capital, and that historical evolution must be hastened by political revolution. Marx at times and Lenin more consistently balanced the fatalist implications of the grand dialectical scheme with a considerable dose of organizational voluntarism.

Some American social scientists examining the problems of modernization such as Apter, Black, Deutsch, Huntington, and Hirschman, have shown a keen awareness of the importance of political choices.[10] But most of their colleagues have been preoccupied instead with the social, economic, and psychological causes of political phenomena. They have sought the requisites of democracy in literacy or in affluence. They have traced the ambivalent attitudes of Burmese officials to crises of personal identity. They have ascribed the Middle Easterner's response to newspapers and radio programs to his capacity for empathy or his familiarity with city life. They have attributed economic growth to changing methods of toilet training.[11] Heedless of all that Lenin, Nkrumah, and others have preached about the primacy of politics, they have relegated politics to the position of dependent variable. No one will mourn the sterile legalism of Wilson's days; but today's generation of scholars has been in danger of throwing the political baby out with the institutional bathwater, of letting their interdisciplinary enthusiasm carry them to the point of self-effacement as political scientists.

[10] See for example, David E. Apter, The Politics of Modernization (University of Chicago Press, 1965); Cyril E. Black, The Dynamics of Modernization (Harper, 1966); Karl W. Deutsch, "Social Mobilization and Political Development," American Political Science Review, Vol. 55 (September 1961), pp. 493-514 and especially Deutsch et al., Political Community and the North Atlantic Area (Princeton University Press, 1957); Samuel P. Huntington, "Political Development and Political Decay," World Politics, Vol. 17, No. 3 (April 1965), pp. 386-430; and Albert O. Hirschman, Journeys Toward Progress (Twentieth Century Fund, 1963).

[11] For these several themes see the writings of Coleman, Lipset, and Pye cited in note 5, p. 140; Daniel Lerner et al., The Passing of Traditional Society: Modernizing the Middle East (Free Press, 1958); and Everett E. Hagen, On the Theory of Social Change (Dorsey, 1962).

The final danger is a confusion between correlation and causation. If the statistics show a correlation between democracy and certain levels of economic performance and if this correlation is too consistent to be accidental, this may suggest that affluence helps produce democracy; that democracy is conducive to affluence; that both are promoted by some third set of factors; or indeed that several of these hypotheses are true, each for part of the empirical material.[12] To cite a related example, a high degree of literacy is often held to be a prerequisite of effective democracy. Yet contemporary Latin American and African evidence suggests that universal franchise without literacy requirements is one of the most effective means of forcing governments to expand education and hence promote literacy.

Politics, economics, sociology, and psychology are so many different aspects of the same seamless web of social reality abstracted for the observer's convenience (or, sometimes, inconvenience). The relation between them must therefore be seen as one of multiple, circular interaction. A good case, furthermore, can be made for asserting that most of man's political activities—the joining of a party, the drafting of a constitution, the seizure of power by military coup—are more deliberate than his economic pursuits, his social habits, or his psychological predispositions. Economics, in Lionel Robbins' classic definition, is concerned with the allocation of scarce means to given ends.[13] In politics the ends are never given. If the social scientist is to help illuminate the range of

---

[12] Although Lipset explicitly acknowledges the two-way interaction of democracy and its socio-economic correlates (*Political Man,* p. 74), and speaks of "requisites" rather than prerequisites, he time and again slips from the language of correlation into the language of causation: "the higher the education . . . , the better the chances for democracy", "the contribution of education to democracy"; "comes close to being a necessary [condition]"; "the more well-to-do a nation, the greater the chances that it will sustain democracy." Pp. 50f., 55, 56, 57. Rostow attacks Marx's economic determinism but still chooses economic criteria for his evolutionary stages. On the distinction between correlation and causation, see W. G. Runciman, *Social Science and Political Theory* (Cambridge, England: University Press, 1963), pp. 91-97.

[13] Lionel Robbins, *An Essay on the Nature and Significance of Economic Science* (London: Macmillan, 1932), p. 15.

human choice, he must be sure to examine politics not only as effect but also as cause.

In attempting a classification of contemporary systems of government, the political scientist must avoid the fallacies of determinism, anachronism, and ethnocentrism; he must acknowledge politics as an independent as well as a dependent variable; and he must not confuse correlation with cause. Indeed, if the classification is to help him in understanding dynamic relationships in the real world, he would do well not to short-circuit the empirical investigation by introducing evolutionary assumptions into his definitions. While awaiting the development of a comprehensive and dynamic political theory, he would do best to start with a more modest set of categories that stay close to the observable features of states engaged in a variety of processes of modernization.

VARIETIES OF GOVERNMENT IN A MODERNIZING WORLD

Among the well-established modern national states, many are democracies and some are totalitarian regimes—the extant ones communist, some recent ones of other ideological hues. Neither democracy nor totalitarianism in their familiar forms can exist in a traditional, pre-modern society.[14] Hence there is no valid reason for asserting that either regime as such is more modern than its rival.

Modernization, it was suggested earlier, is morally ambiguous: as it extends man's mastery over nature, it makes him more dependent on other men; and democracy and totalitarianism each choose opposite horns of the modern political dilemma. But this is a modern dilemma and a choice between two modern systems.

[14] Barrington Moore, Jr., has examined "Totalitarian Elements in Pre-Industrial Societies" in *Political Power and Social Theory*, 2d ed. (Harper, 1962), pp. 30-88. Whether his examples are accepted depends largely, of course, on one's concept of totalitarianism.

Neither the Bolshevik revolutionaries of November 1917, who erected a totalitarian system on the ruins of Kerenski's parliamentary regime, nor the Hungarian revolutionaries of the fall of 1956, who tried to replace Stalinist autocracy by a more nearly democratic regime, can fairly be characterized as traditional, anti-modern movements. The Bolsheviks did not restore the Tsar or peasant serfdom, and the Hungarians, had they succeeded, would not have gone back to Horthy, the landed magnates, or the Habsburg monarchy.

Most developing countries today, however, are ready to reproduce neither democracy nor communism. The path of modernization that would carry them closer to either regime is the same path for some considerable distance, with the crucial fork still in the haze of the future. This, of course, is the reason Americans and Russians have been able to compete in wooing semitraditional countries with similar programs of economic and technical assistance.

The surviving traditional regimes may thus be singled out as one contemporary form of government. These today still include such countries as Afghanistan, Nepal, Paraguay, Haiti, and (at least until the outbreak of the civil war in 1962) Yemen. In addition, such countries as Libya, Saudi Arabia, Cambodia, Jordan, Thailand, Morocco, and Iran may be considered semitraditional. Yet the number in either category has been declining steadily. At the modern end of the spectrum, not one but two forms must be distinguished, democratic and totalitarian; and the question "Which of these is more modern?" must be answered not by advance definition or current theory but by empirical assessment of future development.

It should here be remembered that all three terms—traditional, democratic, totalitarian—are to be taken in a conventional rather than a strictly logical sense. Tradition, as noted in an earlier chapter, is largely a residual concept—a category including a large variety of social systems that become similar only when contrasted with modernity. Democracy in the real modern world necessarily falls short of its supreme ideals of political equality and universal participation. The concept of totalitarianism seems to rest on three tenuous assumptions: that there is a finite and fixed number of functions in society, that these are all known at present, and that in a given society the totality of these functions is performed by one giant organization controlled from a single center. A more logical labeling has been suggested by T. H. Rigby. He distinguishes "traditional societies" based on the principle of custom, "market societies" based on the principle of contract, and "organizational societies" based on the principle of command. The only disadvantage of this set of terms for purposes of political analysis is the exclusively economic flavor of the middle one.[15]

The threefold distinction of traditional, democratic, and totalitarian regimes (or traditional, market, and organizational societies) does not, of course, exhaust the empirical possibilities in today's modernizing world. Indeed, it leaves out most of the countries of Asia, Africa, and Latin America that are the special concern of this study. Nor can this gap be filled by summarily classifying such countries as "transitional"—for the concept of transition hardly does justice to the long duration of the process or to the magnitude of the choices that it involves. Surely a "transition" that in some Latin American countries has lasted a century and a half and the direction of which still is far from certain deserves some analysis in its own right.

Among the many forms of government in the recently modernizing countries, there are three that seem distinct enough and have occurred with sufficient frequency to be added to the first three, namely personal (or "charismatic") regimes, governments installed by military coup, and single-party regimes of a nontotalitarian variety sometimes referred to as "authoritarian." What

[15] "Traditional, Market, and Organizational Societies and the USSR," *World Politics*, Vol. 16, No. 4 (July 1964), pp. 539-57. Rigby derives his scheme from an adaptation of Weber's triad, which will be discussed presently.

thus emerges is a sixfold classification of regimes in the world today:

A 1 Traditional
B   Modernizing
   2 Personal (Charismatic)
   3 Military
   4 Single Party (Authoritarian)
C   Modern
   5 Democratic
   6 Totalitarian

Several caveats, however, should be borne in mind. First, the classification is based on groupings of empirical phenomena rather than on abstract logical distinctions; and the order of listing within groups (B) and (C) does not imply any hypothesis as to evolutionary sequence. Second, there are many possible mixtures among the six forms. Paraguay today displays both military and traditional features; the Mexican one-party system includes some democratic elements; and those under Nkrumah and Touré were partly charismatic, partly traditional, and at times veered toward totalitarianism. Third, regimes change their character over time. The Turkish Republic originated in a military regime in the early 1920's, evolved into an authoritarian one-party system, and lately has moved toward democracy—although there was a second military interlude in 1960-61. Finally, there is always a seventh possibility—that of the absence of any coherent form of government, as, for example, in the former Belgian Congo after 1960. But with all these qualifications and cautions, the claim may be made that this sixfold scheme allows an orderly grouping of governments as they are found in the mid-twentieth century.

Charisma and the Founding of States

To Max Weber social scientists owe the insight that men may willingly obey from habit, from interest, from devotion to a person—or, more commonly, from some combination of the three. Relations between a people and its rulers (or more generally, followers and their leaders) based on obedience from habit he called "traditional authority," those based on obedience from interest "rational authority," and those based on obedience from personal devotion "charismatic authority." The three categories, Weber asserts, exhaust the possibilities of *legitimate* authority, legitimate not by some standard formulated by himself but rather in the eyes of the subjects. He deliberately excluded situations of pure coercion.[16] Military rule, therefore, is not covered by his scheme, except as it transforms itself into something more than compulsion. Single-party, totalitarian, and democratic regimes would be included mostly under "rational authority." In a traditional system, authority is considered legitimate because it is exercised as it has been from time immemorial. In a rational (or, as Weber often says, rational-legal) system, authority is considered legitimate because it is exercised according to stated rules and because it is to the subject's advantage to abide by these. In a charismatic system, the subject obeys because of the divine gift of grace, or a similar quality, that he sees embodied in the leader.

WEBER'S THEORY

Here is what Weber, in his most complete exposition of the concept, has to say about charisma and its workings:

> . . . The term "charisma" shall be understood to refer to an *extraordinary* quality of a person, regardless of whether this quality is actual, alleged, or presumed. "Charismatic authority," hence, shall refer to a rule over men . . . to which the governed submit because of their belief in the extraordinary quality of the specific *person*. . . . The legitimacy of charismatic rule . . . rests upon the belief in magical powers, revelations and hero worship. The source of those beliefs is the "proving" of the charismatic quality through miracles, through

[16] Cf. Peter M. Blau, "Critical Remarks on Weber's Theory of Authority," *American Political Science Review*, Vol. 57 (1963), pp. 305-16 at p. 306.

victories and other successes, that is, through the welfare of the governed. Such beliefs and the claimed authority resting on them therefore disappear, or threaten to disappear, as soon as proof is lacking and as soon as the charismatically qualified person appears to be devoid of his magical power or forsaken by his god. Charismatic rule is not managed according to general norms, either traditional or rational, but, in principle, according to concrete revelations and inspirations, and, in this sense, charismatic authority is "irrational." It is "revolutionary" in the sense of not being bound to the existing order: "It is written — but I say unto you. . . ."[17]

This last theme is emphasized in another passage where Weber says that "Charisma is the one great revolutionary force in epochs bound to tradition."[18]

Charisma probably is not a very apt term in political discourse; yet it has become firmly established since Weber's day particularly in reference to dictators and to political-cultural changes in postcolonial states.[19] The word originally referred to the gift of "speaking with tongues" as described in the letters of Saint Paul— that is, to a palpable if unusual behavior trait—and Weber himself

[17] H. H. Gerth and C. Wright Mills, eds., *From Max Weber: Essays in Sociology* (London: Routledge, 1947), pp. 295-96; for other Weberian definitions of charisma, see *ibid.*, p. 79, and Max Weber, *The Theory of Social and Economic Organization*, A. M. Henderson and Talcott Parsons, eds. (New York: Oxford University Press, 1947), pp. 328, 358.

[18] Max Weber, *Wirtschaft und Gesellschaft*, 4th ed., by Johannes Winckelmann (Tübingen, J. C. B. Mohr, 1956), p. 142. For a slightly different translation see Weber, *The Theory of Social and Economic Organization*, p. 363.

[19] For discussions of charisma in new states see, for example, David Apter, *The Gold Coast in Transition* (Princeton University Press, 1955), pp. 30-31, 320-24, 329-30; Edward Shils, "The Concentration and Dispersion of Charisma," *World Politics*, Vol. 11 (October 1958), pp. 1-19; Pye, *op. cit.*, pp. 29-30; Manfred Halpern, *The Politics of Social Change in the Middle East and North Africa* (Princeton University Press, 1963), pp. 273-74, 284-85; Seymour Martin Lipset, *The First New Nation: The United States in Historical and Comparative Perspective* (Basic Books, 1963), pp. 16-23. For criticisms of the concept cf. Arthur M. Schlesinger, "Democracy and Hero Worship in the Twentieth Century," *Encounter*, Vol. 15 (December 1960), pp. 3-11; Carl J. Friedrich, "Political Leadership and the Problem of Charismatic Power," *Journal of Politics*, Vol. 23 (February 1961), pp. 3-24; and K. J. Ratnam, "Charisma and Political Leadership," *Political Studies*, Vol. 12 (October 1964), pp. 341-54. For the Pauline antecedents of the term see for example, Daniel Bell, "Sociodicy: A Guide to Modern Usage," *The American Scholar*, Vol. 34, No. 4 (Autumn 1966), pp. 696-714, especially 702-06.

encouraged a common misconception when he defined charisma as "a certain quality of an individual personality by virtue of which he is set apart from ordinary men."[20] But in his more careful moments, as in the longer passage just cited, Weber makes it quite clear that charismatic authority is a process of interaction between leader and followers and that the decisive aspect is the followers' belief. Since Weber's day, a good deal of writing by social scientists on leadership in general and charisma in particular has emphasized that these are relational properties rather than personal traits.[21] As beauty is said to be in the eye of the beholder, so the leader's charisma is in the mind of the follower.[22] In Weber's scheme, so long as his followers attribute to the leader superhuman traits of prophecy, or magic, or heroism he is by definition a charismatic figure. The followers' attitude in turn (empirically rather than by definition) is influenced not so much by specific personal qualities common to all charismatic leaders, but rather by the magnitude and improbability of the results he obtains. No results, no belief; no belief, no charisma.

Since Weber intended charismatic authority as an "ideal type," it is misleading to ask whether a given system of authority is charismatic in Weber's sense; the only meaningful question is to what extent it is—or rather to what extent at a given time. Nor of course is charisma synonymous with dictatorship or limited to societies in process of rapid transition from tradition to modernity. Many dictators have relied on coercion or on organizational power (that is, rational-legal power) more than on personal ap-

[20] Weber, *The Theory of Social and Economic Organization*, p. 358.
[21] Cf. Muzafer Sherif, *An Outline of Social Psychology* (Harper, 1948), p. 458; David B. Truman, *The Governmental Process* (Knopf, 1951), pp. 188-93; Sidney Verba, *Small Groups and Political Behavior: A Study of Leadership* (Princeton University Press, 1961), p. 121; Amitai Etzioni, *A Comparative Analysis of Complex Organizations* (Free Press of Glencoe, 1961), pp. 203-04; Ann Ruth Willner and Dorothy Willner, "The Rise and Role of Charismatic Leaders," *Annals of the American Academy of Political and Social Science* (March 1965), p. 79: The leader's "charisma resides in the perceptions of the people he leads."
[22] Erikson has aptly spoken of the "charismatic hunger of mankind." Erik H. Erikson, *Young Man Luther: A Study in Psychoanalysis and History* (Norton, 1958), p. 16.

peal. Conversely, even in a democracy, party founders such as Disraeli and crisis leaders such as Roosevelt in 1933 and Churchill in 1940 are likely to assume a largely charismatic role.[23]

Indeed, since Weber's threefold distinction among types of legitimate authority is meant to be exhaustive, one may infer that the charismatic element is more prominent the weaker the traditional and the rational elements. This is the chief reason Weber's concept is so widely applicable in situations of decolonization, where both traditional and rational-legal elements of authority are suddenly dissolved and the entire weight of legitimacy may come to rest on a single leader and his personal reputation. But in the same context it is well to recall that while charisma *may* provide a regenerative force in such transitional societies, it is also possible (in the absence of "routinization" of charisma or of its continual reassertion through magic successes) that charismatic legitimacy may break down. Anarchy and dissolution of the political system into smaller geographic units are limiting situations which, like coercion, remain outside Weber's scheme.[24]

Charisma, like all leadership, is a mutual relation between leaders and followers. More fully considered, it is a fourfold relationship between leaders, followers, circumstances, and goals. Nobody is a leader unless he has followers, and nobody can be either a leader or a follower unless together they are going somewhere. The four important questions about leadership are: Who is leading whom from where to where? Weber's term charisma places the emphasis on the first question. But, generally, the other three are easier to answer, and those three together tend to shed more light

[23] Joyce Cary's posthumous novel *The Captive and the Free* (London: Michael Joseph, 1959) depicts in vivid detail charismatic authority as exercised by a faith healer in twentieth century Britain.

[24] For further interpretations of Weber's concept see Reinhard Bendix, *Max Weber: An Intellectual Biography* (Doubleday, 1960), Chap. 10; W. G. Runciman, "Charismatic Authority and One-Party Rule in Ghana," *Archives Européennes de Sociologie*, Vol. 4, No. 1 (1963), pp. 148-65; Karl Loewenstein, *Max Weber's Political Ideas in the Perspective of Our Time* (University of Massachusetts Press, 1965); William H. Friedland, "For a Sociological Concept of Charisma," *Social Forces*, Vol. 43, No. 1 (October 1964), pp. 18-26.

on the first question than would an examination of the leader's personality in isolation. Charismatic situations can be more readily identified than charismatic qualities. Different circumstances, different goals, and different followers put a premium on different personal qualities in a leader. The personal characteristics of an individual, moreover, tend to become sharply transformed as he assumes a position of leadership. Leadership qualities develop as they are exercised. Charisma is as charisma does. In short, the phenomenon of leadership is three parts setting and one part personality. The leader at times is the script writer but more often the *souffleur* of the historical drama.[25]

The primary task of a leader may be interpreted as one of mediation, synthesis, or integration: among the various individuals and groups that make up his following, between the realities of the situation and the aspirations of the followers, between an unsatisfactory present and visions of a better future. Note that this task of multiple reconciliation remains even when there are no human opponents to be battled—for example, for the chief of a nomadic tribe who must find a ford across the river during the trek from summer pasture to winter pasture.

CHARISMA IN NEW STATES

The founding of a new state in the process of transition from colonialism to independence is one of the most arduous and delicate tasks of political leadership. Beyond the usual tensions between conflicting interests of followers and antagonists, among different groups of followers, and between aspiration and reality, it involves a number of closely related factors.

First, there is a sharp tension in time perspectives. The task of forming a new political identity, as shown previously, must be rapidly accomplished. In any unification or secession movement,

[25] Arthur F. Bentley, using a similar metaphor, once said that it was difficult to establish whether in passing a given bill "the legislature was Moses the lawgiver or merely Moses the registration clerk." *The Process of Government* (University of Chicago Press, 1908), p. 163.

including the secession of colonies, a steady or even accelerating momentum must be maintained, lest unique opportunities be irretrievably lost. Yet the results of such urgent and rapid action must prove durable. The founding of a new state entails risks and sacrifices which its would-be citizens will not undertake unless the resulting structure may be expected to last for generations to come. To found a state for only a decade or a half-century clearly is not worth the toil and the anguish. The necessary combination of time perspectives—of resoluteness and durability—is not likely to result solely from collective deliberations, let alone to emerge spontaneously among an unstructured or disorganized group of people. On the contrary, it requires an organization headed by a single, personal leader.

Second, there is a reversal of the usual inverse proportion between weightiness and urgency of political issues. In a well-established commonwealth, and outside of revolutionary situations, most of the basic decisions of domestic politics can be allowed to mature the longest. This tends to be true whether the prevailing issues relate to social reform, to political equality, to economic production or distribution, or what not. There always are early warnings to signal the approach of a major issue. A final decision usually can be postponed until the conflicting claims have been registered, clarified, and tested, the possible alternatives fully explored, and until the pressure for ultimate action has become irresistible. In the meantime, a tentative policy can be tried out. If the remedy proves excessive, it can be scaled down. If it proves inadequate, it can be enlarged. If it fails altogether, a new solution can be devised. In short, most domestic issues can be divided into parts, the parts can be variously combined, and the combination constantly readjusted. The entire operation can turn into a more or less orderly process of experimentation and learning. Only crises of foreign affairs, and especially of war, confront established states with questions as urgent as they are weighty; and in times of foreign crisis, even democracies tend to suspend their constitutional procedures and to invest their leaders with plenary powers.

During the formation of a new state, by contrast, domestic and foreign affairs are more closely intertwined than at any other time: the whole task consists in drawing a new and viable geographic boundary around the new state—that is, a boundary between the domestic and foreign spheres. In the founding of a state, a whole host of problems are closely entangled: the process presents a major problem of indivisibility in the economist's sense of that term. Only a single leader can successfully discharge the responsibility of tying up and delivering the entire package.

Third, there is a sharp and well-known contrast between the political attitudes appropriate immediately before and after independence. In the last stages of colonial rule, the aim of the independence movement is to demonstrate as clearly as possible the inadequacy of the existing order. All issues tend to be politicized and all conflicts are exacerbated. Sabotage and destruction, divisiveness and intransigence become a way of life. On the morrow of independence, economic issues move to the top of the agenda, and the passwords are unity, hard work, and sacrifice. Meanwhile, the demise of the old regime has weakened the structure of authority and left a vacuum of expertise. With all offices open for reassignment to natives, the claimants and hence the jealousies multiply overnight. And the masses who have successfully sought the political kingdom insistently clamor that all else be added unto them at once. This abrupt reversal of policy, this sudden shift of attitudes is difficult to accomplish in the best of circumstances. Without centralized and respected leadership a smooth transition becomes impossible.

Fourth, the founders of new states more than any other political leaders must combine involvement and detachment. The leader must be sufficiently remote to discourage rivalry and disputes over his leadership position. Yet to devise solutions acceptable to his followers, he must be intimately familiar with their present (and their likely future) mood, as well as keenly cognizant of the realities of their situation.

The first and fourth of these considerations—the combination of opposite time perspectives and of involvement and detachment—

have been admirably summed up by Rousseau who, following
Plato, called the founder of a state the "law-giver," and described
his ideal qualifications in the following eloquent passage:

> To discover those rules of association that would best suit each
> nation there is need for a superior intelligence acquainted with all
> of men's passions but liable to none of them; wholly detached from
> our nature yet knowing it to the full; its happiness independent from
> us yet willing to be concerned with us; able, in the pursuit of future
> glory in the course of time, to toil in one century and to reap in
> another. Only a god could give laws to men.[26]

Note that Rousseau, like Weber, stresses the need for superhuman, seemingly divine characteristics, but that he goes considerably further in specifying what these extraordinary qualities are.

A fifth, and summary, consideration may be adduced to explain
the need for personal leadership at times of rapid and fundamental transition such as the birth of a new state. Man is adaptable
and his adaptability can be heightened in some situations. Yet
there is no doubt that the human capacity for change has finite
limits. Change in human politics can consist of a change of leaders or of a change of institutions, and it follows that the more institutions are in flux, the more there is a need for continuity of
leadership. This basic insight, too, was expressed with great clarity by a French political philosopher almost two centuries before
Weber offered his discussion of charisma. "At the birth of societies," Montesquieu said, "it is the leaders of the commonwealth
who create the institutions; afterwards, it is the institutions that
shape the leaders."[27]

Montesquieu's statement points to the more general characteristics of charismatic situations. If a political order is to endure,
political man must find stability either in leaders or in institutions. The more the legitimacy of institutions is in question, the
more is there a need to find legitimacy in persons. At moments

---

[26] Jean Jacques Rousseau, *Contrat Social* (1762), Book 2, Chap. 7.
[27] *Considérations sur les causes de la grandeur des romains et de leur dé-
cadence* (1734), Chap. 1; Rousseau quotes the same passage.

when the entire order of political institutions is to be changed—as in the attainment of independence or generally the founding of a new state—the entire burden of legitimacy is on the person of the leader in the transition. The relationship can be expressed in a simple, though not quantifiable, equation:

$$\text{Political Stability} = \text{Legitimacy of Institutions} + \text{Personal Legitimacy of Rulers}$$

Stability, that is to say, can be maintained if an increase in legitimacy of rulers compensates for any loss of legitimacy of institutions, and vice versa.[28] The formula restates a central part of Weber's theory. Since institutions may be either traditional or modern ("rational-legal" in Weber's language), or a combination of the two, Weber's hypothesis can be summed up in a second formula equivalent to the first:

$$\text{Political Legitimacy} = \text{Traditional Legitimacy} + \text{Rational-Legal Legitimacy} + \text{Charismatic Legitimacy}$$

To obtain the same amount of political legitimacy, any decrease in one of the terms must be compensated by an increase in one or both of the others. The mathematical expression makes it clearer perhaps than does Weber's text that the personal legitimacy accorded to rulers (just like the legitimacy of institutions) is a matter of degree and hence subject to variations, whether gradual or sharp, over time. Charisma (or rather charismatic situations) are an ideal type—a matter not of either-or but of more-or-less.

THE LEADERSHIP SITUATION

Charismatic situations in the last few paragraphs have been described, for the sake of brevity, in terms that might suggest a teleological view of causation or a "great man theory of history."

[28] For a specific instance, see my chapter in Lucian W. Pye and Sidney Verba, eds., *Comparative Political Culture* (Princeton University Press, 1965), p. 197.

Before proceeding, it will be well to clear up any misconception on either of these counts. Neither the success of any venture in state founding, nor the particular program that guides it, nor the choice of the particular leader who directs it are in any way predetermined. Nor, of course, does the leader accomplish his task single-handedly. Each of these points deserves some elaboration.

The tensions of modernization, of nascent nationhood, of the formation of a nation-state present many opportunities for creative leadership; but there is no guarantee that the opportunities will be seized, the needs met, or the conflicts and problems resolved. The foregoing considerations merely suggest that *if* the experiment is to succeed, *if* the transition is to be smooth, *if* order and stability are to be maintained, *then* some such process of synthesis, of leadership, of resolution must take place.

In fact, attempts at modernization may miscarry; and like all human history, the early history of nations is full of missed opportunities. In addition to the six types of regime distinguished earlier, there is the seventh possibility of an absence of orderly government. Among the forms of government, anarchy always looms as the last choice, the choice of default.

Furthermore, there are always a variety of formulas by which the resolution of a given conflict may be attempted; for a problem that has only a single plausible solution—a situation that has only one possible outcome—does not, *ex hypothesi,* give rise to conflict, and hence does not create a political situation. These truisms are overlooked by those historians who are tempted to express their findings in providential or determinist language—to suggest that the Tsarist Empire was "doomed" to collapse or that the nineteenth century drive for German unity was "bound" to succeed. In sober truth, knowledge of historic causation is far too sketchy to permit ruling out the possibility that a number of alternative formulas might also have succeeded. One of the prime difficulties of situations of rapid political change is precisely their indeterminacy, the abundance and complexity of alternatives. This need for many choices of goals and of means, of strategy and of tactics, makes concentrated leadership indispensable. Leadership is not the product of inevitability but an instrument of choice. And one of the political scientist's most important tasks is to reconstruct the choices that leaders have confronted in the past.[29]

It may well be argued that among fallible human beings no leader can ever be skillful and perspicacious enough—that "only a god could give laws to men." Yet, whatever the prevailing level of skills, it seems likely that there are several possible candidates at that level.

In the early stages of nationalist organization, for example, there is typically an active competition for leadership, and this competition provides an important test of the qualifications of candidates. Once the leadership is settled in one single person, several important changes occur. The followers become closely attached to the person of the leader, and the leader himself displays new resources of mind and of will which he now applies to his task. Although the question, by its nature, cannot be conclusively answered, it would be difficult to argue that the competitor who narrowly lost out was overwhelmingly less qualified than the one who won; or that, given the opportunity, he would not have developed similar new resources of leadership talent.

The leader tends to be considered indispensable by his followers in direct proportion to the difficulties of the task at hand. This belief generally is encouraged by all the means of publicity available to the movement, and it is of course one of the prime instruments by which a leader will try to enhance and to stabilize his power. Foreign journalists and later historians, too, are notorious for their inclination to endorse the winning faction, to applaud power, and to adulate success. Yet the notion of indispensability

[29] Reinhard Bendix warns of what he calls the "fallacy of retrospective determinism," and rightly insists that we must "conceive of the future as uncertain in the past as well as the present" and "keep the possibility of alternative developments conceptually open." *Nation-Building and Citizenship* (Wiley, 1964), p. 13. For an admirable work of historiography that avoids this fallacy as it recreates for the contemporary reader the full excitement of past political choices, see R. R. Palmer, *The Age of the Democratic Revolution*, 2 Vols. (Princeton University Press, 1959-64).

of a particular leader is due to an understandable optical illusion: it is leadership as such rather than leadership by some particular individual that is indispensable.

In a variety of ways, the leader may be said to be more dependent on the supporting movement than the movement on any particular leader. There can be no leadership without followership, and since the followers must be many, they are in a sense less accidental than the individual leader. There were preparations for Turkish nationalist resistance before Mustafa Kemal appeared in Anatolia to take the lead; the Indian National Congress was founded when Gandhi was a boy; and World Wars I and II that led to the collapse of the Ottoman and British Empires, respectively, were started neither by Kemal nor by Gandhi. In short, there would have been a Turkish and an Indian nationalist movement without Atatürk or without Gandhi, but without these movements neither man would have been a nationalist leader. Many leaders launch or found their own movements, but even then they depend on the readiness of a potential rank-and-file.

It is very well for the followers to attribute the leader's success to magic or to superhuman qualities. It is a different matter for the leader himself, who, after all, is a human being and must achieve the results. If his leadership is to endure, he cannot trust to luck alone. Consciously or unconsciously, he must hit on a program that fits into the real world of causation, and he must display personality traits suitable to his particular task of leadership.

The specific qualifications required of any charismatic leader are suggested by the earlier observation that charisma, like all leadership, is a process of synthesis among leader, followers, circumstances, and goals. The distance between the terms which are to be mediated determines the intensity of the need for leadership; the greater the distance, the greater the need for leadership and for concentration of leadership in a single person. The specific nature of the three other elements—followers, situation, goals—determines the particular qualifications that the leader must bring to his performance. A number of obvious illustrations

THE NATURE OF POLITICAL LEADERSHIP

come to mind. Quintus Fabius Maximus, who employed a strategy of evasion and attrition in defending Rome against Hannibal's long-distance attack, earned the nickname Cunctator, the Lingerer; yet most military leaders, especially those engaged in the offensive, rightly pride themselves on their resoluteness. Dwight Eisenhower, commanding a large-scale invasion by a coalition army, was selected in part for diplomatic skills, of which other generals had far less need. In politics, in an age of face-to-face contacts, the liberator of the Netherlands, William of Orange, was famed as "the Silent." Today, in an age of mass audiences, the great political leaders—Lenin, Atatürk, Roosevelt, Hitler, Churchill, Nasser, Nkrumah, Castro—invariably turn out to be great talkers. If a country acquires its independencce through negotiation, diplomatic talent will be in demand; if independence is won on the battlefield, the martial qualities of a Washington or an Atatürk come into play.[30]

An earlier chapter noted that rapid modernization tends to bring forward programs of "reinforcing dualism" and political actors who "play to two galleries at the same time." Similarly, sweeping changes in social structure bring to the scene dissident aristocrats or bourgeois who apply the intellectual and organizational skills of their upper-class backgrounds to promote the rise of a lower class. Proposals for the redefinition of national identity are most ardently formulated by marginal nationals, individuals who have been through a *Fremdheitserlebnis* (the experience of being a stranger), who have reason to question and then vigorously reassert their personal identification with a nation.

More generally, Deutsch has found that programs of basic political realignment are most effectively pursued by coalitions of the "most outside of the insiders" with the "most inside of the outsiders."[31] Clearly, the most appropriate leader is one who is a one-man coalition of outer inside and inner outside. In each situation, that is to say, the most effective political leaders are those

[30] Cf. Truman, *op. cit.*, pp. 190f., on skills and situation.
[31] Deutsch et al., *Political Community and the North Atlantic Area*, p. 88.

who through personal background and intimate experience have become thoroughly familiar with the terms to be mediated and with the conflict among them—those for whom the resolution of a collective political crisis comes to be congruent with the resolution of an intimate personal crisis. As Erik H. Erikson and Lucian W. Pye have strikingly suggested, the "great man in history" is one who has a "need to settle a personal account on a large scale and in a grand context."[32] The opportunity for greatness beckons when the accounts of a potential mass following are similarly unbalanced and in need of the same settlement.

LEADERSHIP AND COMMUNICATION

All these elements—modernity versus tradition, upper-class origins and championship of the lower classes, *Fremdheitserlebnis* and nationalism, detachment and involvement, ambivalence and resolution—are to be found in recurrent combinations among recent state founders and leaders of "new nations." As I have said elsewhere, so-called charismatic leadership in emerging nations today has a "Janus-faced character,"[33] and the most effective modernizers are leaders of "an elite that serves its apprenticeship under a [previous] order but demonstrates its mastery in building a new one."[34]

Many illustrations of these several themes come to mind among recent Asian and African leaders: Gandhi's stay in South Africa,

[32] Pye, "Personal Identity and Political Ideology," in Dwaine Marvick, ed., *Political Decision-Makers* (Free Press, 1960), pp. 290-310; cf. Pye, *Politics, Personality, and Nation Building*, pp. 52-53 and literature in footnotes. Erikson suggests that it was possible for a man such as Luther "to lift his individual patienthood to the level of a universal one and to try to solve for all what he could not solve for himself alone"; that he "settled a personal account by provoking a public accounting." *Op. cit.*, pp. 67, 250.

[33] Dankwart A. Rustow, *Politics and Westernization in the Near East* (Princeton: Center of International Studies, 1956), p. 29.

[34] "New Horizons for Comparative Politics," *op. cit.*, p. 543.

his appeals for modern mass action on the basis of ancient Hindu symbols, for industrialization through cottage industry, for Hinduism cleansed of untouchability; Atatürk, born in a peripheral area of mixed nationality, acceding to legitimate rule in the traditional manner through victory in war, but performing the traditional role of warrior-ruler-educator for the purpose of replacing dynastic-religious tradition with a modern secular-nationalist order; Hasan II of Morocco, nationalist monarch claiming direct descent from the Prophet but choosing to rule through a plebiscitary constitution; S.W.R.D. Bandaranaike, Christian- and English-educated aristocrat leading the Buddhist lower classes in a triumphant campaign for "Sinhalese Only"; Hastings Kamazu Banda recalled from his detachment as practicing physician in Britain to lead the nationalists of his native Nyasaland (now Malawi)—the examples, the combinations and permutations, could be multiplied almost at will.

What have just been illustrated are some of the specific leadership qualities—the personal tensions and conflicts experienced in a person's life that help him resolve the similar conflicts of large numbers of people throughout an entire society. Naturally, these qualities vary from conflict to conflict, from situation to situation. Beyond these, there are certain general qualities of leaders (including charismatic leaders) in all situations. These are the talents or traits of personality that help them perform the essential leadership activities—the synthesis among followers, circumstances, and goals—in general. The most obvious of such leadership qualities are ambition and an enjoyment of power. But the more rarely found and hence more important leadership quality is an ability to receive, select, and convey information.

Atatürk, when asked how he had won the Turkish War of Independence, replied "With the telegraph wires"—and indeed the control of the army's secret and rapid communications system, which he most tenaciously defended in his contest with the sultan, was one of the prime ingredients in his leadership in the nationalist movement.[35] And one of the chief uses of information to the leader is to enhance not only his foresight in regard to the consequences of various courses of action, but more especially his resourcefulness—his ability to formulate new alternatives when plans go wrong. For leadership, particularly in its incipient stages, inevitably involves a gradual learning process through trial and error.

An orderly, phased flow of information provides the indispensable link between leader, followers, circumstances, and goals in the leadership process. "All leadership takes place through the communication of ideas to the minds of others. . . ."[36] The "underlying structure of events" has been described by Conrad M. Arensberg in a hypothesis that seeks to account for the empirical findings of comparative leadership studies by anthropologists and social psychologists in the last several decades:

It is (1) personal acts of followers (B, C, . . .) taking information or other impulses to the leader (A). It is (2) delayed response by A. Then it is (3) an invitation to action issued by A to the followers, evoking (4) a joint, common, unified, or simultaneous response from them. A leads B and C, has followers, if this drama, or process, unfolds event by event *in the order indicated* and not otherwise. Needless to say, the information must be accurate, the delay appropriately long or short, and the outcome must be "successful."[37]

It seems likely that a comprehensive and accurate theory of political leadership will emerge from further empirical studies taking account of Erikson's hypothesis of congruence of experience between leader and followers and Arensberg's hypothesis of a phased flow of information between them, and generally making full use of the analytic tools of the theories of learning and communication.[38]

[35] See D. A. Rustow, "The Army and the Founding of the Turkish Republic," *World Politics*, Vol. 11 (1959), p. 519.

[36] Charles Horton Cooley, *Human Nature and the Social Order*, rev. ed. (Scribner, 1922), p. 328.

[37] Letter to the writer, December 22, 1964.

[38] For further suggestions along these lines, see Karl W. Deutsch, *The Nerves of Government: Models of Political Communication and Control* (Free Press, 1966).

CHARISMA: SUCCESS AND SUCCESSION

"The outcome must be 'successsful' "—and success recalls Weber's emphasis on the magic or miraculous quality of the results that distinguishes charismatic leadership from traditional or rational-legal leadership. W. G. Runciman, in analyzing the charismatic qualities of Nkrumah and his Convention People's Party in Ghana's transition to independence, surmises that

> Even without a leader of Nkrumah's qualities, the first party victorious [in Gold Coast elections] was likely to remain the embodiment of the charisma derived from achieving the national aim. [The electorate's indifference to opposition,] the control of patronage and propaganda, together with the claim to have forced the concessions granted by the colonial power, meant that the first party to mobilize the necessary electoral support on some sort of national basis would be unlikely to be ousted by any rival national movement. Only a drastic failure to achieve its promulgated objectives could bring this about by depriving it of the manifest and recognized success necessary to counteract the instability inherent in all charismatic authority.[39]

In politics, the likeliest way in which charisma may be demonstrated is by powerful results achieved in the absence of power, for example, through the antagonist's weakness, or of power as previously understood, for example, by the marshaling of hitherto latent resources. The colonial withdrawal from Africa provides an example of the first type of miracle, Gandhi's nonviolent campaign that forced the repeal of the British-Indian salt tax of the second. In either case, the charismatic claims of the first person to achieve such novel results are far stronger than those of any imitators or successors.

Nkrumah's charisma seemed strongest among all African leaders mainly because his country was the first to achieve independence in a continent that was long thought to be doomed to perpetual colonial servitude. Touré's charisma was stronger than that

[39] Runciman, "Charismatic Authority and One-Party Rule in Ghana," *op. cit.*, p. 154.

of any other leaders in former French Africa because in 1958 he was the only one to opt for independence and to defy de Gaulle by compensating for the loss of French economic aid from other foreign sources. Nasser's charisma exceeded that of other Arab leaders because he was the first Arab soldier not only to seize power (1952-54) but also to retain it for more than five years; the first successfully to play out Russia against the United States (1955-56); and the first, after years of mere talk about Arab unity, to achieve the union of two countries (1958). The last example illustrates the need, stressed by Weber and others, for not just one spectacular success but for a whole series of them. "What have you done for me lately?" the proverbial American voter asks his representative. "What miracles have you worked for us lately?" the charismatic followers demand of their leader.

All political leaders, of course, strive for success—and indeed for continuing success—in their pursuit of the art of the possible. But success looms far larger in the purely charismatic system of authority, in one based solely on personal devotion and unsupported by traditional claims or by modern organization. In the game of politics, pure charisma is the gambling table with the highest stakes. Not only the leader's tenure but his very life, the regime he has established, and perhaps national independence itself, are risked on the outcome of each new venture.

Dependent as he is on continual success, the purely charismatic leader's commitment to magic and his aversion to organization imply a weakening of all the normal instruments for achieving success in domestic policy and economic planning. This limitation tends to rechannel energies into propaganda, where spurious successes can be manufactured more or less to order, and into foreign policy, where some magical successes may await him who skillfully exploits the deadlock between two superpowers.

It is no coincidence that those postcolonial leaders whose authority initially derived more from charisma than from organization—Nkrumah, Sukarno, Touré, Nasser—also proved to be the most vociferous and venturesome in their diplomacy. But each propaganda victory that substitutes imaginary for real benefits and each foreign success not based on genuine strength only postpones the final reckoning, and magnifies the ultimate risks. As Weber insisted, it is the "welfare of the governed"—or at least their perception of their welfare—that remains the ultimate test.

Perhaps the risks in the long run are even greater in foreign than in domestic affairs. The crucial international factors all are beyond the charismatic leader's control. Too many new states may be trying to exploit East-West tensions all at once; the superpowers, in any case, may tire of being played upon; and strains in Sino-Soviet or Franco-American relations may blur the bipolar situation and hence reduce the exaggerated leverage of the unaligned. It may prove difficult to insulate domestic propaganda from the corrective flow of international communication. Even the glare of publicity at frequent international meetings can be a mixed blessing. What happens to charisma as fifty inflated egos meet at their summits in Bandung or Belgrade?

For a time, that is to say, foreign successes may be used—deliberately or instinctively—to distract from domestic problems. But in the long run, a charismatically founded regime can be stabilized only at home—and, as Weber pointed out, "routinization" of charisma is the only path to stability. Similarly, the real test of leadership comes not in success but in adversity. Nasser's true stature, for example, emerged not in his early years, but after 1956 when his regime survived defeat at Suez, Syrian secession, and stalemate in Yemen.

Luckily for new states and their leaders, charisma is an "ideal type" rarely if ever found in pure form in politics—so that some routine elements are usually mixed in with charismatic authority from the very start. Charisma, after all, is a religious concept fully embodied only in leaders whose realm is not of this world. Gandhi concentrated more than any other non-Western nationalist leader on the kind of revolutionary inward transformation of which Weber spoke. He refused consistently to become entangled in the day-by-day affairs of the Congress movement. He kept his charisma pure—avoided the need for routinizing it—by leaving routine matters to the party. But if Gandhi contributed the spirit, it was the organization of the Indian National Congress that provided the necessary cohesion in the transition to independence and political stability afterward. Other leaders have combined personal or charismatic appeal more directly with organizational efforts—including Nehru in India itself, Atatürk, who quickly transformed the local remnants of the Committee of Union and Progress into a new nationwide party, and Nasser, who after his military seizure of power came to rely increasingly on the support of a vast bureaucratic establishment. Atatürk's early political career also illustrates his constant endeavor to create new institutions while disguising the novelty of the institutions he created[40]— in short to minimize the instability of the charismatic, the personal, and the "miraculous" elements in his authority.

Success and succession are the two words that sum up the instability of charisma. It has been suggested in these pages that the political leader is from the start more dependent on his followers than the followers on him; he is doubly dependent on them in the end. A charismatic leader whose appeal remains purely personal and magical and who, with great good fortune, sails from success to success in his lifetime will inexorably founder on the succession problem. An acute succession crisis can be avoided only if well in advance of his death he has encouraged a complex and comprehensive organization, a set of structured institutions, perhaps a formalized ideology—in short if he himself has seen to the "routinization" of his charisma. Charisma must achieve its final success by transforming itself into something more stable and less miraculous than pure charisma. Only with a movement to lend him support and to continue his work beyond

[40] See D. A. Rustow, "Origins and Consolidation of the Turkish Nationalist Movement," summarized in the proceedings of the 25th International Congress of Orientalists, *Trudy Dvadtsat' Piatovo Mezhdunarodnovo Kongressa Vostokovedov* (Moscow, 1963), Vol. 2, pp. 483ff.

his lifetime can the founder of a state "toil in one century and reap in another."

Among the characteristic forms of government in today's developing countries, charismatic authority is legitimate but unstable. Before examining other, more stable forms of legitimate rule, such as authoritarian single-party systems, the discussion will turn to a form of regime that is unstable because at the outset it is illegitimate—that is, one based on military seizure of power.

CHAPTER SIX

MILITARY REGIMES

For such authority is to trump in card-playing, save that in matter of government, when nothing else is turned up, clubs are trumps.
HOBBES

I had imagined that our role was to be this commando vanguard. . . . Then suddenly came reality. . . .
NASSER

A soldier's duty cannot be performed with talk and politicking.
ATATÜRK

ARMED SEIZURE OF POWER and other forms of military interference in politics have been frequent and widespread in modernizing countries. In the year 1958, the Middle East and Southern Asia reverberated with the political activity of soldiers. Coups overthrew civilian governments in Burma, Pakistan, Iraq, and the Sudan; one military faction deposed another in Thailand; army officers were deep in the complex maneuvers that joined Syria with Egypt in the United Arab Republic under Colonel-President Nasser; the Arab Legion of Jordan, with the temporary help of British units, shored up the regime of King Hussein; and a smoldering civil war in Lebanon abated when the major factions offered the presidency to the commander-in-chief, Fuad Shihab. Meanwhile, the armed forces provided crucial support for the governments of Presidents Rhee in South Korea, Diem in South Vietnam, and Sukarno in Indonesia, of the Shah in Iran, and of Premier Menderes in Turkey; but within the next few years the same armies overthrew Rhee, Diem, Menderes, and Sukarno.

170

In Latin America, there was a similar rash of coups in the early sixties: in Peru and Argentina in 1962; in Guatemala, Ecuador, the Dominican Republic, and Honduras in 1963; and in Brazil and Bolivia in 1964. Even in Tropical Africa, where most governments ventured on independence with military forces of no more than battalion or regiment strength, prolonged civil wars broke out in the Congo (Leopoldville) and the Sudan; there have been coups or attempts at coups in Togo, Dahomey, Mali, Congo (Brazzaville), Gabon, Ghana, and elsewhere; mutinies threatened the newly established governments of Tanganyika, Kenya, and Uganda, and the Nigerian coup of 1966 set off an ethnic conflict in which army units were involved on each side. Nor was the period from 1958 to 1964 in the Middle East and Latin America an isolated wave. "Between independence and World War I," by one specialist's count, "the Spanish-American republics experienced 115 successful revolutions [that is, violent overthrows of government] and many times that number of abortive revolts"[1]—which averages out to one successful coup per republic about every fifteen years—and in Syria there have been as many as three coups in a single year.

The Legacy of Violence

Soldiers have been prominent in Middle Eastern and Latin American politics throughout history. The Middle East, because of its location at the juncture of three continents, has long been a thoroughfare for conquerors. Naguib and Nasser were merely the first indigenous officers to seize power in a country that had been ruled by soldiers from the days of Cambyses (525-522, B.C.) to those of General Wavell (1940-45, A.D.). Islam, one of the most martial of world religions, was imposed on the area by the Arab conquest of the seventh and eighth centuries; the last period of

[1] Edwin Lieuwen, *Arms and Politics in Latin America* (Praeger, 1960), p. 21. In Mexico alone there were over 1,000 military uprisings between 1821 and 1914. *Ibid.*, p. 101.

political unity in the Middle East resulted from the Ottoman conquests of the fourteenth to sixteenth century. The Ottoman sultans, as indicated in a previous context, introduced their Westernizing reforms first into the army and were in due course overthrown by officers who had embraced Western notions of representative government and nationalism. To this day Middle Eastern military officers are closer in their ethos to the Bonapartist than to the Junker tradition.[2]

The interlude of British and French rule in the Arab countries from the 1880's to the 1950's served to reinforce the tradition of violence in politics. Imperialism came to the Middle East much later than to Asia and Africa—at a time when Westerners had begun to feel somewhat apologetic about it. But in its disguise as temporary occupation or mandate government, foreign rule was doubly odious to educated Middle Easterners, and the result was a dreary pattern of nationalist uprising and imperial repression. In the judgment of the leading British historian of the region:

> There is a case to be made for as well as against the imperial peace . . . as a stage in the development and spread of civilizations; [yet] there is little that can be said in defence of the so-called imperialism encountered by the Middle East in the first half of the twentieth century—an imperialism of interference without responsibility, which would neither create nor permit stable and orderly government.[3]

The militarist tradition in Latin America is of equally long standing. The modern culture of Spain and Portugal was forged in eight centuries of bloody warfare (722-1492) in which the Christian principalities of the northern mountains ejected the Moorish rulers from the remainder of the Iberian peninsula. The first troops that Spain dispatched to the Americas, significantly, were veterans who had just completed this *reconquista* with the capture of Granada. In North America, English colonists settled

[2] Cf. D. A. Rustow, "The Military in Middle Eastern Society and Politics," in Sydney Nettleton Fisher, ed., *The Military in the Middle East: Problems in Society and Government* (Ohio State University Press, 1963), pp. 3-20.

[3] Bernard Lewis, *The Middle East and The West* (Indiana University Press, 1964), p. 59; cf. D. A. Rustow, "The Political Impact of the West" in *The Cambridge History of Islam* (forthcoming).

fertile spaces with little resistance from scattered and diminishing tribes. But the Spaniards to the South subdued the powerful Aztec and Inca empires and established themselves as a military and landed oligarchy over the Indian peasantry. To this day manly virtue, both in Spain and in Hispanic America, remains a boisterous and bellicose ideal.

Independence and modernization reinforced this military tradition. The colonial system came to an end with Napoleon's conquest of Spain. The Spanish settlers, or creoles, at first sided with the Bourbons but then forcibly resisted the reestablishment of royal authority. During the protracted wars of independence (1810-26), representative assemblies convened to draft liberal constitutions. Yet military men such as Bolívar, Santander, Sucre, O'Higgins, and Iturbide emerged as the actual rulers—at least for a time.

Further fragmentation soon set in. Bolívar's Gran Colombia dissolved into three states. Central America seceded from Mexico and was further subdivided into five units. Lengthy civil wars ensued in Mexico, Peru, Uruguay, and Chile, and in many parts political power devolved on local caudillos with their private armies. At times the prolonged rule of a single military dictator provided a spell of political continuity.[4] Centralization and professional training of the armed forces toward the turn of the century in countries like Chile, Argentina, and Brazil, broke the power of the caudillos without removing the military from politics. "The arms revolution . . . may be considered as having made the national forces a great source of strength to the state, but not necessarily to the parliamentary form of government."[5]

Whether in the Middle East or in Latin America, the political prominence of the military is no momentary lapse from precedent. Rather, it is the intervals of peaceful rule by civilians that have

[4] For example, Santa Ana and Díaz in Mexico, 1833-55 and 1876-1910; Rosas in Argentina, 1829-52; Francía and the two López's in Paraguay, 1811-70; Gómez in Venezuela, 1909-35.

[5] John J. Johnson, The Military and Society in Latin America (Stanford University Press, 1964), p. 248.

been the exceptions. In Latin America such intervals occurred in Chile from 1831 to 1924, in Argentina from 1853 to 1930, in Uruguay from the beginning of this century, and in Mexico since the 1930's. In the independent countries of the Middle East, there has been civilian government in Turkey from 1923 to 1960, in Lebanon since 1945, and in Israel since 1948.

Parallels to these Middle Eastern and Latin American themes could be found in other regions: the military impulse to modernization in Japan and Thailand; United States "imperialism of interference without responsibility" in the Caribbean; the warlord tradition and the same irresponsible imperialism in China; protracted guerrilla wars preceding independence in Indonesia, Vietnam, Algeria, and Cyprus.

Because of their very abundance and variety, however, these precedents prove both too little and too much. In the Middle East, the martial character of Islam may have contributed to militarism; but in Catholic Spain and Latin America the same effect has obtained; and there have been repeated coups in Burma and Thailand with their tradition of Buddhist otherworldliness. The same signs of military politics are appearing in Tropical Africa which was largely spared the intense violence accompanying colonialism elsewhere.

Military modernization may have propelled the soldiers onto the Egyptian and Turkish political stages, but General Stroessner of Paraguay, the Somoza family in Nicaragua, and the late Generalissimo Trujillo of the Domican Republic can hardly be accused of the same reformist zeal that animated Mahmud II of Turkey or Muhammad Ali of Egypt. Conversely, Mexico between 1910 and 1929 experienced as turbulent a period of civil war and anarchy as any Latin American country, yet since that time has consolidated a civilian structure of government. And experiences such as the Bolshevik coup in Petrograd in 1917, the Kapp Putsch of 1920 in Germany, the fall of the Fourth Republic in France, and the many coups in East-Central Europe between the world wars should remind us that armed seizure of power is not limited to countries south of the Tropic of Cancer.

Clubs Are Trumps

The true explanation must be sought not in the history of armies or of wars but in the relationship of the military with the remainder of the political structure. Military interference becomes possible wherever distinct civilian and military organizations have emerged within the structure of government. In primitive societies, where warfare is the sole business of government, or where it is inextricably blended with other political functions, military takeovers are *ex hypothesi* impossible. Even in more complex political systems—in the early Roman and Ottoman Empires, in Europe in the feudal and absolutist eras, in the Spanish kingdoms of the *reconquista*, and in colonial Hispanic America—the same merger of functions may persist. The army *is* the government and hence cannot usurp it. But where citizen armies personally commanded by the rulers give way to mercenary troops hired by palace potentates, the possibility of praetorian coups is ever present —as under the Roman emperors, the Arab caliphs, and the Ottoman sultans in their respective periods of decline.

In modernizing or modern societies, civilian and military functions become necessarily distinct. Where once knights supplied their own horses and grooms for armies that "lived off the land," soldiers now are systematically recruited, troops paid in cash, and citizens required to pay taxes. The more elaborate division of labor in society, the expanding scope of government, and the mounting complexity of warfare and administration all reinforce the distinction between soldiers and civilians. The possibility of military coups and other forms of armed interference in politics now arises. Indeed, as political participation spreads beyond a small ruling circle, such upheavals will involve ever wider groups of the populace as prime contestants or as secondary supporters.[6]

---

[6] Samuel E. Finer, in the most comprehensive survey of the problem to date, attributes military intervention primarily to two conditions: the professionaliza-

What turns the possibility of interference into a probability is not the strength of the military but the weakness of the civilian structure. The postwar political role of armies illustrates the point. Soldiers are likely to seize power or otherwise emerge as the arbiters of politics not after victory but after defeat: in Turkey after the Balkan War and World War I; in Greece after the Anatolian debacle of 1919-22; in Syria and Egypt in the aftermath of the Palestine War of 1948; in Bolivia after the loss of the Chaco War of 1932-35; in Russia after 1917; in Germany after 1918; in France in 1958-61 after the defeats in Indochina and Algeria. By contrast, Turkish victory in the War of Independence was followed by 37 years of military withdrawal from politics, and Israel, the only Middle Eastern country to win any recent battlefield victories, has also been the only one immune to military coups.

Military politics in the defeated countries tends to follow a typical pattern. The army, to be sure, has shown its inadequacy on the battlefield, but the civilian government that led the country into the war, that had charge of supplies, and to which the soldiers were responsible, must bear most of the odium of defeat. Keenly sensitive to the shame of its own humiliation, the army is likely to join the government's most vehement critics. Not all commanders are as disingenuous as General Ludendorff, Germany's virtual dictator in 1917-18, who first peremptorily ordered the civilian politicians to conclude an armistice and a few years later joined those who denounced them for stabbing the undefeated army in the back. Yet the same scapegoat motif recurs in attenuated form in Nasser's reminiscences of the rout at Faluja in

---

tion of the officer corps and the rise of nationalism and the nation-state. (*The Man on Horseback: The Role of the Military in Politics*, Praeger, 1962, especially p. 207.) This statement seems too narrow, for it does not account for the praetorianism of earlier periods; yet it is sounder than Lieuwen's view that "the rise of professionalism . . . offered some prospect of curbing militarism." (*Op. cit.,* p. 31.) For a broader application of the concept of praetorianism see David C. Rapoport, "A Comparative Theory of Military and Political Types," in Samuel P. Huntington, ed., *Changing Patterns of Military Politics*, International Yearbook of Political Behavior Research, Vol. 3 (Free Press of Glencoe, 1962), pp. 71-101.

1948.[7] In the atmosphere of recrimination resulting from defeat, armies too weak to beat the enemy at the frontiers still retain ample strength to overwhelm their unarmed opponents in the capital. And more often than not, they will be applauded by the populace: The army is beaten, long live the army. Seizure of power at home beckons as the defeated army's consolation prize.

That weak governments, not strong armies, account for the prevalence of military coups is further demonstrated by the recent situation in Tropical Africa, where diminutive armed forces —at times mere platoons with a few submachine guns—have ousted governments that lacked any organized sources of civilian support. In tracing the etiology of coups, the student of civil-military relations therefore would do well to concentrate on the inadequacies of the civilian government.

Politics, Thomas Hobbes suggested long ago, is like a game of cards: the players must agree which card is to be trump. With this difference, he added, that in politics, when no other card is agreed upon, clubs are trumps.[8] The basic reasons for military intervention are the lack of a sense of legitimacy of the government and the disparity, as Karl Deutsch might say, between the capabilities of government and the loads it has to carry. Disagreement on constitutional procedures, inexperience with government by discussion, a precarious feeling of national identity, lack of technical qualifications among civil servants, a general dearth of educated personnel, atrophy of political parties, diffuseness of economic interest groups—all these reduce governmental capability. Deep-seated ethnic conflicts, exaggerated economic expectations of newly aroused masses, rapid changes in the social structure,

[7] "I would say to myself: Over there is our country, another Faluja on a larger scale. What is happening to us here is a picture in miniature of what is happening in Egypt. Egypt too is besieged by difficulties and enemies; *she* has been deceived and forced into a battle for which *she* was not ready, *her* fate the toy of greed, conspiracy, and lust, which left *her* without weapons under fire." Gamal Abdul Nasser, *Egypt's Liberation: The Philosophy of the Revolution* (Public Affairs Press, 1955), p. 23

[8] "A Dialogue . . . of the Common Laws . . . ," *English Works*, Sir William Molesworth, ed., 11 vols. (London: J. Bohn, 1839-45), Vol. 6, p. 122.

foreign dangers that lurk from the old colonialists of the West and the new colonialists of the East, at times defeat in war—all these add to the burdens. John Johnson, in the light of the Latin American evidence, sees in militarism a form of political decay, a result of "the disciplinary breakdown of an institutionalized fighting force."[9] The factors of weakness and decay just listed are largely the same as those that create a need in new or rapidly modernizing states for charismatic leadership and for comprehensive nationalist parties. It is the absence of such leaders and parties or their manifest inadequacy that creates an atmosphere where violence becomes not only the ultima ratio but all too often the prima ratio of politics, where juntas secretly prepare to seize power, where the ambitious subaltern carries in his knapsack not the marshal's baton but the ruler's scepter.

Two typical situations of susceptibility to military interference may here be singled out: new states that have just been released from colonial rule and unpopular governments that must rely on the armed forces for their continued rule.

Only a few of the post colonial states of Asia and Africa have had to fight for their independence, and in most of these (for example, Indonesia, Vietnam, Algeria) the army has been at the center of the political stage from the beginning. Elsewhere, the transition to independence has been essentially peaceful, the result ultimately of the abdication of the imperial power. Invariably, in line with concepts of legitimacy prevailing in their own Western tradition, the imperial rulers surrendered power to civilian successors. But a majority of those successor regimes established ten or more years ago have in the meantime succumbed to the military.

In the Middle East, the regularity of timing of the initial military coups has been remarkable. Iraq was released from mandate status in 1932; in 1936, General Bakr Sidqi executed his military coup which, in the next five years, was to be followed by six others. In Syria, French occupation was withdrawn early in 1946;

[9] Johnson, The Military and Society in Latin America, p. 17.

in 1949, there were three successive military coups under Colonels Zaim, Hinnawi, and Shishakli. In 1947, the British discontinued their wartime occupation of Egypt proper, concentrating their remaining troops along the Suez Canal; in 1952, the Free Officers seized power under General Naguib and Colonel Nasser. The Sudan attained independence early in 1956 and by the end of 1958 succumbed to a coup under General Abbud. In the Middle East, it took from three to five years for civilian institutions in new states to become sufficiently discredited and for army officers to grow sufficiently restive to set the stage for a first coup. In other countries, the time span has been somewhat longer—ten years in Burma, eleven in Pakistan. African experience, in turn, has conformed closely to the Middle Eastern timetable: 1960 was the great year of independence; 1965 and 1966 were great years of military coups.

Both in former colonial and noncolonial countries military coups frequently follow periods of internal unrest in which an unpopular government has come to rely on armed forces to maintain itself in power. On this point, examples from the Middle East abound. The formative experience of the Young Turk conspirators of 1908 was the losing fight which Abdülhamid's government was carrying on against rebellious subjects on the Balkans and defiant vassals in Arabia. Reza Khan, before his 1921 coup in Iran, had distinguished himself by suppressing the secessionist Gilan Soviet Republic. General Bakr Sidqi of Iraq became a popular hero by his ruthless suppression of the Assyrian uprising in 1933 before seizing power in Baghdad three years later. The Egyptian revolution of 1952 was preceded by fours years of near civil war. And the military revolutions in Iraq in 1958 and in Turkey in 1960 were preceded by several years of forcible suppression of political opposition; the Turkish upheaval clearly reflected the army's refusal to let itself be used any further as a tool of Menderes' repressive policies.

Civilian rulers who rely on the armed forces for protection from popular unrest sooner or later will come up against the fateful question that Presidents Ebert of Germany and Bayar of Turkey had to put to the soldiers of their entourage. Ebert in September 1923, facing run-away inflation, French occupation of the Ruhr, and the threat of secession in Bavaria asked the Chief of Staff, General Hans von Seeckt, where the army stood. Seeckt, who was to maintain an ambiguous attitude throughout most of the Bavarian conflict, preserved his sphinx-like expression behind the customary monocle: "The army, Mr. President, stands behind me."[10] A generation later, Bayar's anxious query to a private of his presidential guard met with the same evasive insolence. Would the troops defend him against popular attack? "Yes," replied the private, "if our officer commands us to do so."

Seeckt's army did not have to seize the government; the very next day President Ebert transferred full executive powers to the minister of war, Otto Gessler, and a few weeks later to Seeckt himself. Although cabinet government resumed at the end of the acute crisis, civilian control over the armed forces was restored only by Hitler well after the fall of the Weimar Republic. In Turkey in 1960, General Cemal Gürsel had just resigned as commander of the land forces with a pointed appeal to the troops not to become involved in politics—that is, not to take the part of the Bayar-Menderes government against civilian demonstrators. The commander of the presidential guard, to whose orders Bayar was referred, turned out to be a key supporter of the junta that under Gürsel's leadership seized power on May 27, 1960.

In sum, military seizure of power does not come as a sudden isolated departure. More commonly it is the climax of a long period of military involvement. Repeated proclamations of states of siege or of martial law in the major cities or in rebellious provinces, frequent use of troops to disperse civilian demonstrators, appointment of the armed forces as guardians of the honesty of

---

[10] Friedrich von Rabenau, Seeckt: Aus seinem Leben 1918-1936 (Leipzig: Hase and Koehler, 1940), p. 342. For the context of the Turkish episode, see Robert E. Ward and D. A. Rustow, eds., Political Modernization in Japan and Turkey (Princeton University Press, 1964), p. 367.

disputed elections, a prolonged and indecisive fight against rebellious guerrilla forces—all these are danger signs. Note that in these situations, it is the civilian government itself that propels the army onto the domestic political stage. As a result of this growing involvement, the army acquires much experience in domestic coercion; yet the more deeply the army becomes involved, the more frustrated it is likely to be. To use force against civilians is a distasteful task at best; to fight a prolonged and losing battle against the government's domestic opponents is doubly galling. In the coup, the army vents its accumulated frustration. The government, with its civilian support dwindling and its ineffectiveness apparent to all, is helpless against the army's *volte-face*. Where survival of a civilian government depends on armed power, a coup in which the army switches sides must, *ex hypothesi*, succeed.

To the deposed government, a military coup appears to be the result of treachery within its security forces. For the population, it may beckon as a last and desperate resort when dissatisfaction can find no peaceful means of forcing a change in government. Any army coup needs civilian support to succeed, and the civilians will hesitate to lend such support until simpler and less risky avenues have been blocked. Hence military coups are the proven antidote to traditional despotisms and to modern dictatorships— including those installed by previous coups—as well as to oligarchies that have thwarted the parliamentary and electoral procedures decreed by the constitution.

The Technique of the Coup

Latin Americans, with their unparalleled opportunity for prolonged and comparative observation, have been fascinated with the classification and nomenclature of seizures of power. The most general term, *golpe,* or coup, refers to the physical ejection of a government by force. A *cuartelazo,* or barracks coup, starts with the uprising of a particular garrison. A *pronunciamento* consists of the action of key military (or, for that matter, civilian) leaders in "pronouncing" their shift of allegiance to a new government. A *telegráfico* consists in the telegraphic pronouncement of major provincial commanders against the incumbent government and, like the *pronunciamento*, results in its peaceful withdrawal.

Middle Eastern terminology is less elaborate, but the region's experience, beginning nearly a century later, is beginning to rival that of Latin America in richness and variety. The Young Turk Revolution of 1908, for example, closely followed the *telegráfico* pattern. Its two known victims were a young officer whom the conspirators suspected of having informed on them and one of the sultan's generals sent to suppress the incipient mutiny but shot in daylight in the market square of Monastir. The constitutional revolution itself was accomplished by a flood of telegrams released on the sultan's palace by army commanders, political committees, and provincial governors throughout Macedonia. A year later the Macedonian army marched on the capital to quell a counterrevolutionary mutiny among the Istanbul garrison.

A uniquely painless way of accomplishing a military coup was devised in Iraq in 1938: a discreet ultimatum whispered into the premier's ear at a social gathering resulted in the cabinet's resignation a few hours later.[11] At other times, a determined show of force by the army is required to overthrow the government. Bakr Sidqi's coup, for example, involved five airplanes dropping quantities of leaflets over Baghdad—as well as four bombs that caused seven casualties.

There are certain technical features, however, that all successful coups must share. A military coup d'état is the seizure by force of threat or threat of force of the machinery of government. To reach their objective, the plotters must oust the incumbent rulers and occupy the seat of power. As Major Goodspeed has shown in a brilliant comparative analysis, "no coup which does not strike directly at the heart of a government can hope to

[11] Majid Khadduri, *Independent Iraq 1932-1958*, 2d ed. (London: Oxford University Press, 1960), p. 133.

achieve its aims."[12] Hence the conspiracy must include the commanders of units closest to the capital which can occupy road junctions, the royal or presidential palace, the government offices, and the radio station. Naval units can play a crucial role in countries where the capital is on the shore, as in Argentina, but not elsewhere. The cooperation or neutrality of the air force is important everywhere, but only land troops can capture the capital. The ideal starting point for the plot is among those officers in the general staff who can assign their fellow conspirators to these crucial commands.

The degree of violence during the military phase of a coup depends mostly on the attitude of the armed forces. If the military establishment acts as a unit—if the coup is led by the chief of staff, or if the higher echelons remain neutral—there will be little bloodshed. Who but fools or martyrs will barehandedly oppose machine guns, tanks, and bombers?

Even if the armed forces are divided, the forcible clashes are likely to be brief. To fire on fellow soldiers is even more distasteful—or, at any rate, far more dangerous—than to fire on civilian fellow citizens, and once clubs become trumps no one is better able to count the trumps than veteran military card-players. The armed forces, therefore, are likely to rally quickly around the leader with the stronger battalions. The bloodier phases of a military revolution are more likely to result from deliberate subsequent action, as Bakr Sidqi's murder of the previous war minister and the death sentences imposed on Menderes and a few associates after a year's trial, or of an enraged civilian mob tolerated by the army, as in the ferocious massacre in Baghdad in 1958.

An important distinction is that between the first military coup after prolonged civilian rule and later ones that are part of a long series. Unless the deadlocked civilians abdicate to the army (for example, by entrusting it with the supervision of elections), a first coup will have to involve a determined show or application of

[12] D. J. Goodspeed, *The Conspirators: A Study of the Coup d'Etat* (Viking, 1961), p. 65.

force. The ritualized *telegráficos* are likely to come later as one junta displaces another. Significantly, Bakr Sidqi's coup of 1936 was the first in Iraq, whereas the coup by whispered ultimatum in 1938 was the third.

But the seizure of the incumbent rulers and their offices is only the first part of the conspirators' task. To ensure ultimate success, power must be consolidated and exercised. Tanks rumbling through deserted streets in the small hours of the morning constitute the climax of the first phase; the triumphant breakfast communiqué read over the radio to the awakening populace marks the opening of the second.

Such a communiqué tends to follow a standard pattern because it performs a number of essential functions in the military bid for power. (1) It announces that power already is in the hands of the new rulers, concedes perhaps that mopping-up operations are still under way, but leaves no doubt that further resistance would be futile. (2) It then must detail the composition of the new ruling group. If the coup was planned by a conspiracy of colonels and majors, they will have done well, for this occasion and for the task of further consolidation, to secure the adherence of a senior figure whose name is widely known both in the armed forces and among the public at large. A respected general who has earlier spoken out against an unpopular government, a Muhammad Naguib or Cemal Gürsel, is the ideal choice. If the chief of staff and the ranking commanders themselves have planned the overthrow, they will become key members of the junta. (3) The initial communiqué or some later pronouncement also must give the citizenry an idea of the program and aims of the new military rulers. The old government's inefficiency, corruption, and unpopularity will be duly castigated. Positive measures for the immediate restoration of tranquillity, for the rooting out of subversion, for speedy reform of the administration, for salvaging the currency and redressing the balance of payments, for friendly relations with foreign powers will be promised. (4) Finally, the sponsors of the coup will protest that they did not wish to seize power but acted in a moment of national emergency under extreme duress and provocation. They depict their coup as a neat act of surgery that once and for all will cure the lingering ailment of the body politic.

Some sponsors will remain in the background, insisting only that the despised civilian government will be replaced with another more to the army's liking. Others will take governmental power but promise to divest themselves of it at the first opportunity—when the parties have been cleansed of corrupt elements, when truly free and honest elections can be held, when the economy has recovered, or the danger of subversion averted. In short, the communiqué is likely to commit the soldiers to what may be termed the one-shot theory of military intervention.

The Soldiers in Power

This peroration should not be dismissed as a show of false modesty. Rather, the soldiers' disclaimers reflect the truism that government can never rest on force alone. The tanks and machine guns deployed before dawn are an excellent instrument for ousting the old rulers: they are quite useless for the task of governing a society. In an age when states are formed by right of national self-determination, and when the popular masses are crowding the political stage, the soldiers will try to legitimize their coup by invoking nationalist and democratic symbols. To proclaim their rule by right of force rather than by some accepted principle of justice would be an invitation to the populace to resist the junta's decrees and to other officers to test its coercive strength. "As soon as force makes right," Rousseau has said, ". . . any force that overcomes the first one inherits its right. As soon as one can disobey with impunity one does so legitimately; and since the strongest is always right, all anyone needs to do is to see to it that it is he who is the strongest."[13] Where loyalties among civilians have broken

[13] *Contrat Social* (1762), Book 1, Chap. 3.

down, force can triumph; but unless some new principle of legitimacy emerges, force may continue to displace force in a steady succession of coups.

Nor is there much profit in speculating about the sincerity of the soldiers' professions of democracy and reform, in tracing their "ideological formation" to their high-school textbooks or to the spare-time reading matter of their years in the staff college. To issue promises of reform is mandatory even for those who may not intend them; to carry them out is difficult even for those who do. In the turmoil of the political contest, mere intentions count for little. A junta's desire to retire to the barracks after a brief stay on the political stage will lead to nothing but frustration: the one-shot theory will quickly have to be abandoned.

Gamal Abdul Nasser was the chief engineer of a coup that at first did no more than replace a gluttonous and lecherous monarch with a regency for his infant son and invite the civilian parties to rid themselves of corrupt elements. His recollections vividly picture a junta's rapid disillusionment.

Before July 23rd [1952], I had imagined that the whole nation was ready and prepared, waiting for nothing but a vanguard to lead the charge against the battlements, whereupon it would fall in behind in serried ranks, ready for the sacred advance towards the great objective. And I had imagined that our role was to be this commando vanguard. I thought that this role would never take more than a few hours. Then immediately would come the sacred advance behind us of the serried ranks and the thunder of marching feet as the ordered advance proceeded towards the great objective. I heard all this in my imagination, but by sheer faith it seemed real and not the figment of my imagination.

Then suddenly came reality after July 23rd. The vanguard performed its task and charged the battlements of tyranny. It threw out Farouk and then paused, waiting for the serried ranks to come up in their sacred advance toward the great objective.

For a long time it waited. Crowds did eventually come, and they came in endless droves—but how different is the reality from the dream! The masses that came were disunited, divided groups of stragglers. At this moment I felt, with sorrow and bitterness, that the task of the vanguard, far from being completed, had only begun.

We needed order, but we found nothing behind us but chaos. We needed unity, but we found nothing behind us but dissension. We needed work, but we found behind us only indolence and sloth. . . .
. . . We set about seeking the views of leaders of opinion and the experience of those who were experienced. Unfortunately we were not able to obtain very much.

Every man we questioned had nothing to recommend except to kill someone else. Every idea we listened to was nothing but an attack on some other idea. If we had gone along with everything we heard, we would have killed off all the people and torn down every idea, and there would have been nothing left for us to do but to sit down among the corpses and ruins, bewailing our evil fortune and cursing our wretched fate.[14]

Vanguard, feet marching, ranks serried, battlements, charges, the great objective: the imagery is the familiar one of the proving ground and of the infantry attack. Command and discipline, direction and momentum count for everything; the objective is given and remains unquestioned or even unknown. Surely, if the ills of the body politic could have been cured so easily, the occasion for a military coup would never have arisen. The political arena is not a defile. Civil servants cannot administer laws by advancing in serried ranks. Economic planners cannot augment production by charging battlements. Free and honest elections cannot be secured by simple marching orders. Above all, the objectives in politics are always in question. Any junta of field-grade officers that expects to reach a sacred but unspecified political goal—and to reach it by storm in a few hours or even weeks—is in for an awakening as tearful and wretched as Nasser intimates.

The disillusionment of the junta's civilian allies is likely to be just as keen. The soldiers' most valuable asset in rallying the opposition against the old government was their reputation for technical competence and efficiency, for honesty and patriotism—a reputation built up during years of service, in the barracks or at the front, for the clear-cut objectives of national defense. But this reputation is a rapidly wasting asset. Thrown suddenly into the

[14] Nasser, *op. cit.*, pp. 32-35.

vortex of political ambitions, confronted brusquely with unexpected domestic and international crises, the members of the junta may quickly lose their footing. Their intentions may be the best, but their skill and experience in political affairs are sure to be deficient. Hence their prestige will tarnish rapidly and their civilian support before long may melt away.

The distinction drawn earlier between coups accomplished by the armed forces as a whole, under the command of the chief of staff and other top ranking officers, and coups resulting from a colonels' conspiracy again becomes relevant. The chief of staff, the minister of defense, and other top generals are likely to have participated in cabinet meetings, to have dealt with problems of national transport, of industrial procurement, of economic planning, of foreign military aid. The senior commanders, in short, have not spent their entire lives in the barracks and on the proving ground: even under the old regime, their most recent professional activity was largely political and administrative. Hence a junta of top-ranking generals and admirals may be expected to bring to the tasks of government more experience and sophistication than the conspiratorial colonels and majors. On the other hand, as military servants in good standing of the deposed regime, the top commanders will have a harder time justifying their coup to the troops and the citizenry, formulating a distinctive program for their own government, and rallying the opponents of the old regime around it.

In contrast, the colonels' oppositional credentials are likely to be more authentic in inverse proportion to their previous political experience. As the victorious conspirators grapple with the old but unaccustomed problems of civilian politics, moreover, they may find that their coup has created a number of new and thorny problems in the ranks of the military.

First, growing fissures may appear within the junta itself. Faced with mounting political problems, some members will wish to retreat, to return the government to civilian hands at the first opportunity. Others will wish to escape forward into greater radicalism, to transform the military coup into a political and social revolution. Rival ambitions may accentuate these and other latent differences. The cleavage between the moderates and radicals may coincide with that between the older general or generals co-opted just before the coup and the younger colonels who planned the original conspiracy. Recent Middle Eastern experience indicates that either side may win. In Egypt, Nasser ousted Naguib in 1954 after a prolonged see-saw contest. In Turkey in 1960, General Gürsel obtained support from the majority of the junta in exiling Colonel Türkeş and thirteen other radicals. In any case, a junta's tenure in office is likely to produce some dissidence and attrition in its own ranks. Once the army gets into politics, it is impossible to keep politics out of the army.

Second, a conspiratorial coup by middle ranking officers is bound to undermine discipline in the armed forces. No general will cheerfully take orders from a junta member who only yesterday was his adjutant at division headquarters. Hence the junta may see itself forced to retire nearly every officer senior in rank to its members.[15] While such a mass purge removes some immediate obstacles to discipline, it also releases passions of rivalry, ambition, and vindictiveness that further strain the army's cohesion. The net result is likely to be a drastic loss in military efficiency.

Third, the junta, because of the very success of its conspiracy, will have to surrender to other officers the command positions in and near the capital that launched it into power; for no one can direct at one and the same time the ministry of economics and a tank battalion or the government information office and an air force squadron. Having played their trump cards, the soldier-rulers will have to deal them to other players, and they may well find themselves challenged to further rounds at the same game.

[15] In Turkey only four months after the coup of May 1960, the junta retired an estimated 3,000 to 5,000 officers, including nearly every general and about half the colonels on active service. The Turkish performance in the NATO maneuvers of the next two years suffered appreciably. See Walter F. Weiker, *The Turkish Revolution of 1960-1961: Aspects of Military Politics* (Brookings Institution, 1963), p. 129; and Dankwart A. Rustow, "Turkey's Second Try at Democracy," *Yale Review*, Vol. 52, No. 4 (June 1963), p. 524.

The Sequels of a Coup

If such are some of the immediate difficulties confronting the soldier-rulers, what is likely to be the ultimate outcome of their intervention? Five sequels are possible. (1) At one extreme the soldiers may retain power for a minimum of time, quickly returning to their barracks and restoring the government to civilian hands. (2) At the opposite extreme, the soldiers may stay in power permanently, inaugurating a stable military oligarchy. Among the intermediate possibilities there are those (3) of a series of military coups leading to a condition best characterized as praetorianism, (4) of a prolonged twilight situation between civilian and military rule, and (5) of a social and political revolution under military aegis which, by removing the conditions that led to the coup, establishes civil government on a new and more secure basis.

BACK TO THE BARRACKS

The "one-shot theory" of military intervention, as already indicated, is as attractive to the draftsmen of a junta's communiqué as it is out of accord with the real setting of most coups. For the body politic as a whole, military seizure of power is a symptom of profound disorder. It takes more than a casual difficulty to overcome an army's inhibition in seizing power, and it takes more than a casual set of decrees to effect a remedy. For the members of a conspiratorial junta, a brief tenure in office is hardly a proper reward for the effort they have expended and the risks they have run. A truly new regime cannot be erected overnight, and under a restored *ancien régime* the conspirators would be criminally liable for high treason. For any civilian successors, the soldiers' rapid and voluntary withdrawal would hold little promise of stability. If they depart for their barracks of their own accord, what is to keep them from reentering the arena at any time of their choosing?

Among the closest empirical examples of the soldiers' rapid withdrawal are the recent military regimes in Peru (1962-63) and in Turkey (1960-61). In Peru, a junta composed of the top service commanders took power during a disputed election and restored it to civilian hands after a new election twelve months later. There was no lengthy conspiracy and no violent seizure of power. The preceding regime itself had appointed the armed forces guardians of the honesty of the 1962 election. In a simple *pronunciamento* they set aside the claims of all the electoral contenders. A general strike called against the coup proved to be far from general. Nor did the military promise any sweeping social or political reforms. Instead, they obtained wide support from the various political groups for a bureaucratic caretaker government under military auspices. There also was strong pressure from the United States, which first threatened to cut off all aid to Peru, but then restored it on condition that new elections would be held in a year's time.

In Turkey, the moderate majority of the junta under General Gürsel saw itself threatened not only by the expelled radicals under Colonel Türkeş, but even more seriously by the newly appointed commanders of the military services. By calling a constituent assembly late in 1960 and appointing an interim cabinet of party politicians, the junta shifted in effect to a civilian basis of support. Yet the restoration of constitutional government in October 1961 did not by any means amount to a full military withdrawal.

STABLE MILITARY RULE

Empirical examples of coups that led to stable military oligarchies are provided by such countries as Nicaragua, the Dominican Republic, and Paraguay. In Nicaragua, for example, United States Marines occupied the country from 1927 to 1932 and on their departure left behind a local security force commanded by Anastasio Somoza. Somoza seized power in 1936 and on his death in

1956 was replaced as dictator by his son Luis Somoza. Significantly, Nicaragua, like some of the other smaller Latin Republics, is at a primitive level of social and political development where, as noted, governmental functions tend to be limited and civil and military activities undifferentiated.

The coups in Thailand that established the military regimes of 1932-44 and since 1951 might be cited as further examples. Here, too, military oligarchy has deep historical roots, and there has been little traditional distinction between army and government.

> Military officers in modern Thailand have their roots in the traditional bureaucracy. Their historical origins are therefore the same as those of the civil officials. . . . All [traditional] political leaders were soldiers in some sense of the word; all were necessarily prepared and able to organize and lead armies. But there was no warrior class. In effect, the ruling group was bureaucratic and official, and all its members—civil and military—were equally subordinate to the throne.[16]

The monarch's withdrawal since 1932 to a figurehead role, the alien and the nonpolitical character of Thailand's Chinese business community, and the somnolent apathy of the peasant population have enhanced the power of the military bureaucracy. Between 1944 and 1951, a group of civilian bureaucrats and "intellectuals" profited from the internal situation to keep the military at bay. During the periods of military rule, there have been repeated clashes among the military factions, for example of army and air force against navy and marines. But in contrast to Syria, Iraq, or Bolivia, where such factions have been closely aligned with rival civilian groups, the Thai incidents may be considered violent reshufflings within a continuous military ruling group.

In sum, the permanent installation of military rulers is likely only in traditional societies or those in the very early stages of modernization. A clean and quick withdrawal of the military is

---

[16] David A. Wilson, "The Military in Thai Politics" in John J. Johnson, ed., *The Role of the Military in Underdeveloped Countries* (Princeton University Press, 1962), p. 254.

altogether unlikely. It is the three intermediate possibilities, therefore, that must be examined in greater detail.

PRAETORIANISM

In countries at more advanced stages of modernization, the difficulties that the soldier-rulers encounter in their conduct of government and in their relations with the armed forces constitute so many open invitations to further military coups. The junta's ardor and inexperience may have done more to aggravate than to resolve the political and economic problems that gave rise to the initial coup. Meanwhile, popular enthusiasm has soured, military discipline has been shaken, and the key commands near the capital have passed into new hands. Having seen how easy it was for one group of colonels to seize power, many majors and captains will now nurture the same ambition. After breaking the spell of loyalties that sustained the old regime, the junta has found no new basis of legitimacy. Might having become right, it remains for some new group of conspirators to possess themselves of greater might.

When the second coup comes, some civilian elements may again applaud it on the illusory assumption that the military are indeed honest, efficient, and patriotic, and that the first junta was merely the exception that proves the rule. But, in fact, a second coup has even less chance of effecting fundamental changes or of restoring legitimacy than did the first. In Bolivia in the 1930's and 1940's, in Syria since 1949, in Iraq in 1936-41, and again since 1958, there has been a long procession of coups, at times several during the same year. In such situations, army purge follows on army purge, unkept promise piles on unkept promise, junta takes over from junta. The armed forces become politicized just as politics becomes militarized. The officer corps is shot through with factionalism. Law-making and administration fall into disarray. Politicians seek power not by rallying popular support but by cultivating military connections. The populace at length withdraws into a sullen apathy, an utter cynicism toward the political process. The country has turned into a praetorian state.

Not every country that experiences a series of coups fits this praetorian model as closely as do Bolivia, Syria, or Iraq. The picture here drawn, nonetheless, seems more realistic than Samuel Huntington's image of a "progression of reform coups."

Reform coups [he has suggested] are the products of the drives for Westernization and modernization. Frequent coups are a sign of change and progress. Not all coups, to be sure, produce reforms, but virtually all reforms are produced by coups. Frequent reform coups d'état should be viewed not as pathological, but rather as a healthy mechanism of gradual change, the non-constitutional equivalent of periodic changes in party control through the electoral process.[17]

The desire for modernization inspires many coups and serves as the excuse for many more, and some coups even produce results in that direction. Obviously, too, each successive junta must try to justify itself by condemning its predecessor and announcing a sharp reversal of the political course. Yet there is nothing gradual about such changes. Above all, the coups that produce modernizing reforms—or indeed any durable results—are not the ones that are part of a rapid series.

CIVILIAN-MILITARY TWILIGHT

The gradual descent into praetorianism can best be forestalled by a military junta in firm control of the armed forces—one commanded by the chief of staff or one made up of middle-ranking officers who manage to restore an effective hierarchy after the indispensable purges. In contrast to an army of rebellious praetorians, such a disciplined force can withdraw to the barracks in a body; yet its withdrawal will remain precarious. The result is likely to be an ambiguous situation in which the military leave the political stage but continue to hover in the wings. The soldiers may entrust to a civilian president or cabinet the daily conduct of

[17] Huntington in *Changing Patterns of Military Politics, op. cit.,* p. 40.

government while reserving to themselves a veto on certain decisions. They may allow elections while banning from participation or victory certain specified groups. In short, the soldiers, in one way or another, continue to assume the role of umpire of the political game, of guardians of the constitution, of guarantors of national unity.

Typical examples of this civil-military twilight are Brazil since 1945, Argentina after 1958, and, to some extent, Turkey since 1961. In Brazil, the military forced the withdrawal in 1945 of Getúlio Vargas after fifteen years of a civilian, semifascist dictatorship and allowed elections to be held on a regular five-year schedule. In 1945, both major parties named military candidates, but in each of the next three elections, the military candidate of one party was beaten by a civilian with strong popular appeal—Vargas himself in 1950, Juscelino Kubitschek in 1955, and Jânio Quadros in 1960. In 1954-55, in a protracted contest with the Vargas movement, the military obtained the dismissal of the demagogical labor minister, João Goulart; insisted on the resignation of Vargas who in a melodramatic gesture committed suicide instead; and replaced Vargas' Vice President, João Café Filho with his next two constitutional successors so as to forestall a plot by Vargas' followers against Kubitschek's accession. In 1961, after the sudden resignation of the erratic Quadros, the military forced Vice President Goulart (their old antagonist of 1954) to surrender most executive power to a parliamentary cabinet before he assumed the presidency.

Throughout the entire period, inflation continued at an accelerating pace, there was recurrent peasant unrest in the drought-stricken Northeast, and communists were said to have gained many controlling positions in the trade unions and the civil service. Following Goulart's restoration to full presidential powers in a plebiscite early in 1963, the military ousted him in a coup in March 1964. The dictatorship of Marshals Humberto Castelo Branco (1964-67) and Arturo Costa e Silva (1967-) has perpetuated the twilight by combining a semblance of elections with widespread repressive measures against opponents and dissident supporters of their conservative regime.

In Argentina, a conspiracy of high officers in 1955 ended Perón's dictatorship which had given South America its sharpest taste of totalitarianism. A first junta under General Eduardo Lonardi was replaced after two months by another under General Pedro Aramburu, who over the next three years strove to restore the economy to a sound footing and to cleanse the administration and trade unions of corrupt Peronist elements. By 1958, national elections were held to which all parties except the outlawed Peronists were admitted. The winner, Dr. Arturo Frondizi, had an impeccable anti-Perón record; yet he owed victory to the exiled dictator's followers and repaid his debt by allowing them to put up their own candidates in the provincial elections of 1962. Again the military intervened by interning Frondizi, setting aside the election results, and installing an interim regime under Senate President José María Guido.

The complex maneuvers of the following year left the Peronists in considerable disarray and secured victory in the 1963 elections for the staunchly anti-Peronist Arturo Illia; yet there was ample evidence that Peronist sentiment continued to run strong, particularly among the masses of industrial workers. In 1965, a further coup under General Ongania unceremoniously disposed of the Illia regime.

In Turkey, General Gürsel's junta submitted a new constitution to popular referendum in July 1961 (fourteen months after the coup); confirmed the death sentences for ex-Premier Menderes and two associates on charges of subverting the old constitution; and scheduled elections for October. Although Menderes' Democratic Party remained outlawed, roughly half the voters cast their ballots for the newly formed Justice Party and other heirs of Menderes. Still, Gürsel's junta and the top military commanders allowed a civilian parliamentary regime to take over on condition that Gürsel be elected president and the Justice Party enter a coalition with the anti-Menderes Republican People's Party under

Ismet Inönü. For the next several years, the military commanders, meeting with the political leaders in the Supreme Military Council or speaking through the Chief of Staff, played a dual role. Repeatedly, they intervened in the political process to prevent public criticism of the military, to delay the process of amnesty for Menderes' followers, or to warn the Justice Party against naming pro-Menderes extremists to its leadership. At the same time, the military rallied to the support of successive coalition governments in suppressing renewed attempts at colonels' coups in 1962 and 1963.

There are striking similarities in these three situations, with some significant variations. In each country, a dictatorial regime had suppressed opposition by a variety of ruthless devices, had plunged the country into inflation, and encouraged corruption in the administration. In each, the military moved in to restore democratic constitutional processes, to clean out corruption, and to halt inflation. Yet in all three countries, the followers of the deposed dictator enjoyed continuing popularity—in Brazil and Argentina among the industrial workers and in Turkey among the peasantry. Of the leading soldiers' dedication to constitutional democracy, there could be little doubt. The Brazilian constitution itself appoints the military guardians of the constitution, and Brazilian officers have taken great pride in that role in contrast to the Spanish-American pattern of military overthrows. Gürsel's appeal to the forces to abstain from politics has already been cited. And Aramburu, in an impassioned public speech, acknowledged the blame that the Argentine military must carry for Perón's rise to power and castigated the corrupt intermingling of military and political affairs. To military activists, the attitude of the three armed forces must have seemed like one of commendable forbearance. What could be more patriotic than to reserve military intervention for situations of extreme danger to the constitution that the soldiers are sworn to uphold? Does not the survival of democracy require the sequestration of popular movements that would install authoritarianism under Vargas, Perón, or their successors?

All this may readily be granted; yet there is another side. In Turkey after 1961, and in Argentina and in Brazil at least until the coups of 1964-65, the military leaders formulated no constructive political programs and shouldered no blame for day-to-day administrative failures. These thankless tasks were left to elected civilians. The military intervened only when the civilians, in pursuit of these tasks, overstepped constitutional limits; but the military remained the sole judges of where these limits lay. When the soldiers did draw the line, it never was easy for them or for their critics to distinguish between military concern for the constitutional order and the self-seeking group interests of the military establishment.

Argentine and Turkish officers, clearly, have been afraid of vindictive civilian groups that would hold them to account for the ouster of Perón and Menderes. Brazilian generals have offered themselves as candidates for the presidency in every election since 1945, and the higher ranks of the administration and the state economic establishments have been filled with generals and colonels drawing military half-pay along with full civilian salaries.[18] The Brazilian army overthrew Goulart only after he had openly encouraged insubordination in the noncommissioned ranks. In Argentina, Colonel Perón himself had come to power with military support. His fellow officers turned on him only when he tried to break up the autonomy of the forces and to integrate them into his authoritarian state. In all three countries, moreover, the dominant moderate factions in the military have had to restrain activist officers, who did not share their dedication to constitutions and democracy. There can be little question that any dictatorship set up by the "red" or activist faction in the Argentine officer corps or by Colonels Türkeş or Aydemir in Turkey would have differed from those of Perón or Menderes more in ideological hue than in ruthlessness.

[18] For details, see Johnson, *The Military and Society in Latin America*, pp. 211-12.

The moderate soldiers themselves have steered a course that has involved them in a succession of sophistries. Democracy is based on majority rule; yet the Argentine people since 1958 have been free to elect by majority any kind of government—except the one that the majority prefers. The constitutions of Brazil and Argentina regulate the succession from president to vice-president to the presiding officers of the chambers of parliament. But they required that power be exercised by Vargas, Café Filho, and Frondizi themselves and not by the legal successors whom the military imposed.

So long as a popular majority supports candidates likely to revive authoritarianism, democracy remains in acute danger. The alternative offered by the military in the three countries has been not one of constitutionalism but of military tutelage. The consequence has been a most unhappy blurring of the lines of power and responsibility that has been demoralizing to officers and civilians alike. Only a reestablishment of clear responsibilities and a reconciliation of the military with the popular majority on the basis of constitutional procedures can resurrect democracy in the long run.

Turkey is the only one of the three countries that has moved in this direction. Here Premier Inönü's prestige as a victorious general of the war of independence and long-time lieutenant of Atatürk has helped to reduce progressively the scope of military intervention. Governments since 1961 have been supported by parliamentary majorities resulting from free elections; no government has been deposed by the military, and no election set aside. And early in 1965, a peaceful transition to a Justice Party government was effected.

REVOLUTION UNDER MILITARY AEGIS

The last possible sequel of a coup is a military revolution that produces fundamental changes in the political institutions and the social structure of a people, erects on those bases a new civilian order, and thus renders further military intervention unnecessary. The difference between military revolutions and nonrevolutionary coups lies neither in the method by which power is seized (which is determined by technical factors) nor in the language by which the seizure is justified (which is determined by the prevailing climate of opinion). All military revolutions begin as coups, and most coups claim to be revolutions. Once power is attained, some coups develop into revolutions: the difference is not in the promise but in the performance. The regimes established by Mustafa Kemal in Turkey after 1919, in Mexico under a succession of presidents between 1920 and 1940, and by Nasser in Egypt since 1952 probably furnish the best empirical examples of such a development.

If a coup is to become the basis of a revolution, it must first meet a negative requirement. The military rulers must not be overthrown in short order; they must have time to carry out a program of basic reform. The initial contribution that a military junta or dictator can make in turning their coup into a revolution consists in preserving or reestablishing discipline within the army. The withdrawal of the military from politics thus begins typically with the forced withdrawal of the soldier-rulers' military rivals. If the head of the regime is a victorious general enjoying wide respect, the process becomes easier; soldiers who do not withdraw from politics out of conviction may do so out of loyalty to their commander.

In Ottoman Turkey, for example, the first law prohibiting military personnel from participating in elections was enacted by a militarily-backed Union and Progress movement eager to forestall the military machinations and intrigues of its federalist rivals. The separation of military and political affairs was fully established only after Kemal's victory in the War of Independence (1919-22). In France since 1958 and in Turkey in 1961-65, the presence of old soldiers like de Gaulle and İnönü at the head of the government has facilitated both the withdrawal of the army into a nonpolitical role and the suppression of those conspirators who refused so to withdraw. In Mexico, after a decade of civil war, the task was harder, but it was courageously tackled by three military presidents, Alvaro Obregón (1920-24), Plutarco Elías Calles (1924-28), and Lázaro Cárdenas (1934-40). Obregón eliminated most of the local military leaders of the civil war period; Calles began the training of a professional officer corps; and Cárdenas eliminated the remaining caudillos, forcing Calles into exile, and defeating a final group of rebel generals in a brief military campaign in 1938.

The same trend may be reinforced by concern not only for political stability but also for military efficiency. Such considerations were particularly prominent in Turkey, which was at war continuously from 1911 to 1922. After the Young Turk military coup of 1913, the older generals who had largely been responsible for the defeats in Libya (1911-12) and on the Balkans (1912-13) were resolutely purged and a German military mission called in to improve the technical training of the rejuvenated army. Throughout World War I, under Union and Progress rule, the connection between political and military affairs remained close, to the detriment of both. But in the War of Independence, leadership was assumed by Mustafa Kemal who, as a professional military man, had sharply criticized Enver Pasha's subordination of strategic considerations to ideological and political goals.

Kemal from the beginning insisted on a clear separation of political and military functions. Having resigned from the army in July 1919, he concentrated on the political organization of the nationalist movement, assuming the supreme command personally only at the time of the decisive campaign against the Greek invaders in 1921-22. Late in 1920, Kemal was faced with a major challenge from Çerkes Edhem, the leader of the nationalist guerrilla forces, whose desire to play an independent political role was a threat not only to Kemal's power in Ankara but also to the orderly conduct of the military campaign against the Greeks. Edhem's desertion facilitated the eventual integration of the guerrillas under the regular command structure. A year later, as a local commander in Thrace made ready to carry his offensive beyond the boundary line laid down in the nationalist political program, Kemal had occasion to state his principle more clearly: "Commanders, while thinking of and carrying out the duties and requirements of the army, must take care not to let political considerations influence their judgment. They must not forget that there are other officials whose duty it is to think of the political aspects. A soldier's duty cannot be performed with talk and politicking. . . ."[19] By "other officials," Kemal meant of course himself as President of the Grand National Assembly and the cabinet set up under his chairmanship by that same body.

The eventual separation of military and political affairs, which was to remain valid for the twenty-seven years of the First Turkish Republic (1923-60), came after the political break between Kemal and his military-political associates of the early War of Independence. It took the form of an understanding of the highest remaining soldiers concerning their future roles. Kemal himself as President of the Republic and Ismet Inönü (who had commanded the Western front against the Greeks in 1920-22) as Prime Minister were to take charge of political matters without military interference. In return, Fevzi Çakmak (Chief of Staff from 1921 until his retirement in 1944) would have a free hand in building up a professional army.

Aside from these negative conditions—restoration of military discipline and ejection of rival soldiers from the political stage—at least two positive conditions must be met to turn a military coup into a military revolution. The first is a program relevant to the major political, social, and economic issues confronting the society. The other is the creation of a civilian organization that can mobilize new sources of support for such a program. The political

---

[19] Atatürk, *Nutuk* (Ankara, 1934), Vol. 2, p. 43. On these and other Turkish developments, cf. D. A. Rustow, "The Army and the Founding of the Turkish Republic," *World Politics*, Vol. 11 (July 1959), pp. 513-52, especially 546ff.; Ward and Rustow, *op. cit.*, pp. 364-66; and George S. Harris, "The Role of the Military in Turkish Politics," *Middle East Journal*, Vol. 19 (1965), pp. 54-66 and 169-76.

aims of the revolutionary regime need not be original. In Turkey, in Mexico, and in Egypt, the military leaders carried out demands widely voiced during the preceding years of turmoil. Most items in Atatürk's program of radical Westernization (including European law codes, expanded and secular schools, a latinized script, the emancipation of women, and changes in dress) had already been advocated or even attempted during the Young Turk period (1908-18). The renunciation of imperial ambition was dictated by defeat in World War I. The social reforms instituted by Cárdenas and his successors in the 1930's and 1940's had already been written into the Mexican constitution of 1917. Demands for British evacuation of Suez, for Arab unity, and even for a high dam at Aswan had been voiced during Farouk's reign or before.

But the Young Turks had been torn among conflicting goals of Westernization, Pan-Islam, and Turanian nationalism, so that most concrete demands for reform were drowned in the ideological hubbub. In Mexico, years of civil war had made impossible orderly administration, let alone social reform. The perennial deadlock among king, Wafd party, and British residency had paralyzed Egyptian politics between the world wars. The decisive contribution of the revolutionary leadership, in short, is not in the formulation of new demands, but in the consolidation of old ones into a consistent and appropriately phased plan of action.

There are situations where the second positive contribution —that of mobilizing effective support for the program of action— may be left to a bureaucracy. This seems to have happened in Egypt. The repeated failure of Nasser's attempts to found some sort of official party or movement, it is true, may be taken as a sign of ineptitude. It also proves that his expanding bureaucracy, including the secret police, has been an adequate instrument for carrying out his program—in conjunction, no doubt, with the proverbial docility of the Egyptian fellah.

A bureaucracy, however, usually reflects closely the vices of any prerevolutionary regime—its indecisiveness, its corruption, its conservatism—and hence cannot be easily transformed into an instrument of revolutionary change without strong outside pressure. In most countries, and this includes both Mexico and Turkey, such pressure has been provided by a civilian political party, the organization of which is thus usually indispensable to the revolutionary success of a military regime and to its ultimate transformation into a new and stable civilian order.

Military regimes, except for the rare ones that manage to preside over a revolutionary transformation, are highly unstable. In concluding this chapter, this military instability may be compared to the instability of charismatic regimes. There is one basic contrast: charismatic legitimacy is strongest at the beginning and later tends to diminish; military legitimacy is weakest at the beginning and increases with time. The power of the charismatic leader over his followers is at a maximum during the miraculous event that dramatically opens his leadership career. It will decline unless he continually reasserts it through new heroic deeds. By contrast, a military regime's difficulties are greatest at the start: a coup d'état at the time it occurs is by definition illegitimate. Force is what brought the soldiers to power, but force is inadequate to keep them in power. Indeed, force can be used by other soldiers in ousting them from power. Yet the longer the first set of soldiers stay in power, the more traditional or rational legitimacy they are likely to acquire.

There also is a basic similarity: neither charismatic nor military regimes can carry on indefinitely on their original basis. Specifically, neither of them can resolve the succession problem without transforming its basic nature. To acquire stability and to ensure a smooth succession, both have to rely on political organization—an organization that is routine rather than charismatic and civilian rather than military. But there is an important variation on this common theme: for a military regime, the succession problem seldom arises before it is overthrown. The most vulnerable period for any dictator (military or civilian) is probably his first four or five years in power. But a second danger point comes for the exceptional dictator who rules until his old age. The certain approach of his death or physical incapacity lessens the terror or awe with which he is regarded. His opponents become more determined in their opposition, and his lieutenants instead of defending his rule start maneuvering for the succession. This would seem to be the explanation of the number of instances in which dictators were overthrown in their old age—Trujillo after three decades of rule, at 71; Porfirio Díaz, who ruled Mexico from 1876 to 1910, and Syngman Rhee of South Korea both in their eighties. It still seems unclear whether Stalin at 73 died a natural death.[20] Similarly, Sukarno's regime in 1965-66 was plunged into coup, countercoup, and near civil war at a time when the dictator's health was visibly failing.

It may be added that many military dictators aspire to building up a charismatic reputation, and that some, like Atatürk and Nasser, succeed. Indeed, their regimes clearly combined military and charismatic (as well as other) features. Kemal, in addition to obtaining a legitimate (though carefully contrived) mandate from the sultan in Anatolia, made good use of his reputation as a victorious general in presenting a charismatic image from the start. Hence he did not have to rely on internal coercion to any great extent. Nasser could acquire a charismatic reputation only after he had resolved the initial instabilities of his military regime, that is, asserted himself against Naguib and the Muslim Brethren. The same would seem to hold for all military rulers who seize power by conspiracy and coup.

The logical way out of the charismatic or military impasse is the creation of a political structure that can provide some organic connection between rulers and subjects and among successive generations of rulers. The only lasting success that either charismatic or military leaders can have is in making themselves

[20] Cf. D. A. Rustow, "Succession in the Twentieth Century," *Journal of International Affairs*, Vol. 18, No. 1 (January 1964), p. 106. Succession struggles in Yugoslavia and China were in progress in 1966 although the septuagenarian dictators survived the early rounds.

superfluous. Normally, the structure that will allow a political system to dispense with charismatic or military heroes will take the form of a political party, or several parties. But again we must guard against a false teleology, a rash assumption of unilinear determinism. There is no inevitable sequence of stages from charismatic or military regimes through one-party system and on to some higher form of evolution. Rather, the analysis indicates that among late-modernizing countries, charismatic, military, and single-party regimes are the most common, and that shifts among the three are frequent.

It also is a plausible hypothesis that it is difficult for any country to move from a charismatic or military regime toward either democracy or totalitarianism except via a single-party (authoritarian) regime. The evidence probably is too limited to allow this hypothesis to be tested conclusively. But even if the statement is true, there is no guarantee that any country will so move. Instead, a country may move from charismatic leader to charismatic leader, from military coup to military coup, or back and forth among charismatic, military, and one-party regimes. And there always is the last resort of a lapse into anarchy—as in Mexico between 1910 and 1920, in China between 1912 and 1927, and in the Congo after 1960.

CHAPTER SEVEN

POLITICAL PARTIES AND MODERNIZATION

. . . a network of new associations through which . . . men come to think of their problems as social rather than personal; as capable of solution by human action rather than part of the natural order.
THOMAS HODGKIN

The moral consensus of a free state is not something mysteriously prior to or above politics: it is the activity (the civilizing activity) of politics itself.
BERNARD CRICK

. . . one perennial problem of opposition is that there is either too much or too little.
ROBERT A. DAHL

POLITICAL PARTIES ARE AMONG the most characteristic phenomena of modern politics. In democracies and under totalitarianism, in developed and in developing countries, they serve as the means for attaining power or a share in power—or on occasion for obstructing the use of power by others. In the four-fold process of political leadership, parties provide crucial links among leaders, followers, circumstances, and goals. There are few obvious similarities between the Republican Party of the United States and the British Labour Party, between the Communist Party of the Soviet Union and the Partido Revolucionário Institucional of Mexico, or between any of these and the Constitutional Union headed by Nuri al-Said in Iraq in 1949-54. Parties, therefore, are among the most elusive subjects for comparative analysis. Yet, because of these complexities, a study of parties

can provide revealing insights into the nature of a political
system.

Nor are parties static. There is no close resemblance between
the Whig Party of Walpole and the Liberal Party of Lloyd
George, or between the Bolshevik Party of 1905 and of 1965. As
the leading student of American parties, the late V. O. Key, has
reminded us, "a conception of the party system must take into account its dimension of time. It may even be more useful to think
of the party system as an historical process than as patterned
institutions."[1] Parties are instruments fashioned for the pursuit of
collective human purposes, and hence their success and failure in
attaining those purposes profoundly transforms their nature. This
time dimension looms especially large in countries undergoing
the rapid and often erratic changes of early modernization.

A discussion of political parties in late modernizing countries,
in short, must deal not only with single-party regimes but can
also illuminate the social forces active on the political stage and
the political patterns by which they can overcome personal or
military rule and, if circumstances are favorable, move toward
democracy.

The Dynamics of Parties, Broad and Narrow

The nature of the power contest is the most obvious variable
influencing the character of political parties. Typically, the
groups that are eager to change the political or social status quo
introduce novel devices of party organization—parliamentary cau-
cuses, organized nominations for elective office, canvassing of voters, or mass propaganda—and the conservatives reluctantly follow
suit. In Europe, the earliest parties originated in the contest between hereditary monarchs and parliaments representing landed
or mercantile interests. In the nineteenth century, the clamor for
a widened franchise caused organized political activity to spill

[1] V. O. Key, Jr., *Politics, Parties, and Pressure Groups*, 4th ed. (Crowell, 1958),
p. 243.

over from the parliament to the country at large. With the advent of mass electorates, parties organized voters in the constituencies for the capture of parliamentary seats, just as they organized members of parliament for the control of government policy and personnel. In the United States, party development followed analogous lines, except for variations resulting from the absence of monarchy, the continued greater independence of the executive from legislative control, and the decentralization implicit in the federal system. But in despotic states such as Romanov Russia and Ottoman Turkey, organized political activity took the form of secret conspiracy at home and of agitation by political refugees abroad; and changes of government resulted from coups and revolutions, not from elections and parliamentary votes. In colonial countries, the first parties emerged toward the turn of the twentieth century in the struggle of modernized elements of the population against the colonial rulers and their local allies.

In countries where there is no accepted concept of national identity, parties may form on a linguistic or ethnic basis with the purpose of redrawing the state's boundaries. In this case, the political contest is not between king and parliament, or between various social groups among the voters, but rather between a national minority and the rest of the population. Most of the parties in the Hapsburg Empire were of this type, and so were the Armenian parties in the late Ottoman Empire, and the organizations supporting the Polish, Danish, and Alsatian members of the German imperial parliament between 1871 and 1918.

Next to the structure of governmental power itself, the most important influence on political parties comes from their social base. In modernizing countries, in particular, an important distinction must be drawn between narrowly based and broadly based political parties. Other terms have been employed; broadly based parties have also been called mass parties, and narrowly based ones have been called patron, or cadre, or elite parties.[2]

[2] See D. A. Rustow in Gabriel A. Almond and James S. Coleman, eds., *The Politics of the Developing Areas* (Princeton University Press, 1960), p. 397; cf. Ruth Schachter Morgenthau, *Political Parties in French-Speaking West Africa*

But whatever the names, it is important to keep in mind that the distinction relates to a spectrum with many shades of grey rather than a black and white dichotomy, and, furthermore, that parties over time can move up and down along this spectrum.

Narrowly based parties are typically competing groups within a small oligarchy. They have been frequent in the independent countries of the Middle East and Latin America, and in some of the colonial countries where an accommodation obtained between imperial rulers and indigenous vested interests. Often such a party is little more than a disguise for the personal ambition of some prominent figure within the ruling class. Taken together, a set of narrowly based parties may serve as master of ceremonies of the game of musical chairs among recurrent groups of oligarchic rulers. An observer of the Iranian scene of the 1940's noted a profusion of parties

. . . formed from above—a few people grouping themselves around some prominent personality or publishing a newspaper with funds provided by an anonymous capitalist. Their programs were virtually interchangeable, and were confined to a series of pious platitudes of which the "integrity and independence of Iran" was usually the first. Their names gave even less indication of their policy. . . . Parties of this type seldom spread their influence beyond their own circle of intellectuals and professional men, and their fortunes, being dependent on the whims of individuals, fluctuated widely.[3]

A Bolivian critic, in a more sarcastic vein, once complained that: "To form a political party only three people and one object are necessary: a president, a vice-president, a secretary, and a rubber stamp. The party can get along even without the vice-president and the secretary. . . . There have been cases in which the existence of only the rubber stamp has been sufficient."[4] The

---

(Oxford: Clarendon Press, 1964), p. 336; Thomas Hodgkin, *African Political Parties* (Penguin, 1961), p. 68; Maurice Duverger, *Political Parties*, translated by B. and R. North, 2d ed. (Wiley, 1963), pp. 63-71.

[3] L. P. Elwell-Sutton, "Political Parties in Iran, 1941-1948," *Middle East Journal*, Vol. 3 (1949), p. 49.

[4] Luis Terán Gómez, *Los Partidos Políticos y su Acción Democrática* (La Paz, 1942), pp. 60-61, cited in Almond and Coleman, eds., *op. cit.*, p. 483.

rubber stamp, surely, supplies the narrowest of all possible bases for a party.

Within a stable oligarchic system, the existing parties will do their best to resist a broadening of the base. In Iraq between 1936 and 1958, for example, a number of political parties emerged that appealed over the heads of the oligarchy to the urban masses. Frequently, however, the successful demagogue who had thus registered some initial success would be absorbed into the ruling class through the timely offer of a cabinet post or other advancement, and his oratorical ardor would markedly cool.

In the modernizing countries of Asia, Africa, and Latin America, broadly based parties have been the by-products of other processes of political modernization, notably of the establishment of a modern bureaucracy, of higher education, and of a modern army—and more indirectly of the growth of cities. The straining of all human resources in the final contest for independence often provided a potent incentive for further breadth. In India, for example, the Macauley report of 1835 provided the impetus for the development of an imperial civil service trained in British-style colleges. In Ottoman Turkey four years later, the Reform Edict of Gülhane inaugurated a similar effort at European-style higher education, for a reformed bureaucracy and army. In both countries, young men from many different regions and social classes henceforth were trained in the capital or other urban centers and sent out to other provinces as district officers, revenue collectors, school teachers, and the like in a comprehensive system of rotation. In both countries, as it happened, the first modern political parties formed fifty years after the initial reform program—the Indian National Congress in 1885 and the Ottoman Society of Union and Progress in 1889. In the early Congress, lawyers, teachers, and journalists predominated; but one of their first demands was for liberalization of the rules whereby Indians could join and rise within the civil service. The Union and Progress Society formed as a conspiracy among the medical cadets—the most specialized and highly trained service within the new army. After a period of activity in European exile, the movement was reconstituted in Macedonia by an alliance of young army officers with teachers, journalists, and civil servants.

The importance of new systems of communication and education for party developments is obvious. The Indian National Congress was formed by a group of graduates of Calcutta University. In the Sudan, the earliest precursor of later political parties was an association of college alumni returning from their foreign studies. The staunchest spokesman of the Union and Progress exiles at the turn of the century was a former director of provincial education. Among the leaders of the revived movement of 1906-08 were a telegraph clerk, a military officer in charge of railroad transport, school teachers, and journalists. The transformation of both the Indian National Congress and of the Turkish movement into well-disciplined nationwide organizations resulted from nationalist activities after World War I—in India Gandhi's struggle against British rule and in Turkey Kemal's War of Independence against Allied partition and Greek invasion.

For Tropical Africa, Hodgkin has noted the importance of the growing towns and cities for the rise of parties.

By mixing men from a variety of social backgrounds they make possible the discovery of new points of contact and interest. Around these interests there develops a network of new associations, through which for the first time men come to think of their problems as social rather than personal; as capable of solution by human action rather than part of the natural order.[5]

In Mexico, the development of the first broad and stable party was closely related to the transition from military to civilian rule. Calles in 1928-29 refused a second presidential term; instead he organized the most important local military figures—the surviving caudillos of the civil war period—into the Partido Nacional Revolucionario so as to control future presidential nominations. Meanwhile, the reforms of Obregón and Calles had created the nu-

[5] Thomas Hodgkin, *Nationalism in Colonial Africa* (New York University Press, 1957), p. 63.

cleus of a professional officer corps, and for the first time officers were rotated in their assignments from state to state. An intensive program of land redistribution began in 1928, and the depression stimulated labor organization. Cárdenas promoted both of these trends and balanced the military in the party (renamed in 1937 Partido de la Revolución Mexicana) with strong agricultural and trade union sectors. Under his successor, the military sector was replaced by a new "popular" sector and the conflict between state and church reconciled. In 1945, the growing stability (some would say conservatism) of the Mexican regime was symbolized by a further change in the party's name—this time to a contradiction in terms: Partido Revolucionario Institucional (PRI).

It is significant that the two countries that successfully overcame a period of intense military interference in politics, Mexico and Turkey, did so through the institution of a single governing party, founded by military leaders but increasingly civilianized. Both the Union and Progress party of 1906-08 and Mustafa Kemal's Republican People's Party (RPP) of 1923 included substantial civilian elements from the start. In the Turkish RPP from about 1935 and in the Mexican PRI from about 1945, the bureaucratic element became predominant. In 1943, for example, three-fourths of the RPP-dominated parliament in Turkey were men whose careers had started in the public service (bureaucracy, army, public education) but only 16 percent of the total were military men.[6] In the "popular" sector of the Mexican PRI, too, military officers gradually were replaced by civil servants. Since 1946, Mexico for the first time in a century has had only civilian presidents: and the last three have risen to the presidency from the post of minister of *gobernación*, which is the capstone of the provincial civil service. Perhaps a third stage can be discerned in both countries, that of the rise of a nonofficial civilian element in

[6] My calculations from the album of the National Assembly. (Cf. Frederick W. Frey, *The Turkish Political Elite*, Massachusetts Institute of Technology Press, 1965, p. 181.) Note that all persons listed by Frey under government, army, and education, most of those under law and medicine (judges, physicians in government hospitals), and religion (muftis and imams) were in public employment.

the two government parties—lawyers, physicians, and journalists in Turkey in the early forties, and businessmen in Mexico in the fifties.

Not only did the single party overcome militarism, it also made possible a solution to the succession problem. Kemal Atatürk in 1938 was one of the rare dictators to be peacefully succeeded. The successor, Inönü, in 1945 took the further unusual step of voluntarily relinquishing his party's political monopoly, and in 1950 became leader of a loyal opposition after an election landslide for the rival Democratic Party. The events of the late fifties, culminating in the 1960 coup, indicated that this transition to democracy may have been premature. Yet after a remarkably brief military interlude, discussed in the preceding chapter, the democratic experiment has been energetically resumed since 1961.

Mexico has had as many as six orderly successions within its one-party system since 1934. In some respects, the Mexican system of government might be described as a monarchy limited to a six-year term and rising on the base of a closely knit yet flexible party oligarchy. It clearly is the only single-party system that has found an institutional solution to the succession problem. The workings of the mechanism are a rather closely guarded secret. Among the apparent ingredients are intense consultations within the party's inner circle, launchings of informal candidacies in the press to test comparative popularities, a decisive final voice for the incumbent president, and a firm closing of party ranks at election time. The memory of the prolonged civil war of 1910-20 and of the frequent coups and disorders up to 1938 helps to keep potential dissidents in line. The critics of the system would charge that the prospect of enrichment at public expense reconciles successive groups of aspirants to the necessary waiting periods.

Legally, opposition parties are free to contest elections, but government patronage and occasional intimidation and fraudulent counting have kept votes for the opposition parties below 20 percent, and their representation to a handful of congressmen. Of the two slogans of the 1910 revolution—"sufragio efectivo; no reelección"—the second has become the cornerstone of the country's unwritten constitution. The growing activity of the opposition party PAN in recent years may indicate that the first also may become increasingly a reality in the future.

In most Latin American countries, party structures have been far weaker and more diffuse than in Mexico, and in most Asian and African countries, party developments lagged by several generations behind those of India and Turkey. But in many of the formerly colonial countries, a number of broad common trends can be discerned. In the British colonies, the establishment of colonial legislatures before or after World War II and the shift from European to indigenous and from appointed to elected members promoted the formation of political parties within the slowly expanding electorates. In French Africa, participation by small groups of enfranchised colonials in the metropolitan elections of the Fourth Republic had a similar effect.

In some of the more traditional regions of the African interior, narrowly based parties formed that relied on local chiefs and often established close working relationships with the colonial administration—for example, the Northern People's Congress led by the Sardauna of Sokoto in Northern Nigeria and some of the parties of the interior of French West Africa. In the more accessible and economically developed coastal regions of North and West Africa, the tendency was toward mass parties: the early Wafd party in Egypt, the Istiqlal party in Morocco, Bourguiba's Neo-Destour in Tunisia, Touré's Parti Démocratique de Guinée, Houphouet-Boigny's Parti Démocratique de la Côte d'Ivoire, Nkrumah's Convention People's Party in Ghana, and the Action Group and the National Congress of Nigeria and the Cameroons in Western and Eastern Nigeria, respectively.

In many Asian countries and in Egypt, party developments go back to the interwar period, and in most of these, World War II provided an important additional impetus to party activity. In

Southeast Asia, the withdrawal first of Western and then of Japanese authority left control in the hands of nationalist groups such as the Partido Nacionalista of the Philippines, the Nationalist Party in Indonesia, and the Anti-Fascist People's Freedom League in Burma.

The broadly based parties of Asia and Africa became what elsewhere I have called "comprehensive-nationalist parties."

> [Their] commitment to nationalism . . . [involved them] in a fight on two fronts — externally, against existing or threatened foreign rule, and domestically, against the traditional political [and social] structure and its defenders. The party's comprehensive character arises from the need to secure support in this two-front fight among the widest possible combination of social strata. But the party is also comprehensive in the further sense that it desires not merely a political regeneration, but, beyond this, a far-reaching reshaping of society. Its major socio-cultural aims commonly are mass education, economic development—particularly of industry—and secularization; in short a hastening of the process of modernization of which the rise of national consciousness itself is but one facet.[7]

The Indian National Congress and the Republican People's Party of Turkey (with its Union and Progress predecessor) may well be considered the prototypes of such parties. The Mexican PRI also fits the model fairly well, even though its struggle against foreign interests was limited to such measures as nationalization of petroleum in 1938; for one of its major concerns has been a gradual bridging of the enormous gulf that has separated the ruling class with its Hispanic culture from the Indian and mestizo majority of the population.

Social Groups in Politics

The comprehensive-nationalist party tries to mobilize all available social strata and all regional groups in the effort at independence and modernization. But the groups that can be mobilized in this

[7] Almond and Coleman, eds., *op. cit.*, p. 399f.

way are not usually the same as those that supported early party movements in Europe or North America. To be sure, there are, in Asia and Africa as in Europe, examples of aristocrats taking up the cause of protest against established authority or championing the rise of lower strata: Mustafa Fazil Pasha who, after being excluded from the Egyptian Khedivial succession, became the patron of the New Ottomans in Turkey; Bandaranaike in Ceylon, the Nehrus and other Brahmin leaders in India; Muhammad Mossadegh (descended on his mother's side from the Qajar royal house) in Iran; Sékou Touré, great-grandson of Samory Touré who fought against the French at the turn of the century.[8]

In fact, a leading student of West African parties has noted a general reversal of social recruitment patterns between the top leadership and the lower echelons of broadly and narrowly based parties: ". . . Mass parties have a surprisingly large number of people with high traditional status as the top national party leaders. And patron parties have an exceptionally large number of prime ministers . . . with low traditional status. . . . It is as if 'princes' fear least the competition of 'captives'; while villagers, first hearing equality preached, learn fastest from 'princes'. "[9] The Mossadeghs, Bandaranaikes, and Tourés, then, are the Asian and African equivalents of the Condorcets, the Arvid Posses, and the Kropotkins.

But there are few parallels in the developing countries to the agrarian-commercial aristocracy that formed the nucleus of the eighteenth century Whigs, or of the independent farmers that supported the party of Jefferson and Jackson. Trade in many parts of Asia and Africa has traditionally been in the hands of groups distinct in language and religion from the agricultural majorities—Chinese in Southeast Asia, Parsees in India, Christians and Jews in the Muslim Middle East, Arabs in Tropical Africa. These groups, as noted in an earlier chapter, were once favored

[8] Samory Touré has been called "the last of the great nineteenth-century Soudanese conquerors." L. Gray Cowan, "Guinea," in Gwendolen M. Carter, ed., *African One-Party States* (Cornell University Press, 1962), p. 150.

[9] Morgenthau, *op. cit.*, p. 345.

by the imperial authorities. With the awakening of national sentiment, they have come to be considered as alien, and hence are
not inclined to compromise themselves further by indulging in
organized political activity.

The alien character of the Western companies that have exploited the mineral and plantation products of colonial or semi-
colonial economies is of course even more pronounced. The size
and international connections of such companies as the United
Fruit Company in the Caribbean and the major petroleum concerns in the Middle East, Venezuela, and elsewhere, have enabled them to deal with governments as from one major power to
another, rather than by the circuitous route of political pressure
through parties or parliaments. The Bolivian example shows that
there is little difference in this respect between foreign-owned
companies, such as Hochschild, which bought into local mines,
and indigenous ones, such as Patiño and Aramayo, which secured their profits by channeling them into investments abroad.

Even the export-import traders, though individually less powerful than the giant mining or plantation concerns, tend to hold
similarly aloof from party politics. Their assets are too large and
their culture is too cosmopolitan for them to feel much affinity to
the masses of urban craftsmen or rural peasants. They find it
more advantageous to use private connections with individual bureaucrats for *ad hoc* relief from the government's multifarious
regulations than to bring collective and public pressure on legislatures for their repeal. A general rule, after all, is not nearly as
troublesome as its specific application.

The fact that Asian and African governments tend to play a
much more active role in the development of industry than did
the governments of Europe at a similar stage of economic growth,
is a result and a further cause of the atrophy of private business
activity. Where socialization and government regulations are the
order of the day, the businessman does better to make his profits
quietly and to channel them abroad rather than risk profits and
capital by attracting attention at home. Only where a fair degree

of commercial and industrial development has occurred under private ownership—as, for example, in Turkey under the Republic, in Mexico since World War II, in the giant free port with its hinterland that is Lebanon, and to some extent in India—have businessmen been an important source of support for party organization.

The situation in agriculture resembles somewhat that in commerce and industry. The large landowners feel aloof from the majority of the population. In the countries where holdings are largest, they form a natural part of the ruling oligarchy, and have no need for elaborate party organization. Aside from the dissident Bandaranaikes and Mossadeghs, the landowners therefore at most participate in narrowly based, oligarchic parties. Between them and the masses of tenant farmers and agricultural workers, the gap is too wide to be readily bridged.

The subsistence farmers, even though they own their land, are equally inactive: they are outside both the economic and the political market-place, and for the same reasons. In the exceptional countries where middle-size farmers grow cash crops—such as the cocoa and coffee growers in Ghana and the Ivory Coast—these have been as active in party politics, or more so, than their equivalents in Europe and North America. In exceptional situations, where vigorously competing parties have exhausted the possibilities of urban and upper-class recruitment, they may proceed to enlist the peasantry. As the Turkish experience of the 1950's shows, such situations provide a strong incentive for government programs of rural development. Where this factor of party competition is absent, the political influence of the peasantry is likely to be weaker or more intermittent, as in Mexico after 1910 and in Bolivia after 1953.

Even the partisan role of high-school and university graduates in Asia and especially in Africa differs from that in nineteenth-century Europe. Almost everywhere in Africa, the number of vacancies in the government bureaucracies vastly exceeds the supply of educated personnel. Hence there is little occasion for such graduates to challenge bureaucratic power by party organization. In many of the African colonies, indeed, there was a tendency for educated young men to rise as high in the civil service as Africans were permitted to rise and for their "contemporaries . . . who had failed the secondary school or college entrance examinations . . . to take part in the crucial first years of post-war political activity, and so [to become] 'founding fathers'."[10] In Asia and the Middle East, where there is a much longer tradition of higher education, lawyers, teachers, and physicians have played prominent roles in the formation of parties—as the careers of Motilal Nehru, of Gandhi, and of Mustafa Kamil (founder in 1897 of the first Egyptian nationalist party) illustrate.

For these groups, too, the attraction of party politics was reduced by the prevalence of government employment. Where the university graduate in nineteenth century Europe looked forward to a career in the "free" professions, the twentieth century Asian has been more likely to become a physician in a government dispensary, a lawyer or engineer in one of the many government economic enterprises, or a teacher in a public institution of learning. In Muslim countries, even the graduates of religious seminaries become muftis and qadis paid from public funds. It would seem that the stereotype of the "unemployed intellectual" applies only to a few Asian and Middle Eastern countries—India, Egypt, Iran—and to none as yet in Tropical Africa. Most intellectuals find employment very readily, and most readily in the rapidly expanding government itself.

Two groups within the Asian and African intellectual middle class must be singled out for their prominent political roles. One is the relatively small group of men returning from studies in Europe or North America. The second are military officers. The returning students have supplied many party leaders—Kwame Nkrumah is an outstanding example. The officers also have played a prominent political role, but the chief instrument of their activity has been not the political party but the coup d'état.

[10] *Ibid.*, p. 335.

There is one social group whose role in Asian and African party politics far exceeds that of its confreres in nineteenth-century Europe, and that is the organized wage earners. It would be grossly misleading to apply to these groups in Asia and Africa the label of "proletarians." On the contrary, they may properly be considered an economic and political elite group. In a country with an overwhelmingly rural population, urban residence gives them a unique exposure to modern influences. In Tropical Africa, they are, together with the urban intellectuals, the main group that begins to live in a national rather than a tribal context. In a country where a majority live in a traditional subsistence economy, their place in the market makes them a distinctly modern group. And in a country where large masses are latently or acutely unemployed, their employment gives them elite status. For all these reasons, trade unions have played a crucial role as key supporters of broadly based parties in many Asian and African countries. The Neo-Destour in Tunisia, the Istiqlal, and more recently the Union Nationale des Forces Populaires in Morocco, and the Parti Démocratique de Guinée are prominent examples.

In the linguistically or religiously heterogeneous countries of Asia and Africa, ethnic or religious groups are important in party politics. The Lebanese parties, for example, have been a mere adjunct to the electorate's main division into Maronites, Sunnis, Shiis, Druzes, and other denominations. The Masjumi in Indonesia is another prominent example of a religiously based party. In Ceylon and Malaya, divisions of language, religion, and party—all three—have tended to coincide. In India before partition, the Muslim League began as the spokesman of the largest religious minority. Its success in creating a state with a mainly religious definition of membership, combined with its failure to create for itself a social base in Pakistan, became one of the reasons for its subsequent sharp decline.

In many African countries, nationalist parties have been a strong factor for integration among the tribes; but in other African countries, parties have been founded mainly on the support of single tribes. This has been true notably in Nigeria, before the coup of 1966, where the Fulani-Hausa supported the Northern People's Congress, the Ibo the National Convention of Nigerian Citizens, and the Yoruba the Action Group; in Kenya, where Kikuyus and Luos were prominent in the Kenya African National Union and the smaller tribes in the rival Kenya African Democratic Union; and in the formerly Belgian Congo. With regard to tribal and supra-tribal support of parties, the same observation can be made as with breadth of social base generally: only parties that are fairly evenly matched can engage in successful competition. In Ghana, for example, one of the chief handicaps of the various opposition groups to Nkrumah's supra-tribal Convention People's Party was that they could offer no alternative but a summation of separate tribal interests.

By and large, religion looms larger in the Muslim, Hindu, and Buddhist parts of Asia and the Middle East than in the predominantly pagan areas of Africa. It was noted in Chapter Two that linguistic conflicts tend to be more tenacious among languages with a long literary tradition. Religious alignments, too, tend to be more clear-cut among the adherents of scriptural creeds than among animists. The elaborate world view of revealed religions, moreover, is more readily translated into political doctrines that can compete, or on occasion blend, with such modern secular creeds as nationalism, democracy, or socialism.

Another important characteristic of many Asian religious-political movements was touched upon in Chapter Four. Movements such as the Muslim Brethren in the Arab countries, the Jamaat-i-Islami in Pakistan, and the so-called "communal" parties in India are ostensibly defending their religious and social traditions against the alien onslaught of secular modernity. Yet the tradition to which these groups nostalgically look back has been disrupted beyond any hope of continuation or restoration. They tend to combine their romaticized image of the past and their denunciation of Western secularism with up-to-date Western-derived techniques of propaganda and of organization. In short, they offer a dynamic blend of tradition and modernity, and it is not very illuminating, as is often done, to refer to them as "conservative," "reactionary," or "primordial."

Single Party Systems

The single party along with the military junta has at this time emerged as the most important ruling agency in Asia and Africa. But typically, the Asian and African single parties are of the so-called authoritarian rather than the totalitarian type.

The struggle for independence creates a strong incentive for unification of all active political forces. Yet it is not usually clear from the start around which groups and leaders this rallying will take place. There often have been rival nationalist groups vying for the role of comprehensive-nationalist party, and the rivalry at times has been bitter. In Tunisia, Bourguiba's broadly based Neo-Destour replaced the more narrowly based old Destour as the spokesman of nationalism. In Ghana, Nkrumah's more radical Convention People's Party broke away from the United Gold Coast Convention. In Algeria, the terrorist activity of the Front de la Libération Nationale was directed not only against French troops and colons but also, and often with particular vehemence, against moderate Algerian groups such as the followers of Hadj Messali and against passive elements of the population.

In much of Asia, World War II and its aftermath shaped the postindependence political movements. In Indonesia, Sukarno's nationalists had revolted against the Dutch as early as 1926, and the Japanese in 1942 were welcomed as liberators. They appointed Sukarno President of the Java Central Council, from which position he moved to that of President of Indonesia in 1945. In Burma, there had been little active opposition to British rule before the war. But here, too, the Japanese were welcomed in the first flush of victory, and U Nu and other nationalists served in a Japanese-sponsored government. As the tide of war

turned, the Anti-Fascist People's Freedom League was formed
with the support of communist, socialist, religious, professional,
and civic groups, although the communists subsequently broke
with the party as they launched their abortive revolt in 1948. In
India, the vast majority of the Congress party took a pro-British
stand during the war, but continued to press its demand for independence. The gulf between Congress and the Muslim League
widened further, and the British negotiated independence with
each group separately. The Indonesian Nationalists, the AFPFL,
the Indian National Congress, and the Muslim League in 1945-48
thus emerged as the predominant groups in their several independent states.

In Tropical Africa, it was not the events of the war or prolonged internal resistance, but rather the psychological pressures
of the Asian and Middle Eastern examples that prompted the
transition to independence in the decade since 1957. The choice
of timing remained largely in the hands of the imperial powers,
although the conditions of the transfer, of course, had to be negotiated with the prospective successor governments. Coleman and
Rosberg have summed up some of the major facets of the transition and defined the groups that became the beneficiaries of this
development:

> During a brief period in the late 1940's, each of these parties was
> more militantly nationalist than its competitors. [In African eyes it
> came to be] thereby endowed with a special mantle of grace. . . .
> Thus the critical element in the legitimating power of revolutionary
> imagery is not necessarily ceaseless struggle and uncompromising
> resistance until the final surrender of imperial power, . . . but the
> establishment by a party of a favorable image in the public mind
> at that point of time when the imperial power seriously launched
> the protracted process of disengagement and withdrawal. Strength-
> ened by an early revolutionary popularity which chastened and in-
> dulgent colonial powers allowed to be kept alive, protected from the
> opposition by the full support of the imperial government, and pro-
> gressively endowed with real power enabling it to consolidate its
> position of primacy within the state, the governing party in many

new states entered the era of independence not only with its aura of legitimacy virtually untarnished, but also with decisive control over the authoritative structures of government.[11]

The "aura of legitimacy" that came to surround the vocal (or formerly vocal) advocates of independence included a strong charismatic element, for the imperial withdrawal in the absence of major internal pressures constituted one of those seemingly magic successes which, according to Weber, are the chief warrant of charismatic authority. Once it has become clear with what group the imperial power will negotiate independence, there is a natural further rallying around that group. After independence, however, this incentive for unity rapidly vanishes, and many divisive issues and ambitions come to the fore.

Amidst these novel pressures, the nationalist party may quickly lose its predominant position. Sukarno broke with his Vice-President, Hatta, and at various times faced mounting opposition from the Masjumi, the communists, or the army. The Muslim League in Pakistan and the AFPFL in Burma crumbled and made way for military regimes. In Morocco, the more militant nationalists and trade unionists formed the Union Nationale des Forces Populaires, whereas the more moderate Istiqlal leaders continued their support for King Hasan's plebiscitary monarchy. A broad social base and close affiliation with the trade union movement enabled some parties, such as Bourguiba's Neo-Destour, to withstand such centrifugal pressures. More frequently, however, a variety of administrative and coercive measures have served the same end.

The transition to independence thrusts into the hands of the successful nationalist leaders and their parties the full power of the administrative machinery of government. Most African countries have elected their legislators by the Anglo-American system of plurality voting in single-member constituencies—a system that overrepresents the most popular party at the expense of its nearest rival, and tends to eliminate third parties altogether unless

[11] James S. Coleman and Carl G. Rosberg, Jr., eds., *Political Parties and National Integration in Tropical Africa* (University of California Press, 1964), p. 660.

they have a strong regional base.[12] The complexities of election administration in inaccessible countries with an overwhelmingly illiterate population further enhance the potential influence of the administrators. It was no coincidence, for example, that when the Congo proceeded to its second national election in 1965, election officials began their four-week tour across the provinces in Premier Moise Tshombe's stronghold of Katanga.

But elections, on balance, are a minor ingredient in the total picture. For the vast array of the government's newly won political, economic, and educational powers—development funds, government scholarships, civil service appointments—is commonly used throughout Africa to reward the followers of the government party and defectors from the opposition. In several countries, indeed, the entire opposition soon after independence "crossed the carpet" to join the government party. In some countries, notably in Ghana under Nkrumah, the recalcitrant opponents, and even dissidents and critics in the government's ranks, have been silenced through coercive measures. These ranged from loss of jobs in the judiciary, the universities, and the civil service, to imprisonment without trial and banishment from the country. In Algeria, the guerrilla war for independence was followed by an equally ruthless internal struggle for power from which first Premier Ben Bella and then his military backer, Colonel Houari Boumedienne, emerged as the victors. By 1965, coercive politics in both Algeria and Ghana had led to military rule.

[12] It may be noted that, whereas most of Latin America today uses some variant of proportional representation, Mexico's single-member plurality system has been a strong buttress to the PRI's predominance. Turkey during its single-party period and until 1960 voted under a multiple-member plurality system (comparable to that used for the electoral college in the United States) that magnified the distortion even further. Until 1945, when no opposition candidates were running, these details did not matter. But in 1954, for example, Menderes' Democratic party obtained 93 percent of the seats in parliament on the basis of only 58 percent of the popular vote.

Difficulties of Democracy

Every one of the fifty or so colonies that attained independence since 1945 was equipped at the outset with a written constitution aimed at a representative and democratic system of government. Yet only in a handful has more than a semblance of democracy survived after a few years. This "erosion of democracy"[13] throughout Asia and Africa, and its difficulties (less serious but of longer standing) in Latin America are so widespread as to mock any explanation that would rely on special circumstances in a particular country or on charges of ill will or incapacity against an individual leader. A phenomenon so general must have more general causes than personal whim and unique circumstance.

In exploring this question, it would be erroneous to assume, as did the American Declaration of Independence and other classic documents of the Western era of revolution, that free or representative institutions are somehow the "natural" form of government that will spring up, like Pallas from the head of Zeus, as soon as the restraints of tyranny or foreign rule are relinquished. Democracy is not a state of nature but a state of civilized society. Nor is it plausible (as departing colonial administrators seemed to assume) that a carefully worded legal text, a few years of parliamentary practice, and the presence of a few expatriate advisers should be enough to transfer representative institutions from Westminster to Accra, Colombo, or Dar es Salaam. Certainly, this was not the way in which constitutionalism or democracy arose in any Western country. In the words of Robert Dahl, we are dealing with "that branch, which of all the arts of government is the most difficult, the art of democratic government."[14] Before asking why democratic institutions have broken down in so many coun-

[13] See Rupert Emerson, *From Empire to Nation* (Harvard University Press, 1960), Chap. 15.
[14] *A Preface to Democratic Theory* (University of Chicago Press, 1956), p. 151.

tries, it will be well to examine briefly some of those countries where they have thrived, or come close to thriving.

SOME HISTORICAL ANTECEDENTS OF DEMOCRACY

A few common features emerge clearly from the history of countries such as the Philippines, Lebanon, Chile, Costa Rica, and Uruguay that can be said to have attained relatively stable democratic systems, and others such as Mexico, India, Ceylon, Colombia, Brazil, and Turkey that have come more or less close.[15]

There has been, first, a history of anywhere from 40 to 130 years of administrative and educational modernization—a factor already discussed in connection with party developments in India, Turkey, and Mexico. Secondly, there has been a stable geographic context for the political system throughout that same period. Even India and Turkey, by virtue of a wholesale transfer of administrative and political personnel, continued the previous context of the British Indian and Ottoman Empires in a way that Pakistan and the Ottoman-Arab successor states did not. Lebanon is no exception, for even under Ottoman rule, it had a continuous history of regional autonomy dating back to the sixteenth century. Largely through foreign intervention, it was the only region that escaped the centralizing tendencies of the Tanzimat and Hamidian periods. Thirdly, there has been a tradition, dating back at least one, two, or three generations, of parties (in Lebanon of religious denominations) that provided some organic link between rulers and subjects, and that were able to involve progressively larger groups in the political process.

A fourth historic condition is equally striking. There have been tenacious and bitter conflicts between major social or political

[15] A series of three successive elections since independence, based on an inclusive franchise, open party competition, and an honest count, and at least one peaceful change of party control may be taken as rough criteria of "stable democracy." Israel and Japan meet the first of these criteria, but have been left out of the above account—the first because of its European-immigrant population, and the second because of its far greater degree of modernization compared to other non-European countries. For further details, see Appendix Table 5.

groups over issues of profound concern to them. From time to time, especially in the earlier stages, these conflicts erupted into violence. But in the end, the losers in any given round of conflict proved strongly enough entrenched, the winners sufficiently unsure of their victory, or sufficiently far-sighted or generous, that the vital interests of no major part of the community were destroyed. Early party developments in India and Turkey, as we have seen, stemmed from such a conflict between a growing colonial or dynastic bureaucracy and rival groups among the graduates of a modern educational system. In the Philippines before independence, as in India, the struggle was between nationalist forces and a colonial ruler. In Turkey, it was at one time between supporters of autocracy and of constitutionalism, at another, between champions of dynastic-religious monarchy and of a nationalist and secularist republic, and at last between the urban educated class and rising elements in the peasantry. In Chile and Uruguay, it has been mainly between entrenched agrarian interests and rising groups in commerce, labor, and the urban professions. In Lebanon, it has been among denominational groups, for the inaccessible Mount Lebanon had for centuries provided refuge for persecuted minorities. In India since independence, it has been mainly among language and caste groups, the pattern of their party affiliation varying from state to state and district to district. What is important is not the stakes of the contest or the identity of the contestants, but the long-drawn and precariously balanced nature of the struggle: for democracy is essentially a matter of political form rather than specific content.

Three of the developments just listed correspond precisely to the quests identified in an earlier chapter as the chief political ingredients of modern nation-statehood: the quests for authority and public service, for geographic identity, and for equality and participation. The fourth condition is the one that channels this development into a specifically democratic direction.

Once again, it should not be assumed that any of these developments run their course inevitably or irresistibly. A number of Latin American examples show that a pattern of constitutional accommodation established within an oligarchic class may break down under the impact of a clamorously rising lower class. In Argentina, there was a period of peaceful constitutional development from 1852 until 1930, in Chile from 1839 until 1925, in Colombia from the 1860's until 1948. All three regimes were based on orderly elections, on peaceful transitions of government in which no president was allowed to succeed himself, and on competing political parties.

But the social base of each system was extremely slender, the franchise being narrowly limited by property or literacy qualifications. In Colombia, political participation was restricted to the Spanish upper class to the exclusion of mestizos and Indians. In Argentina and Chile, where the population consisted almost entirely of European immigrants, large land owners predominated. The oligarchic constitutional balance in all three countries was upset by the economic and social dislocations brought about by World War I and the great depression. It crumbled under the impact of dissatisfied elements among the lower classes, particularly the urban workers and the urban unemployed. In all three countries, elected government gave way to populist dictatorships, military in Argentina and Chile, first civilian and then military in Colombia.

Broadly speaking, the three oligarchic constitutional regimes can be compared to the British system after the constitutional settlement of 1688—with the crucial difference that in Great Britain the pressure of rising lower classes was successively accommodated in 1832, 1867, and 1885. It is clear that no liberal constitutional system is secure unless its basis of representation is widened until it includes the entire population, until it has been fully democratized.

SOME THEORETICAL PRESUPPOSITIONS

What has just been examined in the light of historical examples may be restated in more abstract fashion. Democracy is a modern political system, and it is an egalitarian device. In submitting to democratic elections, the defenders of tradition and of privilege are abandoning the substance of their position. Democracy therefore presupposes that under a preceding oligarchic or autocratic regime the traditionalists have accepted the necessity of modernization, that aristocrats have become reconciled to the inevitability of greater equality. Experience shows that a gradual change of heart follows on such reluctant acceptance, for once the conservative forces conform to the procedures of democracy, their electoral success will depend on it.

Democracy is a method of popular government: it presupposes the existence of a government and of a people. It is a method for settling conflicts: hence it requires that conflicting interests be expressed rather than suppressed, but also that the participants acquire experience in the arts of settling conflict. Democracy requires a relative abundance of skilled administrative and political personnel. Like other modern techniques, it combines continuity and change. It is a device for the temporary rule of changing majorities—or rather their representatives. This ever-present possibility of change of rulers can be entertained only if there is a continuing sense of identity among the subjects. So that governments may change, the people must endure. Finally, democracy is a political technique: specific economic and social conditions are essential to it only insofar as they are required to produce those political ingredients.

Democracy depends on the existence of several parties and the possibility of their alternation in the roles of government and opposition.[16] This implies at least a tripling of trained political personnel. There must be a neutral bureaucracy and at least two competing parties—each with its central organization in the capital and its representatives in every district. The new tendency of African countries (notably Mali and Guinea) to merge their government and party hierarchies throughout the country is in part a result of a shortage of trained personnel.

The temporary nature of the democratic mandate also creates difficulties for developing countries that are not generally appre-

[16] Cf. above, Chap. Three.

ciated. In these countries, too many other aspects of social and political life are in rapid flux for government, also, to be made temporary and changeable in this fashion. Decisions about modernization, geographic identity, and political equality will not be accepted unless they are made for long and indefinite time periods, unless they are thought to be permanent. It is proving difficult enough for Great Britain to nationalize its steel industry after one election, denationalize it after the next, and renationalize after a third. If the process were to be repeated at will, it is doubtful whether any orderly program of private or public investment in steel would ever get underway. To extend this periodic reversal to the entire economy seems unthinkable.

A regime that is thought to be temporary is likely to encourage all forces of basic opposition to it. This is the reason Egyptians felt so bitter about the "temporary" British occupation of 1882 that in one form or another lasted until the evacuation of Suez in 1956, why Syrians resented the French mandate of the interwar period—whereas there turned out to be far greater acceptance of "permanent" colonial rule even in highly civilized societies such as India.[17] If in an African country today the constitution provides that there should be another round at the hustings in only three or four years, why should the opposition not start campaigning on the morrow of the first election? Why should the government not use the full array of its powers to wither the social or ethnic base of the opposition? And since the government party's prospects will be affected by its economic performance in office, why should the opposition not do its best to sabotage that performance? It takes prolonged experience of the dangers of intransigence, of the need for accommodation, and of the rewards of compromise and forbearance to supply convincing answers.

[17] With regard to Egypt, a perceptive British observer has written: "Great Britain had originally refused to undertake fundamental reforms on the ground of the temporary nature of her occupation. The consequences of this refusal gradually came to be used as an excuse for making the occupation permanent. It was, in fact, infinitely more difficult to terminate a 'temporary' occupation than it would have been to terminate a 'permanent' one of the colonial type." John Marlowe, *A History of Egypt and Anglo-Egyptian Relations, 1800-1953* (Praeger, 1954), p. 253.

Whatever the difficulties of the temporary tenure of governments, temporariness of geographic identity would be paralyzing for constitutionalism and democracy. A country that expected to undergo drastic and frequent boundary changes would find it difficult to establish law and order in the interim; and no five-year development plans, *ex hypothesi*, can be applied in boundaries liable to change every three years.

CONSENSUS VERSUS CONCILIATION

There is a common misconception that democracy depends on shared beliefs (either substantive or at least procedural), on common agreements, on consensus. Yet consensus remains one of the more awkward notions to have been introduced into recent political theory.[18] One suspects that theorists who rely on it place too much faith in the power of belief over human action. The history of peaceful transitions from oligarchy to democracy (say in Great Britain between 1832 and 1918 or Sweden between 1890 and 1918) would indicate that opponents of democracy first somewhat grudgingly adjusted their practice, but that within a generation or so they came to believe in what they were doing. Nor is it difficult to explain why men find it easier to adjust their beliefs to their actions than their actions to their beliefs. A new plan of action requires changes in the environment—which may turn out to be very resistant to change; a new set of beliefs requires changes only in the more readily obliging self.[19]

[18] For a spirited and thoughtful critique of the "mirage of consensus" see Otto Kirchheimer, "Private Man and Society," *Political Science Quarterly*, Vol. 81 (March 1966), pp. 1-25, especially pp. 1-3.

[19] For a brief statement of this theorem in relation to economic development see Albert O. Hirschman, "Obstacles to Development: A Classification and a Quasi-Vanishing Act," *Economic Development and Cultural Change*, Vol. 13 (July 1965), pp. 385-93, especially pp. 391ff., who refers to Leon Festinger's *Theory of Cognitive Dissonance* (Stanford University Press, 1957). Tolstoy stated the general proposition that "No man can play an active part in the world unless he believes that his activity is important and good. Therefore, whatever position a man may hold, he is certain to take that view of human life in general which will make his own activity seem important and good." *Resurrection*, Pt. 1, Chap. 44 (tr. Vera Traill, Signet Books, p. 150). Tolstoy proceeds to illustrate the general rule from the life and belief of his prostitute-heroine.

The consensus theory also overlooks that the very essence of democracy is the reconciliation of dissension. Its chief instruments—contests for nominations, elections in the constituencies, divisions in parliament, votes in cabinet or committee—are so many devices for recording disagreement. Only by means of dissension can democracy become a learning and a problem-solving process, a way of finding proximate solutions to insoluble questions.[20] Only through continual expression of disagreement by sharply rivaling groups can political participation be maximized and political equality thus approximated. Agreement and consensus can only be the end-product, not the prerequisite, of the democratic political process—and, of course, as soon as a question is agreed upon, it no longer is a political question. As Bernard Crick has written in his *Defence of Politics:*

. . . it is often thought that for this "master science" to function, there must already be in existence some shared idea of a "common good", some "consensus" or *consensus juris.* But this common good is itself the process of practical reconciliation of the interests of the various . . . aggregates, or groups which compose a state; it is not some external and intangible spiritual adhesive. . . . Diverse groups hold together, firstly, because they have a common interest in sheer survival, and, secondly, because they practise politics — not because they agree about "fundamentals", or some such concept too vague, too personal, or too divine ever to do the job of politics for it. The moral consensus of a free state is not something mysteriously prior to or above politics: it is the activity (the civilizing activity) of politics itself.[21]

If democracy is to evolve, the active participants in a political system must find a tenuous middle ground between imposed uniformity, such as would lead to some form of tyranny, and hostility of a kind that would disrupt the community and throw it into secession or civil war. Hence, as Robert Dahl has aptly put it, "one perennial problem of opposition is that there is either too

[20] Albert O. Hirschman suggests, beyond this, that violence can serve as a signal to policy makers. *Journeys Toward Progress* (Twentieth Century Fund, 1963), pp. 229f., 259ff., 262ff.

[21] Bernard Crick, *In Defence of Politics,* rev. ed. (Penguin Books, 1964), p. 24.

much or too little."[22] On the question of geographic identity there must be rather more than mere agreement and shared opinion; the context within which the political process is to take place must be taken for granted, must be above question and above opinion. On other matters, democracy depends not on consensus, but on disagreement.

A concept almost as troublesome as consensus is tutelage. "Tutelary democracy" is a direct contradiction in terms; it may easily turn into a euphemism to designate certain types of oligarchy. Preparation for democracy must, *ex hypothesi,* begin under a predemocratic regime. But the logical starting point is not autocracy or oligarchy, no matter how benevolent or "tutelary." It is rather the conciliation of vigorously expressed differences of interest, of opinion, of policy.

The crucial turn may come in situations like those in Mexico in 1928-29, in Morocco in 1961, or in Lebanon in the 1860's. The Mexican caudillos (that is, self-appointed local military leaders) had learned in two decades of intense turmoil that their unrestrained activities could lead only to civil war and to periodic assassination of any of them lucky enough to have seized the presidency. Hence they accepted Calles' invitation to form a party that would regulate their competition, that would establish presidential succession by negotiation and agreement rather than by murder. In Morocco, the king and the nationalist leaders who had jointly attained independence broke on major issues of domestic policy. But the popularity of each was strong enough that neither dared destroy the other. The king compensated for his conservative domestic course by adopting some of the more "radical" foreign policies of the left-wing opposition. In Lebanon, the communal war of 1858-60 was followed by a compromise agreement that reinforced an earlier tradition of secular government.[23]

[22] *Political Oppositions in Western Democracies* (Yale University Press, 1966), p. 397.

[23] For details see the lucid discussion by Albert Hourani in Leonard Binder, ed., *Politics in Lebanon* (Wiley, 1966), p. 22.

Clearly, the outcome of these single crises in countries like Mexico, Morocco, or Lebanon can at most supply the germ of the development of democracy. The full growth can result only from a number of further crises overcome with like success. In Mexico, four decades of orderly government followed on the compromise of 1929, and major issues between military and civilian leaders and between church and state have been settled in the meantime. Yet the issue of social equality and political participation for urban workers and for the peasantry are today endangering the political order created by the PRI in the last thirty-seven years. In Lebanon, further compromises were devised in 1926 and the structure reaffirmed after the civil war of 1958.

A single major breakdown of the process of conciliation in any one of the countries may result in a miscarriage of the entire process. On the other hand, every crisis successfully overcome will provide important encouragement for the resolution of the next. The growth of conciliation and democracy is likely to be a slow upward spiral; their breakdown a rapid downward one. It is in the hands of the protagonists in every successive crisis to set the spiral on its upward or its downward course. At any rate, the upward prospects are better in a system that honestly faces its tensions than in one that suppresses them in an artificial unanimity of demagogic propaganda and crude coercion.

Democracy means self-government and hence cannot by definition be imposed. Whatever the contributions of colonial rule or other forms of foreign "tutelage," it is the indigenous participants themselves who must operate the system and by operating come to believe in it. Still, in a tightly interlocking political world, the evolution of a modernizing country into a democratic, or in an opposite totalitarian direction will be a matter of major concern to foreign policy makers. This democratic-communist rivalry in the world politics of the late twentieth century, and the attitudes of countries of the "third world" toward that rivalry will be among the themes of the concluding chapter.

CHAPTER EIGHT

CONCLUSION:
MODERNIZATION
IN A WORLD OF NATIONS

*The nation is the God-appointed instrument
for the welfare of the human race.*
MAZZINI

Wee shall obserue . . . a multitude of wretched and miserable nations.
NATHANAEL CARPENTER (1653)

*. . . the world of nations, or civil world, which, since
men had made it, men could come to know.*
VICO

FIVE OR SIX CENTURIES AGO, modern patterns of thought first took form among people inhabiting the Mediterranean and Atlantic shores of the Eurasian continent. Slowly but steadily, man's ambitious claim to understand his environment changed his relation to nature, to other men in society, and to his own past and future. Scientific discovery prepared technical invention, and technology gave rise to industrial production. Geographic exploration made possible colonial conquest overseas. Meanwhile, in Europe, governments expanded their functions and concentrated their powers. Subjects, feeling the heavier hand of administration, began to clamor for citizenship, first in Europe and later in the colonies. As tribes and principalities were merged

237

and as empires crumbled, civic loyalties came to be refocused within new political boundaries. The nation-state at length emerged as the chief political vehicle of modernization. Today, no society can remain undisturbed in its pre-modern tradition. Half a millennium after the original impulse, the repercussions of modernization are felt in the remote parts of the globe.

More rapidly than ever, man's control over nature is widening, and his interaction with other men is tightening. In space exploration, in automation, and in myriad other ways, the technological and social forces of modernity are proceeding apace. The process is far from complete, and it would be fatuous to look forward to a time when all societies would be uniformly or completely modernized. Modernization faces continuing obstacles. Its progress in various spheres of life is at best uneven. By its very nature, modernization cannot have any fixed goal. Certain logical tensions, moreover, can be readily discerned, some in the concept of modernity itself, and others in its association with the national ideal. In the form of practical difficulties and calamities, these tensions will confront statesmen and citizens of the future.

Modernity enhances man's powers without concentrating them on any one purpose. Science expands man's knowledge without regenerating his will. Technology multiplies his means without specifying his ends. In extending man's control over nature and over other men, modernity does not help him control himself. Indeed, it tempts him to deny his own limits. As modern life liberates him from traditional restraints of scarcity and superstition, it threatens to make him the slave of organization. National loyalty joins men once separated into tribes, or castes, or sects. But it sharply divides those who were loosely united by an imperial allegiance. Modern governments preserve a calmer peace at home—and are equipped to wage infinitely fiercer wars abroad.

The political rhetoric of the late twentieth century resounds with this dissonance. Though increasingly uniform throughout the world, it supplies a verbal arsenal for competition and struggle. Nation, democracy, self-determination, equality, progress, power, unity, revolution—these are intoned, with minor modulations but with equal fervor, by Russians, Chinese, and Americans, by Europeans, Africans, and Asians in one global cacophony. The claim by 130 countries to be regarded as nation-states further attests to the universality of the modern ideal—and to its inner contradiction. The message diffused has been one of sovereignty and power, of national individuality and independence. But the method of diffusion has been one of world-wide interdependence, vulnerability to power, and susceptibility to the influence of others. "Don't let us become a carbon copy nation,"[1] reads the slogan cranked out in 130 copies by history's mimeograph machine. "I am a unique individual," drones the unison chorus of the millions.

The political problems implicit in this contradiction between origin and content of the global message are obvious. "The most intransigent of nationalisms," Professor Emerson has cautioned, "must live in a world of which interdependence has become a central feature; no state acting alone can guarantee its own security or assure its own well-being." Or, as President Senghor of Senegal has succinctly stated it, "Nation is the first reality of the XXth century . . . The second reality . . . is the *interdependence* of races, continents, and nations."[2] The rival and interrelated systems of contemporary political thought—nationalism, democracy, communism—all confront this central dilemma. Without resolving it, no policy can prevail and no political creed endure.

The tensions of modernization are particularly acute in countries where that process began late and where claims to nationhood remain tenuous. What are the prospects for a successful transformation of politics and society in South and Southeast Asia, in the Middle East, in Tropical Africa, and in Latin America? What role will countries of those regions come to play on the world's political stage, and how will older and more powerful na-

---

[1] Sukarno, cited in Paul Sigmund, ed., *Ideologies of the Developing Nations* (Praeger, 1963), pp. 61f.

[2] Rupert Emerson, *From Empire to Nation* (Harvard University Press, 1960), p. 407; Leopold Sédar Senghor, *African Socialism* (American Society for African Culture, 1959), p. 45.

tions react to their intrusive presence? Each question may be re-
phrased as one of the appropriate model. Is the experience of
modernization and of the growth of nationality in countries such
as France, the United States, Russia, or Japan relevant to the late-
modernizing societies, or must they grope for new patterns of
their own? What overall design of struggle or harmony, of growing or decaying order is likely to emerge from the interaction of
old and new states?

Nor can the problems of modernization within nations and of
relations among nation-states be considered separately. Domestic
and foreign policy are as closely intertwined in the late twentieth
century as countries around the globe are interconnected. A civil
war in Katanga is watched with anxiety from Washington and
Moscow, just as a United States election or a power shift in the
Kremlin may seal the fate of governments in Leopoldville.

Their prenatal involvement in world politics led to the proclamation of the new nation-states and inspired them with the ambition to modernize. Their success or failure as modernizing nations
will profoundly affect their postnatal role in the world politics of
the future. Can fledgling nation-states be protected from the rude
shocks bursting on them from beyond their borders? Can the international political system be insulated from disturbances erupt-
ing in the domestic politics of the newer states? Or, if the problems of political order within and among states prove one and in-
divisible, on what principles can such a twofold order be built?
To find even tentative answers will tax the ingenuity and good
will of future statesmen; yet this study cannot conclude without
stating briefly these broad questions of modernization in a world
of nations.

The Prospects of Modernity

Europe's imperial expansion made three contributions to the
world-wide spread of modernity: through the establishment of

colonial rule over much of the globe, through the later emancipation of colonies, and, elsewhere, through reforms intended to ward off the colonialist threat. In Japan during and after the Tokugawa period, some elements of modern civilization might have grown from indigenous roots. But in most other countries, it is impossible to say when if ever modern technology and modern social organization would have evolved without some forcible Western impact.[3] Even in Japan during the Meiji period, the threat of Western power provided the catalyst, and Western science, technology, and administration provided the models for reform.

THE WESTERN IMPACT

The West's impact in each of its three manifestations remained ambiguous. Colonialism modernized some of the technology but few of the social relations of peoples under its sway. On top of traditional distinctions of caste or tribe, it imposed even sharper divisions between subject and alien ruler. Colonial economies catered to the overseas market; yet production on plantations and in mines became dependent on exploitation on an unprecedented scale. Colonial rulers, even as they expanded public functions and strengthened the authority of government, remained firm in denying aspirations for national identity, for political equality, or for participation. Of the three political requisites of modernization, the colonial system supplied at best one. The contradictions, moreover, were inherent in the system itself. Only the self-assertion of colonial peoples could furnish an essential second impulse toward world-wide modernity.

Colonial emancipation also could be ambiguous, though in different ways. In India, two centuries of British rule left behind a far-flung system of public education, a competent civil service, and, as an unintended by-product of these, a well-articulated political party. In the interior of Africa, by contrast, colonialism

[3] Cf. Emerson, *op. cit.*, pp. 7f.

ruled for less than a century—long enough to disrupt traditional society and authority but too briefly to fill the void with viable modern structures or well-trained indigenous officials. In many regions, moreover, notably in Muslim Asia and Africa, colonial administrators formed a close alliance with the most traditional forces—Indian maharajas, nomadic sheikhs around the Persian Gulf, Berber caids in Morocco, and Fulani emirs in Northern Nigeria. During the transition to independence, many of these traditional rulers or ruling classes could thus dispute the claims of modern nationalists. Occasionally, modern conspiratorial or mass organization was effectively adopted by traditionalist groups such as the Jan Sangh in India or the Muslim Brethren in Egypt.

Even where nationalist modernizers were strong enough to overcome these challenges, the danger remained that the new rulers would emulate their colonial predecessors only in their aloofness and arrogance, not in their competence or efficiency. Professions of modernizing ideology, in such circumstances, easily came to have a hollow ring. Indigenous forms of autocracy, oligarchy, and exploitation would soon take the place of earlier, alien ones. In novel and more hypocritical guise, traditional rule would have been restored.

The ambiguity of reform programs such as those of Mahmud II in Turkey or the Meiji emperor in Japan is readily apparent. Defensive modernization was intended to resist, not to advance, the Western impact. Only gradually did new generations of officers, administrators, and teachers, trained in Western-style schools, come to embrace modernization for its own sake. Both the Turkish and the Japanese elites underwent such periods of intensive retraining. Once they did, their earlier cultural and administrative heritage combined with modern techniques and modern orientations to spur them to remarkable advances.[4]

---

[4] Along with these broad similarities, there are important differences. Japan's insular location and ethnic unity, for example, contributed to a far more rapid modernization. See Robert E. Ward and D. A. Rustow, eds., *Political Modernization in Japan and Turkey* (Princeton University Press, 1964), pp. 434-68.

Other noncolonial countries disposed of slenderer political resources and escaped colonial rule more by virtue of their remoteness or their buffer location. In such settings, modernization proceeded more slowly and retained its defensive character longer. In Iran, the stimulus to reform was recurrent imperialist pressure from Russia and Great Britain; and on three occasions —in 1907-09, in 1919-21, and in 1945-47—the country nearly succumbed. Nineteenth-century Thailand offers striking analogies both to Turkey and to Iran. In Saudi Arabia in the 1940's, dramatic changes resulted from the discovery of abundant deposits of petroleum. In Yemen in the 1950's, the arrival of competing foreign aid missions from the United States, the Soviet Union, and China helped undermine the old order, and these were followed, in 1962-65, by military coup, civil war, and Egyptian intervention.

Similar forces are already at work elsewhere: foreign aid and a tightening of dynastic administration in Afghanistan, conspiring officers and bureaucrats in Ethiopia, the disquieting presence of Chinese troops across the borders of Nepal. For the time being, the monarchs of Ethiopia, Nepal, and Afghanistan are among the most conservative rulers in the world, closely followed by those of Morocco, Thailand, and Saudi Arabia. Clearly, however, their regimes are not immune to the forces that have shaken tradition everywhere else.

Meanwhile, the distinction just drawn between former colonies and noncolonies is losing its relevance as the traumas of early independence overshadow even the bitterest colonial memories. Libya, an Italian colony for three decades, experienced the impact of petroleum on tribal monarchy twenty years later than Saudi Arabia but in much the same fashion. Jordan, once a British mandate, and Morocco, once a French protectorate, face problems comparable to those of Iran. Nicaragua and Paraguay, independent for over a century, have regimes as conservative as any Middle Eastern monarchy.

What remains important is that all countries in Asia, Africa, and Latin America have been tied into the modern network of communication, that all are exposed to the same international political and social forces, but that they are very differently equipped to respond to these pressures.

OBSTACLES TO MODERNIZATION

The difficulties of modernization have been noted in earlier chapters. Some of the cultural amalgams of tradition and modernity may hasten the overall transformation, and others may delay it. The pride in this or that historic (or mythological) period which the early nationalist instills in his countrymen may spur them to greater effort or give them an excuse for collective indolence. The example of modern accomplishments abroad may foster a healthy spirit of self-criticism or merely a self-righteous criticism of others. Of the three imperatives "be proud, work, be confident" the first may be taken to heart more readily than the others. Afraid to become a "carbon copy nation," a people may not become a nation at all. Instead of a "reinforcing dualism" that hastens the advent of modernity there may be an enfeebling monism leading back toward tradition.

The cultural malaise characteristic of many late-modernizing countries is aggravated by some tangible economic, social, and demographic factors. Some smaller countries, such as Somalia, Chad, Mauritania, Yemen, and Paraguay, suffer from a lack of known resources. Others depend heavily on a single mineral or a single agricultural product and hence on the vagaries of international prices and on the power of foreign investors. Where there are undeveloped resources, central economic planning may promote their efficient use, but it may also spread the evils of governmental corruption through the economy and the administration.

Many countries that are called "underdeveloped" are in fact overpopulated. The available resources barely suffice to keep the population at starvation levels, and in some Middle American and

North African countries, that population is likely to double every twenty or twenty-five years. It costs only a few cents spent on public hygiene to keep a child alive, but it costs hundreds of dollars to feed and educate him, and thousands more in capital investment to employ him in a modern industrial economy. By such grim arithmetic, populations saved from malaria or the tse-tse fly starve or else survive in malnutrition and unemployment. To give one example, Egypt despite steadily increasing production has long faced the threat of declining standards of living. Only the provision of foreign agricultural surpluses has in recent years maintained a precarious balance. Even the completion of the gigantic High Dam at Aswan, with its benefits of vastly increased crops and ample electric power throughout the country, will at present rates of population increase more likely slow down an inexorable decline of per-capita income rather than produce any dramatic improvement.

The rapid growth of cities is both a help and a hindrance to modernization. The peasant who leaves a remote village or tribal area for the metropolis may acquire a new sense of national identity and a new perspective of purposeful social action, may in short become a modern citizen. But long before such effects are felt on any substantial scale, it becomes clear that the cities have attracted migrants at a precipitous rate; that even the best intentioned and most vigorous municipality cannot keep abreast of the demand for public utilities, transport, and schooling; that the newcomers' dream of a better life may be snuffed out in the squalor of a shantytown; and that their first political act may be the shouts of a surging, raging mob.

Education from the grammar school to the university remains the chief instrument by which a country must train the workers and managers for its modern industry and the clerks and political leaders for a modern government. Yet without trained teachers, adequate classrooms and textbooks, and above all, some concept of education responsive to the country's needs and opportunities, these benefits may turn into disadvantages. Teachers and students, as heirs to a traditional or a colonial caste system, may indulge in sterile legal or metaphysical conceptualism while looking down their noses at the scientist and the engineer. Instead of training workers or managers, citizens or rulers, the schools and universities may graduate half-educated young men with an avid taste for the products of the machine but unskilled in its operation, too ignorant to take any effective part in government but too restive to be governed by others.

The foreign relations of late-modernizing societies add to this list of mixed blessings. Once again, psychological, economic, and political aspects can be distinguished. The late-comer's psychological problems include the humiliating sense of backwardness, the compulsion to catch up with others, the mixed feelings of hate and admiration both for the foreigners in more modern countries and for his own history and culture. Nor are this ambivalence and these frustrations likely to disappear with the mere passage of time. Too many development schemes rest on the comforting illusion that in twenty or thirty year's time Ruritania will be fully caught up—if only the advanced countries will stand still in the meantime. But the so-called "developed" peoples of Europe, North America, Russia, and Japan are not standing still; in fact, they are, along many different scales, progressing much faster than Asians, Africans, or Latin Americans. While minimal standards of health and perhaps of literacy are becoming the common possessions of mankind, the gaps in economic productivity, in military power, and in overall effectiveness of social organization are growing wider.

The world-wide spread of the nationalist ideology has intensified the frustrations. The proliferation of claims to nationhood, like any inflation, has cheapened that particular currency. When Germany and Italy a century ago became nation-states, they joined at once the ranks of the half-dozen major powers of the day. Even Ghana in 1957, though not about to become a major power, could take pride in being the first to attain independence in a region long regarded as colonialism's preserve. But only a decade later, countries like Sierra Leone, Burundi, and Singapore are comparatively insignificant names on the ever-lengthening roll of the United Nations General Assembly. Their situation suggests the keen disappointment of the freshman at Harvard or Princeton who in his hometown without much effort had always ranked first in his class, but now finds that someone must be the two-hundred-and-fifty-ninth.

A modern nation, it was noted earlier, must be of a certain minimum size to make possible the division of labor that is the foundation of modernity. It is striking to note, therefore, that the countries most recently independent also tend to be the smallest in population. The median population of all states independent before 1776 is today 22.6 million, of those emerging from the first anticolonial revolution and the dissolution of dynastic empires (1776-1945) 5.2 million, and of those that won their independence in the last two decades only 3.4 million. There may be some disagreement on the optimum size of a nation-state, but there is little doubt that it is above three or four million. The very size of the newly proclaimed states, particularly in Africa, makes it difficult for them to realize those aspirations of modernity and power, of dignity and prosperity, which their leaders profess.[5]

DEVELOPMENT OR DECAY

Reacting against an earlier spate of optimistic writings which suggested that modernization meant steady, unilinear progress, recent authors have stressed the imbalances and difficulties of the process. Hirschman, still optimistic in his conclusions, has shown that the notion of "balanced economic growth" is an unrealistic mirage, that the only perfect balance is the balance of stagnation,

[5] For details, see Appendix Tables 6-7. The figures refer to present populations. If population at the time of independence had been taken as the base, the contrast would not have been quite as sharp; but global competition for power, wealth, and prestige takes place, of course, among contemporaries. The last section of Table 6 suggests that future proclamations of independence are likely further to depress the median of the most recent group.

and that successful "reformmongers" must creatively use the existing imbalances to achieve advances now in this and now in that direction.[6] Pye's study of the psychological conflicts of Burmese administrators has led him to form "a gloomy view of the prospects of nation-building."[7] Eisenstadt has cited recent developments in Pakistan and elsewhere as instances of "breakdown of modernization."[8] And Huntington, more generally, has warned that modernization (by which he means technical and economic progress combined with social mobilization) is as likely to lead to political development as to political decay.[9]

Valid as these arguments are, they need to be considerably refined. Hirschman is right in asserting that any realistic process of modernization or of economic growth is necessarily uneven. But how much imbalance stimulates further growth, how much represents the inevitable cost of learning by trial and error, and how much will lead to frustration, retreat into fantasy, or general decline? What, in short, is the optimum degree of imbalance?

Similarly, Huntington suggests two strategies for reducing the dangers of political decay implicit in modernization. But the first of these—slowing mobilization—seems today far less applicable than the second—creating institutions.[10] It is hard to imagine contemporary settings where the first type of advice would be acceptable. Is one to persuade Libya to shut down its oil wells so as to preserve the stability of the Sanusi dynasty? Or Iran to stop sending students abroad who may come back full of restless ambition? Or countries of Asia or Latin America to close down their

[6] See Albert O. Hirschman, *The Strategy of Economic Development* (Yale University Press, 1959), and *Journeys Toward Progress* (Twentieth Century Fund, 1963).

[7] Lucian W. Pye, *Politics, Personality, and Nation Building: Burma's Search for Identity* (Yale University Press, 1962), p. 285.

[8] S. N. Eisenstadt, "Breakdowns of Modernization," *Economic Development and Cultural Change*, Vol. 12, No. 4 (July 1964), pp. 345-67. For a similar perspective see Ann Ruth Willner's study of Indonesia, *The Neotraditional Accommodation to Political Independence* (Center of International Studies, Princeton, 1966).

[9] Samuel P. Huntington, "Political Development and Political Decay," *World Politics*, Vol. 17, No. 4 (April 1965), pp. 386-430.

[10] *Ibid.*, pp. 419-24.

universities because a little knowledge is a dangerous thing? Or African countries to withdraw their ambassadors lest they make unflattering comparisons between their home countries and France, Russia, or the United States? The downfall of the tight little oligarchies of Batista in Cuba, Trujillo in the Dominican Republic, Nuri al-Said in Iraq, and Imam Ahmad in Yemen suggest that these are questions not just of ethics but of plain prudence.

The need to channel the forces of modernization, to keep imbalances within fruitful limits, and to avoid the dangers of stagnation or breakdown suggest the importance of plausible models of political development that nascent nation-states in the throes of late modernization can try to follow.

The Western Model and United States Policy

The most obvious models of modernization today, though not the most generally relevant, are the Western democracies and the communist dictatorships. The Western countries were the early pioneers of modernity. They continue to set the standards for a modernizing world not only in economic production and material comfort but also in social organization and political institutions. Universal suffrage, written constitutions, presidents, cabinets, and parliaments, an independent judiciary, separation of church and state, political neutrality of the armed forces, and the vocabulary of nationalism, of egalitarianism, and of sovereignty—all these have been almost universally accepted in principle, however widely they may be abused or disregarded in application. They form as integral a part of the emerging global civilization of modernity as do the telephone, the airplane, the assembly line, the computer, and other Western technical inventions.

Colonial memories for the moment still make it difficult for new states to acknowledge this political debt to the West. The most serious difficulty, however, is not the bitter aftertaste of colonialism, but the enormous and growing gap that separates the West from the late-modernizing countries in economic and political matters. To provide a suitable model, a country must not only be ahead but also seem reachable. The recurrent complaints of neo-colonialism in Africa and elsewhere reflect in large part the frustrations inspired by the unreachable Western ideal.

The difference in size between countries like the United States, Great Britain, or France and most new states of Africa poses an added difficulty. In the West, too, there are small countries, such as Belgium, Switzerland, Denmark, New Zealand, and Austria. But these generally have learned to follow a policy of extreme liberalism in foreign trade and relative passivity in foreign policy. More recently, many of them have turned into ardent proponents of economic and political integration with their neighbors. In various ways, that is to say, they have known how to compensate for their size. By cultivating the most precise specialization within the widest possible network of trade, they have remained in the forefront of technical and economic modernization.

But the postcolonial legacy once again has complicated the corresponding adjustments in Asia and Africa. Most new countries, with their low levels of skill and of capital investment, have found it difficult to export finished products in a highly competitive world market. Emotionally, too, the militant rulers of new nation-states have not been much attracted to economic liberalism, genuine neutrality (as opposed to truculent "neutralism"), or close regional integration.

The West had not much success in promoting its form of government or social organization overseas—except by massive settlement of Europeans in thinly populated lands. Representative institutions, as we saw, took root in but few of the colonial countries, such as India, the Philippines, and Ceylon, and in some noncolonial countries such as Japan and Turkey.

Nor have the large programs of foreign aid undertaken by the United States, and more recently by Western European countries, been very effective in spreading Western institutions. Since economic aid looms so large in United States relations with Asia,

Africa, and Latin America, this is a point that deserves closer examination.

American thinking on foreign aid, understandably enough, long remained under the spell of the Marshall Plan and its enormous success. Capital transfers had stimulated industry, the economic revival had given new hope to democracy, and in its newly found prosperity and strength, Europe had been able to ward off the communist threat. The experience seemed to confirm deep-seated American notions that the economic sphere is relatively autonomous and that political change is a consequence of economic growth and not also its prerequisite.

As the focus of aid shifted to Asia, Africa, and Latin America, United States policy makers were conscious that the problem was not one of postwar reconstruction of modern institutions that had existed for centuries, but rather one of creating modern institutions for the first time. Yet too frequently, officials at the working level continued to assume that economic growth was a financial and perhaps a technical matter, and that it would produce automatic if somewhat nebulous benefits in the political realm.

In appeals to the Congress and the public, moreover, there was a tendency to justify economic aid primarily in Cold War terms. A major portion of the aid program was devoted outright to military aid, and some of the rest labeled "defense support." Stability, it was assumed, was the only political prerequisite of economic growth, and also its further consequence. And political stability came to mean continuation of the government of the day and preservation of the social status quo. In the 1950's, official American pronouncements often extended the term "free world" to colonies of the West as well as to the regimes of a Chiang, Diem, Rhee, Franco, or Trujillo—any dictatorship, in fact, that proved willing to sign one of the mutual security or military assistance pacts so assiduously championed by John Foster Dulles during his tenure as secretary of state. Only when there seemed to be danger that a country might renounce such a pact or otherwise veer closer to the communist bloc—as in Iran in 1953, Guatemala

in 1954, or Indonesia in 1958—was the United States government
ready to surrender stability in favor of violent change as engi-
neered by its Central Intelligence Agency.

The years of the Kennedy administration (1961-63) brought a
fundamental reassesssment. In proclaiming the Alliance for Progress, President Kennedy stressed that "political freedom must be
accompanied by social change." United States aid, it was made
clear, would be used in part to promote such change and not just
to prop up unpopular conservative regimes. Dulles' harsh judgment of the supposed immorality of neutralism was reversed. No
longer was it assumed that all countries not for us were automat-
ically against us. Hence the Kennedy administration was able to
extend aid not only to allies sharing the burdens of a common defense, but also to nonaligned countries to strengthen their friendship with the West, to hostile neutrals to make them more genu-
inely neutral, and even to communist countries like Poland and
Romania, so as to promote their independence from or within the
Soviet Bloc. In one notable instance (Peru 1962), United States
aid was discontinued in an attempt to prevent a military coup
from setting aside a center-left election victory. Although the military junta survived this pressure, it agreed, in return for resumed
aid, to hold new elections within a year.[11]

Already under Kennedy, however, there were important cross-
currents. The headlong drift of the Castro regime toward communism brought the Cold War into the immediate vicinity of the
United States. On at least one occasion, United States aid was
used to obtain a marginal vote endorsing some anti-Castro resolution at an Inter-American meeting.[12] The ill-fated Bay of Pigs
invasion betrayed a nervousness and an ineffectual militancy
otherwise uncharacteristic of the Kennedy regime (and in sharp

[11] On the aid policy of the Kennedy administration see Arthur M. Schlesinger,
A Thousand Days (Houghton Mifflin, 1965), pp. 506ff, 567ff, and 585ff; on Peru,
ibid., 785ff. See also Robert A. Packenham, "Political Development Doctrines in
the American Foreign Aid Program," World Politics, Vol. 18, (January 1966),
pp. 194-235.
[12] Schlesinger, op. cit., p. 782.

contrast to the calm and prudent use of American power in the Cuban missile crisis the following year).

Under President Johnson, there have been further signs of inconsistency. The invasion of the Dominican Republic in the spring of 1965, justified by the alleged presence of some fifty communists in a country of three million, contrasted sharply, with his administration's firm opposition to the use of force by its allies in areas of their major national interest—for example, Pakistan in Kashmir, or Turkey in Cyprus. In Vietnam, where the Johnson administration proceeded to a vast extension of military operations by air in the North and by land in the South, the United States faced a formidable dilemma. The very scale of its military effort was likely to imperil the kind of indigenous social and political evolution that alone could confirm military victory in a guerrilla war; yet the ineffectiveness of the existing regime seemed to make defeat inevitable unless such massive military aid was proffered. Meanwhile, there was a gradual but steady attrition of foreign-aid budgets, thus severely reducing the scope of that instrument of foreign policy even while Americans were still learning about its uses.

The Communist Model and Communist Policy

In the context of the Cold War of the 1950's and 1960's, the West's difficulties in the developing countries often benefited its chief antagonists. The communists, by means of their doctrine, could harness to their cause the very contradictions that were paralyzing the West in Asia, Africa, and Latin America. Their passion for politics seemed more relevant to the problems of the non-Western leaders than the faith of United States aid officials in the magic dividends of economic growth. Communism, moreover, had a clear-cut and definite quality that was not characteristic of the official Western doctrines of nationalism, democracy, or liberalism.

THE ATTRACTIONS OF COMMUNISM

Communism began as a Western creed. "Both Marxism and liberalism embody the ideals of Greece and Rome and Jerusalem: the humanism of the Renaissance, the rationalism of the eighteenth-century enlightenment."[13] Communism, nonetheless, came to power first in Russia, then in China, the two largest countries that had escaped imperial conquest by the West. To Asia, Africa, and Latin America, communism could make much the same appeal as it had to Russia and China. In a single, tightly wrapped package, it combined an intense Westernism with an equally intense anti-Westernism: Westernization of technology, economy, and society —but relentless opposition to the Western powers in the rhetorical, political, and military arenas. Communism's most alluring promise was to resolve the ambivalence of the late-modernizers, to cure their painful love-hate for the West.[14]

The geographic spread of communism confirms this psychological hypothesis. Wherever Western colonial rule was firmly entrenched and then peacefully relinquished—in India, in the Philippines, in much of Africa—communism made little headway. The same was true in countries like Japan or Turkey that accomplished successful programs of modernization under indigenous leadership. But the attraction to communism was at its strongest in the twilight zone of imperialism—among the victims of gunboat diplomacy in China and the Caribbean, among the subjects of Western mandates or military regimes in the Middle East (which combined the fiction of independence with the reality of subjec-

[13] C. Wright Mills, *The Marxists*, Penguin ed. (1963), p. 15.
[14] Spengler and Toynbee have made us wary of broad historical analogies. Still, it might be pointed out that the communist appeal to the lower class in the West and to non-Westerners resembles that of the Shi'ah. Originating as a dissident Muslim faction defeated (in the seventh century A.D.) by the official Sunni establishment, it became a means for self-assertion of sedentary Mesopotamians against their bedouin conquerors and of Persians against intruding Arabs. Cf. Bernard Lewis's study of one of the two major branches of the Shi'ah, *The Origins of Ismailism* (Cambridge: University Press, 1940).

tion), among peoples such as the Indonesians, the Vietnamese, and the Algerians, who had to fight for their independence in long guerrilla or military campaigns.[15]

Non-Westerners embraced communism not only on the rebound from the imperialist West, but also for its positive attractions. The Marxists' claims to scientific truth and tactical certainty, their belief in the primacy of politics and their resourcefulness in organization, their cynicism about the past and their utopianism about the future, above all their single-minded pursuit of power, all found a ready echo in the postcolonial vacuum of authority. Lenin's theory of "imperialism the last stage of capitalism" was the first open proposal of an alliance between communism and the colonial peoples. Efforts such as the Congress of the Peoples of the East at Baku in 1920 and Khrushchev's activist policy in the decade from 1955 to 1965 were intended to consummate it. In the intervening generation, Asian, African, and Latin American leaders who came under the spell of the Marxist doctrine or the Leninist technique of organization included figures as diverse as Sun Yat-sen, Chiang Kai-shek, Nehru, Sukarno, U Nu, Touré, Nkrumah, Senghor, Ben Bella, Haya de la Torre, and Betancourt.

In the postcolonial period several common errors of perspective enhanced the communists' tactical claims. Outside of Indochina, they had not been responsible for the overthrow of one colonial regime. A large number of factors may be adduced to account for the collapse of colonial rule: the growing tenderness of Western consciences in an age of democracy and the welfare state; Europe's exhaustion from two world wars; the Japanese conquests in Southeast Asia in 1942-44; United States pressure for imperial withdrawal from India, Palestine, and Indonesia; the demonstration effect of independence in Asia on colonial rulers

[15] Russia, to be sure, does not fit this generalization. Perhaps it is relevant, though, that after two centuries of modernization from the military establishment downward, Russia in the dozen years before the revolution suffered two humiliating defeats—one, the first to be inflicted in modern times by an Asian on a European people, and the other at the hands of a country that gained its national unity only a generation before.

and subjects in Africa. Yet whatever one's favorite explanation, it seems clear that the communists did not play a decisive or even a major part. Their uprising in Java in 1926 turned into a fiasco. A generation later, they participated in the nationalist movements in Southeast Asia—movements that took power not from the colonialists but from the retreating Japanese; in Vietnam, they assumed the leadership in such a movement. In the Middle East and in Africa, too, they waited for the withdrawal of European imperial power before embarking on a more active course. In the early phases of the Algerian uprising, the French communists opted squarely for repression. Clearly, as the strongest party in the Fourth Republic, they would rather seize power throughout the French empire than hasten its liquidation.

The communists' record, in short, was often opportunistic. Later, however, they sought to claim much of the credit for the anticolonial revolution, even as they worked for the overthrow of postcolonial regimes, as in Burma in 1948, in Syria in 1957, in Iraq in 1958-62, in Indonesia in 1948 and 1965, and in several countries in Tropical Africa in the early 1960's.

In their claims to leadership in economic development, the communists similarly benefited from tendentious statistics that took for their base year Russia in 1921—a low point after three years of foreign war and four more years of internal war set off by the communist coup in Petrograd itself. They benefited also from their ability to allocate resources to widely publicized achievements in military and space technology while shortages in Russia of housing and consumer goods and chronic mass starvation in China received far less publicity. They benefited finally from a misapprehension shared widely by intellectuals both in the West and in developing countries—that economic growth will come about if not by peaceful evolution then by some cathartic process of revolution, that where democracy cannot work, communism can.[16] Those who hold these tenets tended to overlook that some

[16] For a critique of the implications of this fallacy, see Hirschman, *Journeys Toward Progress*, pp. 251ff.

economies may be condemned to stagnation or shrinkage whatever their regime, that democracy and communism are not exclusive alternatives, and that revolutions are not necessarily
cathartic.

The most striking evidence of the communists' failure in economic planning comes from their own periodic reversals of policy. Russian progress in industry has been impressive, but each
one of the successive Soviet programs in agriculture has in due
course been acknowledged as a failure; and so has China's industrial "great leap forward" of 1958-59. Whether communism is
more successful than democracy in promoting economic growth,
or even rapid growth, is a question on which much contradictory
evidence must be sifted. But there can be little doubt that communism has been far more effective in suppressing any discontent
due to the failure of economic development. In the eyes of many
Asian or African leaders, caught as they are in the vise of dwindling resources and exploding populations, this may be a communist asset rather than a liability.

In the political sphere, the strongest force in the non-Western
world proved to be nationalism—the self-assertion of indigenous
elites in the name of a would-be nation—and communism made
most of its gains by assuming a nationalist guise. Newly independent countries, dedicated to an activist or "positive" neutralism,
were tempted to play off Russia against the former colonial powers, and some of them, such as Egypt in 1954-55 and Guinea in
1958-61, had the heady sensation of being wooed by competitive
offers of economic aid from East and West.

The game of playing off the distant against the nearby foreigner is a losing game in the long run, however, for it brings the
once-distant foreigner into uncomfortable proximity. In many
countries, the communists' popularity was highest in the period
immediately following independence. It often diminished as communist embassies became involved in factional politics in their
host countries, as Russian aid equipment proved ill-suited to tropical climates, or as the communists were forced to choose sides in

the many regional disputes among Asian or African countries. Leaders like Touré, Nasser, Kassem, and Kenyatta vacillated or abandoned their earlier tactical alignment with the communists; others like Ben Bella, Nkrumah, and Sukarno were overthrown by their own armies.

THREE RANGES OF INVOLVEMENT

In assessing the effectiveness of communist policies—propaganda, aid, and diplomacy—it is useful to distinguish three ranges of involvement. The first range includes countries immediately bordering on established communist powers and recognized by other powers as within the communist sphere of influence. The third range includes countries under a strong and viable noncommunist or anticommunist regime, that is, most of the countries of Western Europe, their colonies before independence, some of the right-wing dictatorships in Asia, the Middle East, and Latin America, and many other countries. The middle range includes countries where the communists are not in control, but where they and their sympathizers have enough freedom of action to constitute a serious challenge to the existing regime.

The first and third ranges give full scope to the communists' organizational and doctrinal versatility. In Eastern Europe after World War II, for example, they operated through their own parties even while they were infiltrating socialist or bourgeois parties. They demonstrated, they organized associations, they participated in elections, they staged coups; and they seized power in a number of neighboring countries—Poland and East Germany, Hungary and Romania—that had been bitter antagonists throughout much of their history. Any tensions they encountered in the situation itself or introduced by their own changing tactics could be removed in the last resort by communist force—as in Czechoslovakia in 1948 or in Hungary in 1956.

At the opposite end of the spectrum, in the third range, the scope for maneuver is obviously far smaller. Still, a great variety of tactics can be attempted all at once. The communists can try to appeal to restless elements among college graduates, ethnic or religious minorities, trade unionists, landless peasants, and others. Similarly, in a region beyond their reach, they can try to cultivate the friendship of several powers that are themselves at swords' point—as Greece and Turkey in 1964, or India and Pakistan in 1965. As radical and irresponsible opponents of the existing order, the communists need not be consistent. Where in the first range communist force can be employed to cut the Gordian knot, in the third range the power of anticommunist regimes keeps it from being drawn too tightly.

In the middle range, the contradictions inherent in the situation and aggravated by communist tactics come fully into the open. In many cases, these are likely to jeopardize the entire communist program. The Middle East in the Khrushchev years supplies a number of striking illustrations. Where domestic political factions are bitterly feuding—for example, Nasserites, the Baath party, and a variety of military cliques in Syria; or Sunnis, Shiis, Arabs, Kurds, and a variety of civilian and military factions in Iraq—it is difficult for communists to play an active political role without antagonizing most or all of these groups. The same is true of an entangled international situation. In 1948, the Soviets rushed to recognize Israel; as successive Arab countries became fully independent from the West, they courted each in turn; but by the 1960's, they were forced to concentrate their Middle Eastern favors on Nasser as the chief chosen instrument—thereby making his enemies theirs.[17]

POLYCENTRISM VERSUS INFALLIBILITY

The most striking communist failure has been the lack of any theory or settled practice of foreign relations among communist states. In 1917, the Bolsheviks had looked on their revolution as

[17] For an elaboration of these and other Middle Eastern examples, see D. A. Rustow, "The Appeal of Communism to Islamic Peoples," in J. Harris Proctor, ed., *Islam and International Relations* (Praeger, 1965), pp. 40-60, especially pp. 52ff. The essay is also available as *Brookings Institution Reprint* No. 90.

the first tremor in a world-wide upheaval; later they accommodated themselves to the realities of "Socialism in One Country." Under neither arrangement was there any room for international relations among communist states. Even after World War II in Eastern Europe, the situation was not much changed; for Russian troops and Russian control of the secret police for some years ensured a monotonous uniformity. But difficulties arose wherever communist rulers had been installed by their own indigenous strength or at any rate without decisive Soviet help, as in Yugoslavia, Albania, China, Vietnam, or Cuba. Stalin's famous sneer, "I shall wag my finger and there will be no more Tito," showed how little mutual respect or even sophistication had developed in relations among communist leaders.

Tito, of course, refused to vanish; and soon the old monolithic system was brought down by Khrushchev's denunciation of Stalin in 1956, by growing bitterness between Russia and China after 1958, and the eagerness of smaller countries such as Albania and Romania to exploit that conflict to secure greater freedom. The Chinese in Korea in 1950 and the Russians in Hungary in 1956 used armed force to prevent the complete overturn of a neighboring communist regime. But Russia's secret opposition to Communist China's entry into the United Nations, its failure to support China with any nuclear threats in the Quemoy-Matsu crisis of 1958, Khrushchev's direct negotiations with Kennedy about Soviet missiles on Cuba in 1962, Russian and Chinese reluctance or inability to protect North Vietnam from American bombs in 1965, the abrupt ending of Soviet technical aid to China in 1959 and of Chinese economic aid to Cuba in 1966—these and other episodes showed to what extent warm professions of communist solidarity came to be tempered by cold calculations of national interest.

But the cracks in the monolith had more than political significance: they also put in doubt the communists' intellectual and moral claims. Communists are taught to believe that Marxian socialism is a body of scientific truth from which day-to-day practical applications can be deduced. In practice, such a claim to infallibility can be sustained only within a tightly hierarchical organization. Stalin often reversed his political course—from "popular front" to "revolutionary strategy" and back or, most dramatically, in his somersaults of foreign policy in 1939 and 1941. Each of these reversals was bound to strain the credulity of the faithful and to encourage defections, especially outside Russia. Still, so long as there remained a single center of communist power in Moscow, the leaders could rationalize their zigzags as impelled by changing objective circumstances and forcibly restore organizational (and hence ideological) unity.

The Peking-Moscow dispute of the 1960's was quite a different matter—and it was far more damaging to the communist cause in the world than could be any dispute among Washington, Paris, London, or Bonn to the West where disagreements are fully in accord with prevailing liberal and pluralist ideas. As good communists, both Muscovites and Pekinese were bound to state their quarrel in ideological language. Only this time, unlike in Stalin's day, contradictory interpretations would be put forward simultaneously, and put forward with increasing vehemence on both sides. Even if the debate should revert to more civilized tones in the future, the divisive effects are likely to be long-lasting and irreparable. Meanwhile, other communists such as Tito of Yugoslavia, Gheorghiu-Dej of Romania, Castro of Cuba, Togliatti of Italy and their successors could be counted on to add to the variety of ideological positions.

Communism had long appealed to non-Westerners by promising relief from the bewildering skepticism of the Western intellectual tradition and from the crippling ambivalence of late modernization. Neophytes with lingering doubts about the truth of communism had been able to console themselves that it was both broad and pointed; that, even as it explained the universe, the past, and the future, it told you what to do today and tomorrow; that it allowed you to use brute force and low cunning for the highest moral ends; that if you firmly embraced it, it would free you from doubt and worry and anguish of conscience. But now, in the 1960's communism itself was becoming an ambivalent and contradictory doctrine. Each new blast from Peking, Moscow, Bucharest, Belgrade, or Havana was likely to fan the flames of skepticism in communist minds. An infallible and precise doctrine loudly proclaimed in contradictory versions will soon seem neither infallible nor precise. There can be no polycentric infallibility.

Communism came to power through indigenous developments in no more than half a dozen countries: Russia, China, Cuba, Vietnam, Yugoslavia, and Albania.[18] In all of these except Cuba, foreign invasion and prolonged war had gravely undermined the previous political and social order. In Russia and China, moreover, communism could resume and elaborate the tradition of two of the largest and most centralized imperial bureaucracies known to history. Elsewhere—Outer Mongolia 1924, the Baltic countries 1940, East-Central Europe 1945-48, North Korea 1945, Tibet 1950-59, Laos 1960-62—communism was imposed, ultimately, by outside force. In all other countries—Indonesia, the Philippines, Malaya, Iran, Iraq, Syria, Greece, Guatemala, and Guyana —their various bids for power have so far failed. Cuba thus remains the sole country in Asia, Africa, or Latin America to go communist in a purely internal revolution. Generally, the tried and proven recipe has been internal subversion supported by Russian or Chinese bayonets.

It seemed possible at various times in the 1950's or 1960's that developments like nationalization of industry and commerce in Egypt or collective agriculture in Algeria might impel a late-modernizing country in a communist direction. Yet the task of setting up a totalitarian party in a traditionally disorganized country must not be underestimated. In the Congo, it has been said facetiously, the Russians found that even they were not able to sub-

---

[18] In the last two, the communists received outside assistance not from Russia but from the West; see Cyril E. Black and Thomas P. Thornton, eds., *Communism and Revolution: The Strategic Uses of Political Violence* (Princeton University Press, 1964), p. 82. The book provides the most thoughtful account of empirical conditions of communist success and failure; see especially Black's conclusion, pp. 417-49.

vert total anarchy. Each new communist party that did emerge was apt to sponsor its own brand of Titoism and would thus hasten the polycentric trend. And the experience of Egypt, Iraq, Guinea, Ghana, and Indonesia suggested (as did that of Turkey and Iran a generation earlier) that nationalist leaders could quickly get over their communist flirtations provided they remained safe from communist military pressure and met with some understanding from the West.

By the 1960's, the problem, long unrecognized or postponed, of relations among communist states came to haunt the movement. As a result, not only its political strategy but also its spiritual appeal were in grave disarray. The perplexities arising two decades after the seizure of power in China and Eastern Europe were almost sure to recur in the unlikely event that other countries (say Algeria or Syria, not to speak of large countries like Indonesia, India, or Brazil) were to go communist in their turn. For the communist leaders of the post-Stalin era, the most pressing task was to foster a sense of international community among their several states. Otherwise their troubles might continue to multiply in geometric proportion to the number of states under their sway. In the late twentieth century, international communism was in danger of becoming a victim of its mid-century successes.

The New States and the Cold War

The foregoing summary suggests that neither democracy nor communism has proved readily transferable to late-modernizing countries. The older communist regimes emerged from the confusion of defeat in war, the more recent ones were imposed, with one exception, by force from the outside. The spread of democracy in some cases also involved outside force—colonial or military occupation as in India and the Philippines or more recently in Germany and Japan; yet these have been exceptions. In a world where military deterrence is closely balanced, neither communists nor democrats had much hope of propagating their systems by conquest.

THE SUSPICIONS OF SMALL STATES

In fact, the means currently applied by large states in their relations with smaller ones are ill-suited to reshaping the smaller countries' internal politics. Transfers of public capital, visiting missions of technical experts, shipments of obsolescent weapons, the signing of alliances, favorable or adverse votes at international gatherings can make for intricate patterns of diplomacy, but are unlikely to refashion governments or society in the smaller countries.

Alliances and arms shipments, whatever their international effects on the prospects of war or peace, tend to further the domestic ambitions of the military; and within the weak civilian structure of most Asian and African countries, military commanders were natural contenders for power. Regimes installed by armed coup were, *ex hypothesi*, undemocratic; usually they turned out to be staunchly anticommunist as well. In Seoul, Saigon, Karachi, Ankara, and in many Latin American capitals, Sherman tanks made in the United States rumbled through deserted pre-dawn streets to bring down elected or pro-American governments. In Algiers, Akkra, Damascus, Baghdad, and Jakarta, Russian-made T-34s did as much for neutralist dictators with pro-communist leanings. The guns that Americans and Russians so generously gave away had a deplorable tendency to backfire.

Civilian aid, whether economic or technical, has posed other difficulties, some of which were already noted in connection with the American program. The Russians, with smaller aid budgets, with fewer kinds of aid to offer and more patently political in their motives, faced even greater difficulties. Poorer countries in Tropical Africa, the Andes, or around the Caribbean were often too short of trained personnel to put large amounts of aid to rational use. If social reform was made a condition of aid, this presupposed the virtual self-abdication of conservative legislatures and bureaucracies. Even where spectacular economic results were achieved, the immediate beneficiaries often were *nouveau riche* entrepreneurs or corrupt government and party officials.

What was said earlier of the three ranges of communist involvement applies with suitable variations to any set of dynamic political relations. In the closest range, a major power may seek to establish dominion by the time-honored policy of divide and rule; or a group of smaller powers may resolve their differences within a growing network of mutual relations as in Western Europe in the last two decades. At the other extreme, in the most distant range, a government may cultivate a variety of friendly relations regardless of antagonisms among its various partners.

Foreign aid, however, places a country in the intermediate range—and particularly if it is intended as an instrument of political or social change. In this middle range, conflicts, contradictions, and resentments are likely to be most intense. The greatest difficulties are psychological. No self-respecting country likes to think that it is revamping its government or social system in response to foreign blandishments, that bribery or extortion have made it yield up its heritage of ideals and institutions. Hobbes stated the matter succinctly three centuries before foreign aid became a standard item in the diplomatic repertoire.

To have received from one, to whom we think our selves equall, greater benefits than there is hope to Requite, disposeth to counterfeit love; but really secret hatred; and puts a man into the estate of a desperate debtor, that in declining the sight of his creditor, tacitely wishes him there, where he might never see him more. For benefits oblige; and obligation is thraldome; and unrequitable obligation, perpetuall thraldome; which is to ones equall, hatefull. But to have received benefits from one, whom we acknowledge for superiour, enclines to love; because the obligation is no new depression: and cheerfull acceptation, (which men call *Gratitude*,) is such an honour done to the obliger, as is taken generally for retribution. Also to receive benefits, though from an equall, or inferiour, as long as there is hope of requitall, disposeth to love: for in the intention of the receiver, the obligation is of ayd, and service mutuall; from whence proceedeth an Emulation of who shall exceed in benefiting; the most noble and profitable contention possible; wherein the victor is pleased with his victory, and the other revenged by confessing it.[19]

It is not hard to imagine what sort of advice one of Hobbes's disciples might give today to an American or Russian director of foreign aid. Wherever possible, place aid in a broader context of cooperation among equals, as in the progressive association of Spain, Greece, and Turkey with the European Common Market. If there is to be an "Alliance for Progress," make it more nearly a true alliance by allowing committees of Latin Americans to allocate the funds and by moving the headquarters from Washington to some Latin city. Remember that, for aid-receiving countries afraid of dependence, there is safety in numbers; therefore, diversify the sources of aid by welcoming the efforts of Israel, Japan, Brazil, Yugoslavia, Czechoslovakia, Kuwait, India, and others. In short, start up a general and most noble emulation. Channel a maximum of funds through regional organizations or through the United Nations and its agencies—for these, any country can readily acknowledge superior.

Where bilateral aid is to continue, do not offer ready gifts, much less spectacular gifts, but concentrate on joint projects, jointly planned and jointly financed. If you expect material advantages for yourself from a given arrangement, such as increased trade or shipping, do not hide behind a false façade of generosity; for mutual advantage removes the thraldom of unrequitable obligation. Always remember that all foreign aid imposes a double burden, financial on the giver and moral on the receiver, but that the receiver's burden is the heavier by far. Don't be surprised, therefore, if his accumulated resentment now and then comes into the open. If you wish to promote political and social changes in the recipient country, concentrate on encouraging changes for which there already is some solid support.

That new and weak states should prove suspicious of large and established powers, should come as no surprise to Americans. For

[19] *Leviathan* (1651), Book I, Chap. 11.

over a century American policy remained under the spell of George Washington's warning in his *Farewell Address* against "interweaving our destiny with that of any part of Europe." For generations, American statesmen had extolled the virtues of neutrality and isolation. As rivalry between Great Britain and France had helped the thirteen colonies, as French invasion of Spain had given the Spanish colonies their chance of liberation, so Asian and African colonies on their way to independence profited from wars and rivalries among Germany, Japan, Great Britain, France, the Soviet Union, and the United States. The close involvement of several major powers gave colonial countries the longed-for opportunity to get disinvolved from all of them.

Today, when it takes airplanes six hours to cross oceans that sailboats traversed in six weeks, there is little prospect of complete isolation; yet basic psychological attitudes are not greatly changed. Of the eleven noncommunist Asian states that are, or were at one time, allied with the West, for example, only five are former colonies; but of the sixteen neutrals as many as thirteen.[20] In the mid-twentieth century no less than in the late eighteenth, abstention from entanglement remains the policy, both instinctive and rational, of new states toward old.

DISENGAGEMENT OF THE SUPERPOWERS

By about 1955, both Russia and the United States had come to apply a fair amount of caution in their direct dealings with each other. The United States, despite much talk in the 1952 election campaign of "rolling back the Iron Curtain" and of the "immorality of containment," did not help the Hungarians in their desper-

---

[20] Asian countries which in the fifties signed military agreements with the United States or Great Britain included Iran, Japan, South Korea, Taiwan, Thailand, and Turkey, which had not been Western dependencies, and Kuwait, Malaysia, Pakistan, the Philippines, and South Vietnam, which had. Neutral states included Afghanistan, Saudi Arabia, Yemen, and the former dependencies of Burma, Cambodia, Ceylon, India, Indonesia, Israel, Jordan, Laos, Lebanon, Nepal, Singapore, Syria, and Iraq—the latter briefly (1955-58) a member of the Western-oriented Baghdad Pact.

ate effort to shake off Russian domination in 1956. Khrushchev several times postponed his 1958 ultimatum over Berlin and that same year did not back up China in the crisis over Quemoy and Matsu. The type of miscalculation on both sides that had led to the Korean War in 1950 was not likely to recur. There were thus the beginnings of a détente along clearly drawn geographic lines in Europe and East Asia.

Further to the South, however, there were no such lines of demarcation, and it looked as if the postcolonial vacuum of power might suck both superpowers into its vortex. Egypt in 1954, the Congo in 1960-62, Cuba in 1961-62 each offered a highly volatile combination of a weak and ambitious government with a strategic location or mineral assets of international importance. The high stakes were likely to encourage the worst gambling instincts in Moscow, and the murkiness of the local situation created risks of miscalculation in both Moscow and Washington.

The Cuban missile conflict of 1962, which brought the world closer to a third world war than any other crisis since 1945, may have had the net effect of extending the harder, cooler type of calculation further to the South. By the late 1960's, the two major powers seemed to be reducing or even abandoning their earlier efforts at proselytizing the smaller countries. Khrushchev's flamboyance had given way to Kosygin's more methodical tactics. The Chinese sounded as bellicose as ever, yet their attempts to set up client states in Africa by cajoling or subverting the postcolonial regimes—for example, Kenya, Burundi, Congo-Brazzaville—had brought few impressive results. Among the lesser communist powers, Cuba had obtained no tangible successes in its long-heralded campaign of sedition in Venezuela, Central America, and the High Andes. The Johnson administration soon came to regret its adventure in Santo Domingo in 1965. While American officials seemed determined by all necessary means to redeem their commitment in Vietnam, it seemed doubtful that they would willingly take on comparable commitments elsewhere in the future. To these changes in big power attitude, there corresponded a growing caution on the part of the new states themselves. Africans, in particular, tended to take the experience of the Congo in 1960-62 as a graphic warning of the dangers of direct involvement in the East-West conflict.

The large powers, even as they restrained their own earlier activism, took a number of steps to curb the activism of others. The Sinai-Suez War of 1956, the Cyprus conflict of 1964, and the Kashmir War of 1965 each held important lessons for the conduct of foreign affairs by middling or small powers. In 1956, United States refusal to compensate Great Britain and France for interrupted oil deliveries from the Middle East, together with Khrushchev's talk of missiles on London or Paris, put pressure behind the United Nations resolutions for cease-fire and withdrawal. In 1964, President Johnson, by a blunt message to Premier Inönü, forestalled Turkish military intervention under the 1960 treaty of guarantee for Cyprus; Russia, which first had leaned toward the Greek Cypriotes, soon began to cultivate closer relations with the Turks. In 1965, United States suspension of aid to both India and Pakistan meant that the Pakistani forces soon ran out of ammunition and spare parts for their American weapons; and Kosygin at Tashkent in January 1966 negotiated the cessation of hostilities.

Like any empirical precedents, these three situations remained somewhat ambiguous in their implications. In 1956 and 1965, the countries that resorted to military action were allies of the United States and recipients of American weapons; similarly Turkey, which contemplated intervention in 1964, was generally considered a more important ally of the United States than Greece. Hence in all three situations American action proved decisive in restoring peace. There was no comparable indication whether the Soviet Union would do as much in a local conflict provoked by a country equipped with Russian arms—for example, in case of an attack by Egypt on Saudi Arabia, by Algeria on Tunisia, or by Somalia on Ethiopia. If not, the possibility of great power involvement on opposite sides of a local conflict and of escalation by inadvertence obviously remained. In view of the inevitable slowness of diplomacy, moreover, it was doubtful whether the superpowers or the United Nations could reverse any *fait accompli*—say the complete conquest of one African country by another if accomplished within 48 or 72 hours.

Such episodes as the dispatch of Russian missiles to Cuba or of United States marines to Santo Domingo proved that the superpowers in restoring peace at Suez or in Kashmir did not act from any sudden access of pacifism. On the contrary, in deterring the military action of lesser powers, they seemed to reserve to themselves a world-wide monopoly (or rather duopoly) of mischief-making. But regardless of its motives, American and Russian solicitude for the territorial status quo was sure to find a warm response among postcolonial governments haunted by the specters of sedition, secession, and foreign infiltration. The response was if anything warmer in the United Nations—an organization that could justify much of its rhetoric and its very constitution only if it were supposed that each member state were indeed a nation and as such sovereign and inviolable.

Communist China, of course, remained staunchly opposed to any lessening of tensions in the developing regions. The brief military campaign in the Himalayas in 1962 suggested the ominous possibility of a headlong Chinese drive of military expansion; and observers did not seem sure some years after the event just what considerations had restrained Peking from pouring its troops into the plains of Assam and Bengal. The fact still remained that in 1962 as in 1958 China had acted cautiously. Even in Vietnam, Chinese military support of the communist war effort remained limited to materiel. It remained to be seen, therefore, whether communist China under Mao or his successors would be willing or able seriously to threaten the United States-Soviet Union condominium—or what response each of the superpowers would make to such a challenge.

Perhaps the most serious threat to the current equilibrium was the possibility that in the next decade countries like Israel, India, Pakistan, or Egypt might develop nuclear bombs and effective delivery systems. The consequences of such a development would be hard to calculate, and the Israeli-Egyptian arms race seems to be particularly ominous.[21] One may only hope that the superpowers, whether they are willing to agree to controls on their own nuclear weapons, will find effective ways to keep them out of the hands of less responsible powers. In the sphere of nuclear weapons, an enforcement of the superpowers' monopoly on mischiefmaking may be the only effective guarantee of peace.

If present trends of American and Russian policy continued undisturbed by Chinese expansionism or by nuclear proliferation, it was possible to foresee a time when the underdeveloped regions would no longer be, as in 1955-65, at the very center of the Cold War arena. This is not to say that the Cold War would cease, or that Russians and Americans would explicitly coordinate their actions. In some important countries, such as now in India and Egypt, the superpowers would continue to compete for the sympathies of governments or peoples. Left-wing coups d'état would still be hailed in Moscow as people's revolutions, and right-wing countercoups in Washington as victories for liberty and economic progress. In some regions, each major power might still have its own local protégés; occasionally, these might switch sides or embroil their sponsors in their quarrels. Generally, local wars such as that in the Congo in 1960-64 might become more frequent. Neither Moscow nor Washington, however, would be likely to invest large amounts of weapons, personnel, or prestige in such adventures, and there would thus be far less danger that they would escalate into full-scale conflicts between them.

Both powers might reduce their foreign aid budgets and con-

[21] Israel has far greater technical skills at its disposal and probably is refraining from bomb production because of the opprobrium this might incur and because it has (as the wars of 1948 and 1956 showed) conventional superiority. At the same time, Israel presumably is determined to remain one step ahead of Egypt. Egypt's pace toward nuclear weapons therefore remains the key to the situation. For an elaboration of these arguments see D. A. Rustow, "Israel and the United Arab Republic," in Edgar S. Furniss, Jr., and T. Alden Williams, eds., *Political Problems of Nth Country Nuclear Arms Choices, 1966-1980* (Columbus, Ohio: Mershon Center for Education in National Security, 1965, multilith), pp. 1-18.

centrate available funds on a few specific tasks, such as birth control, technical education, and development of mineral resources. They also might favor a few recipients considered economically promising or politically important. Russia would not set out to convert states far beyond its borders to communism. The United States would not consider any shout raised for neutralism or against "neocolonialism" an affront to its dignity. If the superpowers continued to expect a showdown in their Cold War, they would no longer expect to have it in the southerly regions of the globe.

Further Models, Seen and Unseen

In an atmosphere of reduced tensions, the countries of Asia, Africa, and Latin America might find themselves with fewer external resources, but also under less outside pressure in coping with their problems of late modernization. Patterns of modernity would become relevant not as outsiders tried to cajole or coerce them into joining this bloc or endorsing that ideology, but as they themselves looked for models to suit their needs.

THE UNREACHABLE IDEALS

The great industrial powers would not prove very suitable, both because of the gap that separates them from the late modernizers and because of the innate suspicion of new states toward old. Countries that had more recently solved some of their problems of modernization would be a more logical choice; yet there are several obstacles to such mutual emulation among the late modernizers.

First, the global network of communications—airlines, diplomatic missions, journalists' assignments, exports and imports—radiates outward from the major centers of modernity and power. The quickest way to fly from Lagos to Tunis is via Rome and to

Bogotá via London and New York. Newly independent countries in Africa appoint their first ambassadors to the United Nations, and to Washington, Moscow, Paris, or London; next to other African capitals; and often not at all to Latin America or South East Asia. Newspapers in Mexico City reprint much of their Latin American news from such sources as United Press International or Agence France Presse. The young Indian intellectual is more eager to go to Oxford or Cambridge, to New York or Moscow than he is to travel to other Asian capitals—or for that matter to the interior of his own country. Animosities, snobberies, and prejudices thrive in such absence of tangible contact. Asians are proud heirs of some of the oldest cultures; Latin Americans will not be lumped with non-Westerners or new states; neither of them like being compared to Africans. Even in the same region, the more charitably new nationalists might judge their own country, the more cynically they are sure to appraise their neighbors.

Second, the developing countries share memories of colonialism, fears of becoming victims of the Cold War, and a wish to make their views prevail at the United Nations. Beyond that, they do not constitute any natural economic or political bloc of their own. As producers of raw materials, they compete for markets, and as capital-poor countries for investments. The few that have seen some solid economic advance are understandably engrossed in their own problems and opportunities. Few of them have given any thought to the possibility of lending technical aid to others.

Third, there is the same dilemma that rules out the United States, Western Europe, or even Russia as practical models. Those countries that have advanced farthest—say Japan, Israel, Brazil—seem thereby farthest beyond the reach of others.

Japan tells *the* success story of rapid modernization. Its per capita income by now is as high as that of Italy, and it is one of the world's foremost industrial powers. But Japan began its intensive modernization a century ago, and even before that had assembled some important building blocks of modernity. Its protected location, its unity of language, its traditions of central authority and feudalism, its high level of education, and its habit of cultural borrowing from overseas provided starting points for the Meiji program of modernization that none of today's latecomers can easily reproduce.

Israel emerged as a thriving, modernizing society within only a generation after the arrival of the first wave of settlers. Its lush citrus groves and green forests are a visible token of modern man's control over nature and contrast starkly with the barren hillsides beyond its borders. Israel's army has proved a match to those of all its neighbors. But Israel is a country founded by European immigrants. Its people are the bearers of a distinctive tradition of community that had survived two thousand years of dispersion and persecution—a tradition that spiritually attached them to the land they now occupy. Much of Israel's development capital, moreover, was provided not from the usual foreign government sources but from private donations reflecting the worldwide solidarity of that same community of religion and descent.

Brazil has developed, around São Paulo, the largest industrial complex south of the Equator. Although its politics remain suspended between military and civilian rule, it is one of the few countries that has a genuine federal system. Brazil also is one of the largest countries and one of the richest in natural resources; its internal market is as large as that of two dozen African countries combined. There are steep class gradations in its society (somewhat correlated with skin color), but there is an old and refined national culture without racial or ethnic barriers.

The list could be much extended. There are many countries that have made impressive advances in some aspects of modernization, though they may have lagged in others. India has a far-flung educational system, a well-trained public service, and a national party that blends together in pragmatic fashion a myriad of local grievances and aspirations. Mexico and Turkey overcame militarism through the founding of single-party systems, and Mexico has a unique record of orderly succession of rulers in such a system. Chile and the Philippines have vigorous multiparty systems.

Other countries such as Venezuela, Turkey, and Ceylon have continued their democratic traditions despite obstacles and setbacks. The Lebanese system of representation harmonizes the interests of a dozen religious communities. Egypt is one of the few countries that has stabilized a military regime on a bureaucratic base. Tunisia has rapidly secularized an ingrained religious tradition. The list could be extended even further by a reexamination of the history of Western countries between the sixteenth and nineteenth centuries. The problems of modernization of Nehru, Lumumba, and Castelo Branco are somewhat more similar to those of Cromwell, Jefferson, Robespierre, or Bismarck than they are to those of Clement Attlee or John F. Kennedy.

Each of the success stories among modernizing countries could give rise to discouraging reflections. When one starts searching for causes, a country's rapid progress will always turn out to be closely related to very special and very favorable circumstances in its location or heritage. The most admirable achievement seems least susceptible of imitation. What is encouraging is the length and diversity of the list. There clearly is no single pattern of modernization. Modernity is interrelated in its various aspects, but it is not an all-or-nothing package deal. There is no one universal and indispensable prerequisite of modernization. Imbalances may prove helpful and stimulating, as long as they do not slow down the overall momentum. Where so many different paths have pointed toward the goal, other paths as yet untried may promise equal success. The one thing that the countries mentioned earlier have in common is that they have made the most of some particular opportunity that could be seized at each one's unique starting point.

DIVERSITY OF PATHS

The lesson for other latecomers is plain. There is no reason to search for a single universal recipe, and even less to despair if any of its alleged ingredients is missing. Instead, each country must start with a frank assessment of its particular liabilities and assets; and each will be able to learn most from those countries whose problems most closely resemble its own.

A second lesson might perhaps be derived from what was said in Chapters Three and Four about the advantages of various sequences among the tasks of political modernization. The most favorable sequence of tasks, it was suggested, is *unity—authority —equality*. This presupposes a historical heritage of unity in premodern days which has been most clearly present only in some Western European countries, in their overseas off-shoots, and in Japan. Hence a second sequence, *authority—unity—equality*, was identified as the one most widely applicable and most likely to lead to an early and effective completion of the modernization process. A third sequence, where the quest for equality is taken up before unity and authority are achieved, was said to be likely to lead to a breakdown of government into anarchy or civil war.

A future theory of political modernization might therefore distinguish among (1) those countries where the immediate need is for the building up of responsible authority and dedicated public service, (2) those countries that have, in their bureaucracies or party organizations (or both), an effective instrument of national unification but have not yet arrived at an accepted definition of their geographic identity, and (3) those that have solved the problems of authority and unity and are therefore free to concentrate on matters of political and social equality.

It is easier to define these categories in the abstract than to apply them to specific countries. A few observations on the typical problems of various developing regions may be in order.

In most countries of Tropical Africa, the primary need is for the building up of a qualified bureaucracy dedicated to impersonal public service. Once this has been achieved, a firmer kind of national integration will become possible, very likely involving a redefinition of national identities and a redrawing of boundaries. Social equality, representative government, and (on the economic side) rapid industrialization will be feasible only after the other two desiderata have been accomplished. Meanwhile, the practical choice would seem to be among personal, party, or military dictatorships that do or do not promote public service and national unity.

In the countries of Latin America, on the other hand, basic national identities have become well-established and accepted in the last century and a half. Some of them are linguistically homogenous (for example, Argentina, Brazil, Chile, Uruguay, Costa Rica); even in those with large groups that do not speak Spanish (mainly the Andean countries and Guatemala), the language problem is not so much one of clear-cut regional divisions but may largely be subsumed under the problem of political-social equality. On the other hand, Latin American countries differ widely in the degree of effective authority and public service they are able to offer—with Argentina, Chile, and Mexico at the higher and Bolivia, Paraguay, and Haiti at the lower end of the spectrum. Only in the former group can the issue of equality be successfully pushed to the top of the political agenda.

The Arab countries also differ widely in the degree to which public service and effective authority are developed—the spectrum ranging from Kuwait and Egypt to Yemen—and the question of unification had preoccupied them for several decades. Yet no tangible results were achieved, except for the interlude of unification of Egypt and Syria in 1958-61. Unless the drive for unity is soon resumed, the existing states will be consolidated in their national characteristics.

The German and Italian examples would indicate that a successful unification must rely more on a blending of interests across borders and less on coercion and intrigue. On the other hand, if the long-accepted psychological theorems about frustration and aggression have any validity, it may be assumed that a unified Arab state engaged in constructive work on the problems of internal political unity and integrated economic planning would be less truculent in dealing with Israel and other outside powers than are the divided and competing Arab states today.

In some of the Asian former colonies such as India, there is a tradition of public service comparable at least to the better-administered Latin American countries. In others, such as Indonesia, administration is in complete disarray. In many of the Asian countries, the question of linguistic diversity is thorny and potentially explosive and will complicate and delay any developments toward genuine democracy.

In drawing these broad distinctions, however, what was said earlier about the interrelation of the three quests should be kept in mind. For example, the countries of Tropical Africa will have to continue for some time a process of gradual and selective expansion of their educational system so as to produce a more nearly adequate body of bureaucrats and military officers. Meanwhile, the language or languages adopted for the primary and secondary schools will have a crucial bearing on the future possibilities of national unity. A solution of these educational problems will have a more important long-range impact on political (and hence economic) development in these countries than the construction of hydroelectric dams or experiments in electoral government.

One last lesson derives from a comparative look at the experience of late-modernizing countries. There is nothing automatic about progress to the foremost ranks of modernity. Latin America in the nineteenth and the Balkans in the early twentieth century provide appropriate deterrent models of political modernization —or rather of political stagnation and confusion—in the first, a dreary sequence of coups, rebellions, and ideological revolutions each with its own emotional hangover; in the other, a pattern of ethnic animosity, governmental instability, and reckless foreign policy.

To encourage a mutual exchange among developing countries of their experiences in political development would be a task worthy of the best efforts of international organizations such as the Organization of American States, the Organization of African Unity, and the United Nations. It would be a more promising task than that of making neutralist countries into a "third force" among the great powers, or that of organizing some sort of cartel among countries producing major raw materials.[22] Whereas economic development puts a premium on advisers from technically advanced countries, the political field is one where the United Nations could effectively use talent from the underdeveloped countries that make up a majority of its members.

An effort of this type might address itself to practical problems of immediate and long-range self-interest of governments of developing countries. It might include specific programs of advice and mutual assistance in the development of local party organizations and of trade unions, in the conduct of elections and of legislative meetings (including parliamentary procedure and the technique of legislative drafting), in the development of a competent civil service that transcends ethnic and regional cleavages, in the planning of an educational system in a multilingual state. Experts from the developed countries might well be invited under any such program; but in the obvious interest of both sponsors and beneficiaries, communist party cells and agents of the Central Intelligence Agency should be kept out. The popularity of Israeli and Yugoslav technical assistance programs indicates what can be achieved with slender resources in a context free from great power rivalries.

More generally, the task is not just one of interchanging available knowledge but of extending the knowledge that is available. Any of the programs just suggested would greatly benefit from the development of research by Asian, African, and Latin American social scientists into the needs of their own countries and regions. In the field of scholarship on modernization, the opportunities for insight are not restricted by political boundaries, diplomatic rivalry, or ideological positions—for scholarship has its own tests of validity and accuracy.

[22] The conferences at Bandung (1955), Belgrade (1961), and elsewhere might be cited as examples of the first; the Organization of Petroleum Exporting Countries (OPEC) and the proposals by Raul Prebisch and others at the World Trade Conference (Geneva, 1964) as examples of the second.

The most complex and urgent task for future thinking will remain a clarification of the relationship of nationhood to modernity. In Asia and Africa today, nationalism is fighting a two-front battle against constraints from abroad and disruptive forces of caste, tribe, or sect, at home. The more strenuously the leadership fights the internal divisions, the more likely it is to become a divisive force on the international scene. In Europe, the national boundaries drawn in the first few centuries of modernization are now acknowledged as impediments to further modernization. In the Western Hemisphere, the Central American Common Market and the Latin American Free Trade Association are promising beginnings of integration. In Africa, it would be utopian to try to bypass the nation-state, to seek the social integration required for modernity on a continental, Pan-African basis. Yet it seems doubtful that the present pattern of poor and diminutive countries can become the basis of successful modernization. One possible answer would be a series of movements for unification on a less-than-continental scale. The first African leaders to train a truly dedicated and competent cadre of public servants with a supra-tribal allegiance may well find themselves cast in the role of a Cavour or a Bismarck.

FATHERLANDS AND HUMANITY

Cavour's countryman, Giuseppe Mazzini, had dreamed of a map of Europe redrawn entirely along national lines. "Nationalism is what God has prescribed to each people in the work of humanity." "The nation is the God-appointed instrument for the welfare of the human race . . . Fatherlands are but workshops of humanity." "Nationalities are sacred and providentially constituted to represent, within humanity, the division or distribution of labor for the advantage of the peoples, as the division or distribution of labor within the limits of the state should be organized for the greatest benefit of all the citizens. If they do not look to *that* end, they are useless and fall. If they persist in evil, which is egotism, they perish; nor do they rise again unless they make atonement and return to good."[23]

Mazzini was keenly conscious of the human suffering inflicted by despotic monarchs in suppressing popular aspirations or in starting dynastic wars. His analogy of the division of labor within and among nations alludes to a recurrent theme in the study of modernization. But from the suffering that nations might cause through their own forms of oppression or aggressiveness, Mazzini turned away in a transport of quasi-religious enthusiasm. The Great Playwright had written a happy ending for every scene and act: if a nation persisted in garbling its lines, it would be sent backstage till it properly memorized the script. Mazzini's faith was reminiscent of Adam Smith's and David Ricardo's trust in an Unseen Hand that would turn private greed to public benefit.[24] Luckily for the classical economists, they could take for granted a national political order in which the constable, the justice of the peace, and the debtors' gaol were visible enough in their own day —and in which such agencies as the Food and Drug Administration and the Securities and Exchange Commission would one day become more visible still. The problem Mazzini ignored was that of order *among* such nation-states, and there were few comparable institutions then or now to preserve *his* illusion of automatic harmony.

The demand for national boundaries has been met not only in Europe but over the entire globe. Colonial emancipation has solved what used to be the internal problems of empires, often at the cost of transforming them into foreign problems among newly proclaimed nations—as in Palestine, Kashmir, or Cyprus. Even if

[23] Quoted in Carlton J. H. Hayes, *The Historical Evolution of Modern Nationalism* (Macmillan, 1951), pp. 155f., and in Crane Brinton, *Ideas and Men* (Prentice Hall, 1950), p. 420.

[24] On the theological antecedents of this trust see Alexander Rüstow, *Das Versagen des Wirtschaftsliberalismus* 2d ed. (Godesberg: Küpper, 1950). The phrase "invisible hand" occurs in Smith's *Theory of Moral Sentiments* (1759), Pt. 4, Chap. 1, and his *Wealth of Nations* (1776), Book 4, Chap. 2; "private vices— publick benefits" was the subtitle of Bernard de Mandeville's *Fable of the Bees* (1714). Cf. Rüstow, pp. 19, 60f.

the Russian-American conflict should abate in the postcolonial regions, these international problems can be expected to remain entangled with those of governments too weak to control their territories or populations. A common law to regulate the intercourse of nations is only slowly and painfully growing up. The nations have not even begun, in a rapidly changing world of modernization, to devise means of orderly and legitimate change; for surely appointment of governments by outgoing colonialists, perpetuation of accidental boundaries, or overthrow of both by violent *faits accomplis* are insufficient principles of legitimacy. Meanwhile weapons are being accumulated that could instantly destroy entire nations. The rhetoric of the United Nations, though less poetic, sounds at times quite as naive as Mazzini's. As a guardian of order, it remains rather less effective than the proverbial night watchman of Adam Smith's day.

Two centuries before Mazzini, an English geographer named Nathanael Carpenter had somewhat offhandedly sounded what was to become the perennial theme of the critics of nationalism. "Wee shall obserue," he had warned the readers of his treatise, "a multitude of miserable and wretched nations."[25] Will Mazzini's dream come true of a world of nations each making its God-ordained contribution to the common welfare of mankind? Or will it be Carpenter's nightmare of "a multitude of miserable and wretched nations"? More than 130 nations, real or so-called, will each make its contribution to the history of the late twentieth century; but too many of these will be contributions to their own wretchedness or to each other's misery. Much of this future course will seem beyond the deliberate control of statesmen—not to speak of scholars or plain citizens. Yet there indubitably is a margin for human choice. It is the most urgent and the most awesome task of the student of politics to explore the choices in that margin.

[25] *Geography Delineated Forth in Two Bookes*, 2, 3 (1653), p. 53, as quoted in the *Oxford English Dictionary*, s.v. "nation."

APPENDIX TABLES

TABLE 1

Linguistic Unity and Diversity of Countries [a]

Country and Source	Mother Tongue of Largest Group	% of Population	Mother Tongue of Second Largest Group	% of Population
		Europe		
Germany (B)	German	100		
Norway (B)	Norwegian	100		
Portugal (C)	Portuguese	100		
Austria (C)	German	99	Serbo-Croatian	0
Italy (C, F)	Italian	99	German	1
Greece (B)	Greek	98	Turkish	2
Sweden (C)	Swedish	98	Finnish	1
United Kingdom (E)	English	98	Welsh	1
Denmark (C)	Danish	97	Faroese	1
Hungary (A)	Hungarian	97	German	1
Iceland (C)	Icelandic	97	Danish	1
Ireland (F)	English	97	Gaelic	3
Albania (C)	Albanian	95	Greek	2
Malta (C)	Maltese	95	English	2
Netherlands (C)	Dutch-Flemish	95	Frisian	4
Luxembourg (C)	German	93	Italian	2
Finland (A)	Finnish	92	Swedish	7
Poland (B)	Polish	88	German	8
Bulgaria (C)	Bulgarian	86	Turkish	9
France (C)	French	86	German	4
Romania (A)	Romanian	86	Hungarian	10
Spain (C)	Spanish	73	Catalan	17
Yugoslavia (B) [b]	Serbo-Croatian	73	Slovene	9
Switzerland (A)	German	69	French	18
Czechoslovakia (C)	Czech	67	Slovak	27
U.S.S.R. (A)	Russian	59	Ukrainian	16
Belgium (B) [c]	Dutch-Flemish	50	French	44

Sources: In selecting language names for the table, the following sources have been consulted: Center for Applied Linguistics, various mimeographed materials; A. Meillet and Marcel Cohen, *Les langues du monde,* 2d ed., 2 vols. (Paris: H. Champion, 1952); International African Institute, *Handbook of African Languages,* 6 vols. (London: Oxford University Press, 1952–1966); Joseph H. Greenberg, "The Languages of Africa," *International Journal of American Linguistics,* Vol. 29, No. 1 (January 1963).

The letters following the country names indicate the following sources: (A) *Demographic Yearbook 1963* (United Nations, 1964); (B) *Demographic Yearbook 1956* (United Nations, 1957); (C) S. I. Bruk, ed., *Chislennost' i Rasselenie Narodov Mira* (Moscow: Izdatel'stvo Akademii Nauk S.S.S.R., Institut Etnografii, 1962); (D) Janet Roberts, "Sociocultural Change and Communications Problems," in Frank A. Rice, ed., *Study of the Role of Second Languages in Asia, Africa, and Latin America* (Center for Applied Linguistics, 1962), pp. 112–20; (E) Siegfried H. Muller, *The World's Living Languages* (Frederick Ungar, 1964); (F) estimate supplied by Dr. Heinz Kloss, Forschungsstelle für Nationalitäten-und Sprachenfragen, Marburg/Lahn, West Germany.

[a] *Countries:* The table includes all countries that at the end of 1966 were independent and had populations over 100,000 or were dependent and had populations over one million.

Language names: There is no general agreement, especially with regard to Tropical Africa, whether a given form of speech is a dialect, a language, or a group of languages. There is often equal uncertainty about the name by which a language or group is to be called. In the table, hyphens join alternate names for the same language (or for dialects in a dialect cluster), for example, Dutch-Flemish, Malinke-Bambara-Dyula. Names of language groups are given in parentheses (a) after a language name when the group name is more widely known, and (b) instead of a language name when the source does not give separate figures for each language in the group.

Percentages: Percentages have been calculated from absolute figures in the sources above. Where the classification or nomenclature in the source differed from that in the table, the necessary adjustments were made. Where censuses reported in sources A or B list bilinguals separately, these have been added to the speakers of the nonofficial languages, for example, to the Indian languages of Middle and South America. But see note (c).

[b] Alternate estimates, source C: Thailand, Thai-Lao, 74; (Chinese), 18. Yugoslavia, Serbo-Croatian, 65; Slovene, 9.

[c] Flemish-French bilinguals in Belgium and Sinhalese-Tamil bilinguals in Ceylon have been divided evenly between the two groups. Data for Algeria have been adjusted to account for the departure of French speakers since 1962.

284

TABLE 1 *(Continued)*

Country and Source	Mother Tongue of Largest Group	% of Population	Mother Tongue of Second Largest Group	% of Population
	East and South Asia			
Korea (C)	Korean	100		
Maldive Islands (C)	Sinhalese	100		
Japan (C)	Japanese	99	Korean	1
Bhutan (C)	Bhutanese-Bhotia	98		
Thailand (A)ᵇ	Thai-Lao	91	(Chinese)	4
Hong Kong (E)	Cantonese	88		
Vietnam (N & S) (C)	Vietnamese	85	Thai-Lao	4
Cambodia (C)	Cambodian-Khmer	84	Vietnamese	7
China (Mainland) (C, D)	Mandarin	81	Wu	8
Mongolia (C)	Mongolian-Khalkha	78	(Oirat)	8
Taiwan (A)	Fukienese-Taiwanese	78	Mandarin	18
Singapore (B)	(Chinese)	75	Indonesian-Malay	14
Burma (C)	Burmese	71	(Karen)	9
Laos (C)	Thai-Lao	69	Mon	11
Ceylon (B)ᶜ	Sinhalese	67	Tamil	29
Pakistan (A)	Bengali	56	Punjabi	30
Nepal (C, F)	Nepali	49	Hindi-Urdu	28
Indonesia (C)	Javanese	45	Sundanese	15
Malaysia (A)	Indonesian-Malay	43	(Chinese)	36
India (B)	Hindi-Urdu, Punjabi	42	Telugu	9
Philippines (A)	Cebuano-Visayan	24	Tagalog	21
	Oceania			
Australia (C)	English	91	Italian	1
New Zealand (C)	English	91	Maori	7
New Guinea (C)	(Papuan)	69	(Melanesian)	30
	Middle East and Northern Africa			
United Arab Republic (C)	Arabic	98	Nubian	1
Jordan (C)	Arabic	98	Circassian	1
Yemen (C)	Arabic	98	(African Languages)	1
Saudi Arabia (C)	Arabic	96	(African Languages)	1
Somalia (C)	Somali	95	Arabic	2
Tunisia (C)	Arabic	93	French	2
Lebanon (C)	Arabic	92	Armenian	5
Turkey (A)	Turkish	90	Kurdish	7
Muscat and Oman (C)	Arabic	89	Baluchi	4
Libya (C)	Arabic	88	(Berber)	6
Algeria (D)ᶜ	Arabic	87	(Berber)	12
Syria (C)	Arabic	87	Kurdish	6
Kuwait (C)	Arabic	85	Persian-Tajik	9
Mauritania (C)	Arabic	82	Fulani	12
Iraq (A)	Arabic	79	Kurdish	16
Cyprus (A)	Greek	77	Turkish	18
Iran (D)	Persian-Tajik	69	Azerbaijani	12
Israel (A)	Hebrew	66	Arabic	16
Morocco (C)	Arabic	65	Tamazight and Shilha (Berber)	12 each
Afghanistan (C)	Pashto	53	Persian-Tajik	31
Ethiopia (C)	Amharic	49	Galla	23
Sudan (C)	Arabic	48	Dinka (Nilotic)	12
	Tropical and Southern Africa			
Lesotho (C)	Sotho	99	Zulu-Xhosa	1
Madagascar (C)	Malagasy	97	French	2
Rwanda (E)	Rwanda	90		
Botswana (C)	Tswana	69	Shona	9
Rhodesia (C)	Shona	65	Zulu-Xhosa	15

TABLE 1 *(Continued)*

Country and Source	Mother Tongue of Largest Group	% of Population	Mother Tongue of Second Largest Group	% of Population
	Tropical and Southern Africa (Continued)			
Dahomey (C)	Ewe-Fon	58	Gurma-Somba	13
Upper Volta (C)	Mossi	54	Lobi, Bobo, Dogon	13
Sierra Leone (C)	Temne, Bulom, Limba	52	Mende	34
Mozambique (C)	Makua	51	Tsonga	24
Congo (Brazzaville) (C)	Kongo	50	Teke	25
Central African Rep. (C)	Banda	47	Gbaya	27
Gambia (C)	Malinke-Bambara-Dyula	46	Fulani	19
Ghana (A)	(Akan)	44	Mossi, Dagomba	16
Niger (C)	Hausa	43	Songhai	18
Senegal (C)	Wolof	42	Fulani	24
Togo (C)	Ewe-Fon	41	Tem-Kabre	22
Mali (C)	Malinke-Bambara-Dyula	40	Fulani and Senufo	14 each
South Africa (C)	Zulu-Xhosa	40	Afrikaans	21
Guinea (C)	Fulani	39	Malinke-Bambara-Dyula	26
Angola (C)	Umbundu	36	Kimbundu	24
Malawi (D)	Nyanja	36	Nguru and Yao	14 each
Chad (C)	Arabic	33	(Bongo-Bagirmi)	25
Zambia (C)	Bemba	33	Tonga	15
Gabon (C)	Kele, Njabi	31	Fang	30
Liberia (D)	Kru-Bassa	30	Kpelle	25
Kenya (C)[d]	Kikuyu	29	Luhya	19
Burundi (E)	Rundi	28	Swahili	17
Uganda (C)	Ganda	28	Nyoro, Nyankore, Hororo	17
Ivory Coast (C)	Anyi-Baule	24	Bete	18
Nigeria (C)	Hausa	21	Ibo	18
Cameroon (C)	Fang	19	Bamileke	18
Congo (Kinshasa) (C)[d]	Rwanda	17	Luba Lulua	17
Tanzania (C)[d]	Nyamwezi-Sukuma	17	Hehe	7
	The Americas			
Haiti (C)	French	99	Spanish	1
Barbados (C)	English	98	Spanish	1
Brazil (B)	Portuguese	98	German	1
Cuba (C)	Spanish	98		
Dominican Republic (B)	Spanish	98	French	1
Jamaica (C)	English	98	Spanish	1
Colombia (C)	Spanish	97	Chibcha	1
Costa Rica (B)	Spanish	97	English	2
Trinidad (C)	English	97	Hindi-Urdu	2
Nicaragua (B)	Spanish	96	Mosquito	3
Uruguay (C)	Spanish	94	Italian	2
Venezuela (C)	Spanish	94	Italian	1
Honduras (C)	Spanish	93	Mosquito	3
Chile (C)	Spanish	92	Araucanian	4
Panama (B)	Spanish	92	English	8
Paraguay (F)	Guarani	88	Spanish	6
Ecuador (B)	Spanish	86	Quechua	13
El Salvador (C)	Spanish	86	Nahuatl-Pipil	4
United States (including Puerto Rico) (E)	English	86	Spanish	3
Argentina (C)	Spanish	84	Italian	5
Mexico (C)	Spanish	81	Aztec	2
Canada (A)	English	58	French	29
Guatemala (C)	Spanish	55	Quiche	14
Peru (B)	Quechua	47	Spanish	45
Guyana (C)	English	45	Hindi-Urdu	45
Bolivia (B)	Quechua	37	Spanish	36

[d] In addition, 50% in Tanzania, 15% in Congo (Kinshasa), and 11% in Kenya speak Swahili as a second language.

TABLE 2

Linguistic Unity and Diversity, by World Region

Region	No. of Countries by Percent of Population Speaking Main Language									Total 10–100%
	90–100	80–89	70–79	60–69	50–59	40–49	30–39	20–29	10–19	
Europe	17	4	2	2	2	—	—	—	—	27
East and South Asia	5	3	4	3	1	4	—	1	—	21
Oceania[a]	2	—	—	—	—	—	—	—	—	2
Middle East and Northern Africa	8	6	2	3	1	2	—	—	—	22
Tropical and Southern Africa	3	—	—	2	5	8	7	5	3	33
The Americas	15	6	—	—	2	2	1	—	—	26
World Total	50	19	8	10	11	16	8	6	3	131

Source: Table 1.
[a] Not including New Guinea, for which no breakdown by individual languages was available.

TABLE 3
Linguistic States [a]

Language Spoken (1)	Country (2)	% Population in Country Who Speak Language (3)	% of Speakers of Language Who Live in Country (4)
Europe			
Albanian	Albania	95	69
Bulgarian	Bulgaria	86	93
Czech	Czechoslovakia	67	91
Danish[b]	Denmark	97	89
Finnish	Finland	92	85
French[c]	France	86	70
German[c]	Germany (W & E)	100	75
Greek[c]	Greece	98	83
Hungarian[b]	Hungary	97	91
Icelandic	Iceland	97	93
Italian[b]	Italy	99	84
Maltese	Malta	95	93
Norwegian	Norway	100	78
Polish	Poland	88	83
Romanian	Romania	86	85
Serbo-Croatian	Yugoslavia	73	96
Swedish	Sweden	98	81
East and South Asia			
Bhutanese-Bhotia	Bhutan	98	83
Burmese	Burma	71	99
Cambodian-Khmer	Cambodia	84	84
Japanese	Japan	99	99
Korean[b]	Korea (S & N)	100	95
Mandarin[b]	China (Mainland)	81	99
Mongolian-Khalkha	Mongolia	78	100
Sinhalese[d]	Ceylon	67	99
Thai-Lao[c]	Thailand	91	94
Vietnamese[b]	Vietnam (N & S)	85	98
Middle East and Northern Africa			
Persian-Tajik[b]	Iran	69	82
Turkish	Turkey	90	96
Tropical and Southern Africa			
Malagasy	Madagascar	97	100
The Americas			
Portuguese[d]	Brazil	87	86

Sources: Column 3 from Table 1; column 4 calculated from source C, Table 1, pp. 418–50. Note that this source tends to underestimate the proportion of speakers of European languages resident in their home country, since overseas emigrants and some of their descendants are often attributed to their native or ancestral language. Figures for Persian and Mandarin in column 4 calculated from estimates by Center for Applied Linguistics.

[a] The table includes all those groups who constitute two-thirds or more of their country's population as well as two-thirds or more of the speakers of their language—that is, all language-country pairs for which the figure in each column is 67 percent or more.

[b] This language also is spoken by the second largest group in one or more other countries. See Table 1.

[c] This language is spoken by the largest or second largest group in one or more other countries. See Table 1.

[d] This language is spoken by the largest group in one or more other countries. See Table 1.

TABLE 4

The Scope of Government Authority [a]

Country	Government Revenue as % of GNP	Civilian Government Employees as % of Population Ages 15 to 64	Country	Government Revenue as % of GNP	Civilian Government Employees as % of Population Ages 15 to 64
Europe			*Asia* (Continued)		
Sweden	51.8	11.5[b]	Burma	28.1	
Austria	43.1		Taiwan		3.2
Netherlands	42.7		Thailand	14.2	1.2[b]
West Germany	41.3	7.2	India	13.7	2.5
United Kingdom	41.1	10.6	Pakistan	12.7	
France	40.0	7.8	Jordan	11.2[b]	
Norway	39.6	5.9	Philippines	9.2[b]	
Finland	38.9		South Korea		1.7
Italy	37.3	3.1	Afghanistan	7.0[b]	
Ireland	30.9		*Africa*		
Denmark	29.2	9.8	Ghana		5.8
Belgium	28.0	3.7[b]	Egypt	37.1[b]	
Switzerland	25.0		Congo (Kinshasa)	25.5	
Portugal	24.3		Kenya	22.9[b]	4.5
Greece	23.3		Uganda	19.6[b]	2.7
Spain	20.7		Tanganyika	14.9[b]	1.7[b]
Other Industrial Countries			Ivory Coast		1.5
Japan	44.9	4.5	Nigeria		1.2
New Zealand	43.4	12.9	*Middle and South America*		
Canada	32.9	3.3[b]	Trinidad		9.1
South Africa	30.4	4.8[b]	Venezuela	21.9[b]	
Australia	28.5	12.5	Barbados	17.2	
United States	27.4	8.1	Brazil	17.2	
Asia			Mexico		3.2
Malaya		5.5	Jamaica	14.3	
Iraq	32.3[b]		Peru	12.4[b]	
Israel	30.9[b]		Bolivia	11.1[b,c]	
Turkey	28.4[b]		Argentina	9.8[b,c]	

Source: Bruce M. Russett et al., *World Handbook of Political and Social Indicators* (Yale University Press, 1964), pp. 64, 67f., 70f. Figures refer to revenues and to employment of government at all levels, national, state, and local; social security revenues and revenues from and employment in public enterprises are included.
[a] Government revenue and government employment in selected countries about 1959.
[b] Includes national government only.
[c] Does not include social security revenues.

TABLE 5. Contemporary Democratic Systems:

Country	Origins of Political System				Participation		
	Present Territorial Identity Since	Year of First Constitution	Year of Current Constitution	Continuous Popular Elections Since	Potential Voters as % of Total Population		Actual Voters as % of Voting-Age Population
					c. 1909	c. 1950	c. 1960
	(1)	(2)	(3)	(4)	(5)	(6)	(7)
United States	1776	1787	1787	1788	16.3[a]	39.5	64.4
Norway	c. 1000	1814	1814	1814	33.9	63.5	78.8
Belgium	1830	1831	1831	1831	23.5	65.4	87.6
United Kingdom	1603	1688[b]	1832[b]	1832	17.0	67.7	78.0
Netherlands	1588	1795	1815	1848	14.6	49.9	92.1
Switzerland[c]	1513	1798	1874	1848	24.3	30.1	28.0
New Zealand	1907	1852	1852	1852	61.1	58.8	86.4
Denmark	c. 1000	1849	1953	1855	17.8	58.7	84.0
Sweden	c. 1000	1720	1809	1866	20.4	68.4	83.1
Canada	1867	1867	1867	1867	25.3	58.3	74.2
Iceland	1918	1874	1944	1874	14.1	50.7	86.6
Luxembourg	1839	1841	1868	1868	—	—	71.1
Australia	1901	1900	1900	1900	63.3	61.5	85.3
Finland	1918	1919	1919	1906	45.9	43.5	72.8
Mexico	1822	1814	1917	1920	—	13.6[a]	34.6
Ireland	1921	1922	1937	1921	—	60.0	71.6
Lebanon[d]	1943	1926	1926	1926	—	—	48.0
Ceylon	1948	1912	1948	1931	—	39.6	58.8
Chile	1818	1811	1925	1932	—	12.0	37.4
Uruguay[c]	1828	1830	1952	1942	—	39.0	58.3
Austria	1918	1920	1945	1945	19.9	63.5	90.4
France	843	1791	1958	1946	28.9	61.9	89.4
Greece[d,e]	1830	1844	1911	1946	—	22.9[a]	73.3
Italy	1860	1848	1948	1946	24.2	58.6	92.9
Japan	c. 600 B.C.	1889	1946	1946	2.9	51.0	71.2
Philippines	1946	1935	1935	1946	3.0	26.4	55.1
Israel	1948	1948[b]	1948[b]	1949	—	43.2	88.0
West Germany	1945	1848	1949	1949	22.2	66.7	86.9
Costa Rica	1839	1825	1949	1949	—	33.0	57.6
India	1947	1950	1950	1952	—	50.6	52.6
Colombia	1830	1819	1886	1958	—	24.8	40.2

Sources: Col. 5: W. S. and E. S. Woytinsky, *World Commerce and Governments* (Twentieth Century Fund, 1955), p. 596; Karl Braunias, *Das parlamentarische Wahlrecht*, 2 vols. (Berlin: de Gruyter, 1932). Col. 6: United Nations, *Demographic Yearbook; Statesman's Yearbook; Statistical Abstract of Latin America* (U.C.L.A., 1963); and statistical yearbooks of individual countries. Col. 7: Bruce M. Russett et al., *World Handbook of Political and Social Indicators* (Yale University Press, 1964), pp. 84–86. Cols. 8–14 are based on lists of heads of government in Bertold Spuler, *Regenten und Regierungen der Welt*, vols. 3, 4, and supplement (Würzburg: Ploetz, 1962–1967; Raymond Fusilier, *Les monarchies parlementaires* (Paris: Editions Ouvrières, 1960); supplemented by *Statesman's Yearbook;* Council on Foreign Relations, *Political Handbook of the World; Encyclopaedia Britannica; Keesing's Contemporary Archives;* and monograph sources.

[a] Actual voters as percent of total population.
[b] Date of unwritten constitution.
[c] Multiparty plural executive.
[d] No clear party alignments.
[e] A military coup in April 1967 superseded the constitutional government of Greece.

Explanatory Note: The table includes all countries which at the beginning of 1967 had regimes based on three or more consecutive, popular, and competitive elections. Periods of democratic government interrupted by dictatorship, military coup, or foreign occupation (e.g. France, 1875–1940; Germany, 1919–1930; Czechoslovakia, 1920–1938; Philippines, 1935–1942; Turkey, 1950–1960; Brazil, intermittently, 1945–1964) have been disregarded, except where democratic governments continued in wartime exile (e.g. Netherlands and Norway, 1940–1945). Countries have been listed in the order of dates in column 4.

Cols. 1–4: In many countries, particularly in Europe, territorial identity, constitutions, and electoral regimes developed gradually, and different dates might therefore have been selected in many instances.

Col. 4: Elections to estates or those based on a very restrictive franchise (as in Britain before 1832) have been disregarded. Elections to legislatures enjoying substantial autonomy under foreign rule (as in Finland after 1906, Ceylon after 1931, and Lebanon after 1926) have been included.

Cols. 5–7: These figures give some indication of the degree of political equality and participation attained

	Party Changes					
				Length of Continuous Rule by Same Party		
Party Changes of Head of Government			Average Length (Years) (11)	Longest Period		
Number (8)	From (9)	To (10)		Length (Years) (12)	From (13)	To (14)
14	1829	1961	9.2	24	1861	1885
21	1884	1965	3.8	28	1935	1963
16	1845	1958	7.2	34	1884	1918
28	1830	1964	4.7	17	1905	1922
28	1848	1966	4.1	13	1861	1874
—	—	—	—	—	—	—
11	1876	1960	7.4	12	1890	1912
14	1901	1953	4.4	14	1953	—
16	1905	1936	3.6	31	1936	—
11	1867	1963	8.3	18	1878	1896
8	1944	1963	2.6	4	1963	—
3	1867	1926	25.0	48	1867	1915
9	1905	1949	6.2	18	1949	—
33	1919	1966	1.2	6	1937	1943
0	1929	—	—	38	1929	—
5	1922	1957	7.5	16	1932	1948
—	—	—	—	—	—	—
2	1947	1965	6.6	9	1947	1956
3	1932	1964	8.8	20	1932	1952
—	—	—	—	—	—	—
0	1945	—	—	22	1945	—
19	1946	1958	1.1	9	1958	—
—	—	—	—	—	—	—
0	1945	—	—	22	1945	—
0	1948	—	—	19	1948	—
4	1945	1965	5.5	8	1953	1961
0	1948	—	—	19	1948	—
0	1949	—	—	18	1949	—
4	1949	1966	4.5	5	1953	1958
0	1947	—	—	20	1947	—
2	1958	1966	3	4	1958 } 1962	1962 } 1966

through elections to the legislature or its more popular house. The most significant measure would have been potential voters as a percentage of voting-age population, but such figures are not readily available for most countries. Figures in columns 5 and 6 reflect in part a country's age structure, and those in column 7 fluctuations in voting participation. Generally, in column 5 or 6, figures above 40% indicate universal suffrage, figures of 20–35% suffrage for adult men only, and figures under 20% tax or literacy qualifications. Similarly, in column 7, figures under 50% usually indicate that all or most women are disfranchised.

Cols. 8–10: Column 9 gives the year when clearly organized parties assumed control of the government. (In contrast to column 4, periods before independence have not been included.) Column 8 indicates the number of changes of party control, counting the date in column 10 but not that in column 9. Column 10 indicates the last such change before January 1, 1967. In all three columns, the criterion has been the party affiliation of the president or prime minister. Changes from party government to coalition government or from one coalition to another thus are counted only when a new party took over the premiership. For the United Kingdom, for instance, a change of party control was recorded for 1931 but not again until 1945. This method of calculation exaggerates the difference between postwar Italy, where Christian Democratic premiers presided over shifting coalitions of center, center-right, and center-left parties, and France, where the premier's party affiliation shifted along with changing coalitions. If the party affiliation of the largest group of ministers in the coalition rather than that of the premier, had been the criterion, column 8 for France would read 8 and column 11 would read 2.6.

Col. 11: Average period of control by a single party, from year given in column 9 until 1967. Note that this is a measure for *periods* of control rather than for *changes* between such periods; hence the divisor is larger by one unit than the figure in col. 8:

$$(\text{col. 11}) = \frac{1967 - (\text{col. 9})}{(\text{col. 8}) + 1}$$

Cols. 12–14: Longest continuous period of control by a single party. The figures were obtained by subtracting the year of accession from the year of resignation; hence there is a margin of error of ± 1 year.

TABLE 6

The Fragmentation of Sovereignty: Countries of the World by Region, Date of Independence, and Size of Population [a]

(In millions)

Country	Year of Independence	Population	Country	Year of Independence	Population

Independent before 1775

Country	Year of Independence	Population	Country	Year of Independence	Population
Europe			*East & South Asia*		
U.S.S.R.	—	227.7	China (Mainland)	—	689.9
Germany	—	75.4	Japan	—	96.9
United Kingdom	—	54.2	Thailand	—	29.7
Italy	—	51.1	Nepal	—	9.9
France	—	48.4	Bhutan	—	.8
Spain	—	31.3	*Middle East & Northern Africa*		
Netherlands	—	12.1	Turkey	—	30.7
Portugal	—	9.1	Iran	—	22.9
Sweden	—	7.7	Ethiopia	—	22.2
Austria	—	7.2	Afghanistan	—	15.2
Switzerland	—	5.9	Muscat & Oman	—	.6
Denmark	—	4.7			

Independent between 1776 and 1943

Country	Year of Independence	Population	Country	Year of Independence	Population
Europe			*Middle East & Northern Africa* (Continued)		
Poland	1918	31.2	Yemen	1918	5.0
Yugoslavia	1878	19.3	Lebanon	1943	2.3
Romania	1878	19.0			
Czechoslovakia	1918	14.1	*Tropical & Southern Africa*		
Hungary	1918	10.1	South Africa	1910	17.5
Belgium	1831	9.4	Liberia	1847	1.0
Greece	1830	8.5			
Bulgaria	1908	8.1			
Finland	1918	4.6	*Middle & South America*		
Norway	1905	3.7	Brazil	1822	78.8
Ireland	1921	2.8	Mexico	1820	39.6
Albania	1912	1.8	Argentina	1816	22.0
Luxembourg	1890	.3	Colombia	1819	17.5
Iceland	1918	.2	Peru	1821	11.3
			Chile	1818	8.5
North America & Oceania			Venezuela	1830	8.4
United States	1776	192.1	Cuba	1901	7.4
Canada	1867	19.3	Ecuador	1830	4.9
Australia	1901	11.1	Haiti	1840	4.6
New Zealand	1907	2.6	Guatemala	1813	4.3
			Bolivia	1825	3.7
East & South Asia			Dominican Republic	1844	3.5
Mongolia	1921	1.1	El Salvador	1838	2.8
			Uruguay	1828	2.7
Middle East & Northern Africa			Honduras	1838	2.1
Egypt	1922	29.0	Paraguay	1811	2.0
Iraq	1932	7.0	Nicaragua	1838	1.6
Saudi Arabia	1925	6.6	Costa Rica	1838	1.4
Syria	1943	5.2	Panama	1903	1.2

[a] The table includes all countries that on December 31, 1966, were members of the United Nations and other countries with populations over 200,000. Population figures in millions are estimates for mid-1964. United Nations, Statistical Office, *Statistical Yearbook 1965* (1966).

TABLE 6 *(Continued)*

Country	Year of Independence	Popula- tion	Country	Year of Independence	Popula- tion

Independent between 1945 and 1966

Country	Year of Independence	Popula- tion	Country	Year of Independence	Popula- tion
Europe			Tanzania	1961	10.3
Malta	1964	.3	Kenya	1963	1.9
East & South Asia			Ghana	1957	7.5
India	1947	471.6	Uganda	1962	7.4
Indonesia	1949	102.2	Madagascar	1960	6.2
Pakistan	1947	100.8	Cameroon	1960	5.1
Korea	1945	39.4	Upper Volta	1960	4.8
Vietnam	1954	34.1	Mali	1960	4.5
Philippines	1946	31.3	Rhodesia	1965	4.1
Burma	1948	24.2	Malawi	1964	3.9
Taiwan	1949	12.1	Ivory Coast	1960	3.8
Ceylon	1947	11.0	Zambia	1964	3.6
Malaysia	1957	7.8	Guinea	1958	3.4
Cambodia	1954	6.2	Senegal	1960	3.4
Laos	1954	2.0	Niger	1960	3.3
Singapore	1965	1.8	Chad	1960	3.3
Maldive Islands	1965	.1	Rwanda	1962	3.0
Middle East & Northern Africa			Burundi	1962	2.5
			Dahomey	1960	2.3
Sudan	1956	13.0	Sierra Leone	1961	2.2
Morocco	1956	13.0	Togo	1960	1.6
Algeria	1962	11.0	Central African		
Tunisia	1956	4.6	Republic	1960	1.3
Israel	1948	2.5	Congo (Brazzaville)	1960	.8
Somalia	1960	2.4	Lesotho	1966	.7
Jordan	1946	1.9	Gabon	1960	.5
Libya	1951	1.6	Botswana	1966	.5
Mauritania	1960	.9	Gambia	1965	.3
Cyprus	1960	.6	*Middle & South America*		
Kuwait	1961	.4	Jamaica	1962	1.7
Tropical & Southern Africa			Trinidad & Tobago	1962	.9
Nigeria	1960	56.4	Guyana	1966	.6
Congo (Kinshasa)	1960	15.3	Barbados	1966	.2

Dependent in 1966

Country	Year of Independence	Popula- tion	Country	Year of Independence	Popula- tion
North America & Oceania			*Tropical & Southern Africa* (Continued)		
New Guinea	—	1.5	Angola	—	5.1
Papua	—	.6	Mauritius	—	.7
Portuguese Timor	—	.5	South West Africa	—	.6
Fiji	—	.4	Portuguese Guinea	—	.5
			Reunion	—	.4
East & South Asia			Swaziland	—	.3
Hong Kong	—	3.7	Spanish Guinea	—	.3
Ryukyu Islands	—	.9	Cape Verde Islands	—	.2
Sikkim	—	.2	Comoro Islands	—	.2
			Rio Muni	—	.2
Middle East & Northern Africa					
South Arabia	—	.9	*Middle & South America*		
Gaza Strip	—	.4	Puerto Rico	—	2.6
Aden	—	.2	Surinam	—	.3
Spanish North Africa	—	.2	Martinique	—	.3
			Guadeloupe	—	.3
Tropical & Southern Africa			Netherlands Antilles	—	.2
Mozambique	—	6.9			

TABLE 7

The Fragmentation of Sovereignty: Median Population of
Countries, by Region and Period of Independence

(In millions)

Region	Median Population of Countries, Mid-1964			
	Independent Before 1775	Independent 1776–1943	Independent 1945–1966	All Independent Countries
Europe	21.7	8.3	.3	9.1
North America & Oceania	—	15.2	—	15.2
East and South Asia	29.7	1.1	18.2	18.2
Middle East & Northern Africa	22.2	5.9	2.4	5.1
Tropical & Southern Africa	—	9.3	3.4	3.4
Middle & South America	—	4.5	.8	3.6
All Regions	22.6	5.2	3.4	5.0

Source: Table 6.

INDEX

INDEX

Abdullah, Sharif, King of Transjordan, 68

Acton, John Emerich Edward Dalberg-Acton, 28

Africa, 2, 6, 12, 15, 27, 29, 31, 51, 75, 107; multiplicity of languages in 54, 56, 57; patterns of state formation, 62, 67-70; colonial impact on indigenous political systems, 111, 250; political parties in, 215, 216; aristocrats' aid in the rise of lower strata, 217; transition to independence, 244; silencing of dissidents in, 226; developing countries' problems, 276-77

Ahmad, Imam of Yemen, 249

Algeria, 49, 174, 178, 255, 256

Alliance for Progress, 252

Almond, Gabriel A., 4n, 97n, 140n, 216n

Antonius, George, 41n, 45n

Apter, David E., 17n, 80n, 143, 150n

Arab countries, 12, 41; communists' courting of, 259; differences in degree of governmental authority, 277

Aramburu, Pedro, 196, 197

Arensberg, Conrad M., 164

Argentina, 66, 183, 195-99 passim

Aristotle, 136, 139

Asian countries, 2, 6, 15, 27, 29, 31, 51, 56, 75, 107; patterns of state formation in, 62, 67-70; colonial impact on indigenous political systems, 111; political parties in, 215, 216; aristocrats' aid in the rise of lower strata, 217; postcolonial legacy of new states, 250; policy of abstention from entanglement, 267

Atatürk, Kemal. See Kemal Atatürk

Australia, 66, 77

Authority. See Governmental authority

Aydemir, Talât, 198

Balfour Declaration, 49n

Baltic countries, 42, 262

Bandaranaike, S. W. R. D., 86, 163, 217, 219

Bandaranaike, Sirimavo, 118

Batista, Fulgencio, 249

Bayar, Celâl, **180**

Beard, Charles A., 6

Becker, Carl Lotus, 42n

Belgium: ethnic alignment in, 97

Bell, Daniel, 150n

Ben Bella, Muhammad, 226, 255, 258

Bendix, Reinhard, 37n, 152n, 159n

Bentley, Arthur F., 153n

Besant, Annie, 86

Betancourt, Rómulo, 255

Billing, Bishop Gottfrid, 86

Binder, Leonard, 37n

Bismarck, Otto von, 37, 124, 275, 280

Black, Cyril E., 1, 115n, 143, 262n

Blackmer, Donald L. M., 140n

Blau, Peter M., 149n

Bolívar, Simón, 173

Bolivia, 192, 193, 194

Borden, Sir Robert, 88n

Boumedienne, Houari, 226

Boundaries: "natural frontiers" in border disputes, 40; effect of language on, 48; determination of by plebiscite, 58-60; demand for national boundaries, 281, 282

Bourguiba, Habib, 215, 223, 225

Branting, Hjalmar, 86

Brazil, 66, 195-99 passim, 263, 273, 274

Brinton, Crane, 109n

British Empire, 49, 78, 160, 228. See also Great Britain

Bryce, James, 93n, 98n

Bureaucracies: growth of in the Middle Ages, 73; expansion of for wider integration of opinions, 94, 129-30; Russia and China the largest known to history, 262. See also Governmental authority

Burke, Edmund, 93

Burma, 174, 256

Café Filho, João, 195, 199

Çakmak, Fevzi, 202

tic reputation, 205; difficulty of move toward democracy in, 206; undemocratic character of, 264. *See also* Coups d'état

Mill, John Stuart, 20, 21, 22, 93

Millikan, Max F., 140*n*

Mills, C. Wright, 99, 254*n*

Minority groups: degree of national allegiance of, 25; in the successor states to imperialism, 50-51

Modernity: tension between nationhood and, 2; defined, 9; variety of cultural traits in, 10-11; egalitarian pressures of, 80-81; counterpressures from holders of privilege, 81, 82; technological and social forces of, 238

Modernization: defined, 3; perspectives on time, environment, and fellowman, 3-5, 12, 19, 42; aspects examined by social scientists, 5-8; ambiguous effects of, 8-9; meaning of progress in, 8-11; residual tradition in, 11-15, 107, 146; gradualism, uniformity, and variety of, 15-18; political aspects of, 18-20; opportunities for equality in, 82; colonial conquest and resistance as stimuli to, 109; the worldwide march toward, 237-40; tensions in the struggle for, 238-39; success of various modernizing countries, 273-75; intercourse of nations in a modernizing world, 282

—prospects: the Western impact, 241-44; obstacles to fulfillment, 244-47; question of development or decay, 247-49

—Western democracies as models: unreadiness of new states to achieve Western economic, social, and political ideals, 249-50; inconsistencies of U.S. foreign policy, 251-53

--communist countries as models: attractions of communism, 254-58, 261; alignment and nonalignment with communists, 257-58; propaganda, aid, and diplomacy tactics, 258-59

—late-modernizing countries: nontransferability of democracy or communism to, 263-64; suspicions of small states, 264-67, 272; search for new models to suit unreachable ideals, 272-75; diversity of paths in different countries, 275-80; suggested programs for mutual exchange of experi-

ences in political developments, 278-80

See also Political modernization

Monarchies: defensive modernization in, 112-13; direction of reform efforts in, 113-15; present-day conservative rulers of, 243

Montesquieu, Charles de Secondat de, 135, 156

Moore, Barrington, Jr., 145*n*

Morgenthau, Ruth Schachter, 209*n*, 217*n*, 220*n*

Morocco, 225, 243

Mossadegh, Mohammed, 217, 219

Muhammad Ali of Egypt, 45, 106, 112, 174

Muslim League, 25, 221, 224, 225

Naguib, Muhammad, 171, 179, 184, 189, 205

Napoleon, 38, 42, 45, 102, 127, 173

Nasser, Gamal Abdul, 1, 6*n*, 7, 22, 27, 45, 50, 52, 161, 166, 167, 168, 170, 171, 176-77, 179, 186-87, 189, 200, 203, 205, 258, 259

Nation-states: world-wide interdependence of, 3, 239-40; defined, 21, 35; the vehicle of modernization, 29-30, 237-38; political requirements for success of, 35-36; territorial aspects of, 39-40; political integration of, 60-62; scope of public functions in, 73-74; regional organizations formed by, 278. *See also* Nations

National identity: requirements for group consciousness of territory and citizenry, 36-38; the "will of the people" as a criterion, 58-61; and governmental authority, 62-70; shapers of, 65; question of state boundaries, 79-80

Nationalism: uses of the term, 21-22, 25-26, 257; cultural ingredients of, 30, 31; changes in values, 43; search for a suitable past to justify confidence in the present, 41, 44-47, 117; nationalist movements in Southeast Asia, 256

Nationality: the ideal of, 20-21; factors in the formation of, 60-61, 62

Nationhood: the dual revolution of modernity and, 2; tenuous claims to in late-modernizing soceities, 239-40; proliferation of claims to, 246

Nations: definitions of, 20-28 *passim;* fluidity of allegiance to, 24-27; creation of new nations, 25-26; traditional and modern types, 27-31; factors promoting loyalty, 30-31; constituted by human inhabitants, 40; national identity and authority, 62-71; criteria of membership in a modern nation, 70-71; man's welfare in a future world of nations, 280-82

—patterns of formation: post-dynastic states, 63-64; linguistic states, 64-65; countries of overseas immigration, 65-67; postcolonial states, 67-70. *See also* Nation-states

NATO, 189n

Nature: prehistoric and modern control over, 13-14, 19, 238

Nehru, Jawaharlal, 37, 168, 217, 255, 275

Nehru, Motilal, 86, 217, 220

Neustadt, Richard E., 96n

Neutralism, 252, 257

New Zealand: pattern of state formation, 66; social welfare programs in, 77

Nicaragua, 191-92, 243

Nigeria: federal structure of, 69; transition from colonialism to independence, 242

Nkrumah, Kwame, 6n, 7, 22, 42, 143, 148, 161, 165, 166, 215, 220, 222, 223, 226, 255, 258

North American Indians: the term "nations" applied to, 28

Nu, U, 223, 255

Nuclear proliferation: the threat of in a world of nations, 270-71

Nuri al-Said, 207, 249

Obregón, Alvaro, 201, 212

O'Higgins, Bernardo, 173

Oligarchies: means of perpetuating power of, 90; Spain's rule in the Americas, 172-73; military coups as an antidote to undemocratic oligarchies, 181

Ongania, Gen. Juan Carlos, 196

Organization of political power: modern man's need for, 19; threats to universal participation in, 91; in constitutional democracies and in communist regimes, 92-104. *See also* Communism; Democracy

Organization of African Unity, 278

Organization of American States, 278

Ostrogorski, M. I., 93n

Ottoman Empire, 11, 29, 39, 45-46, 49, 65, 79, 160, 175, 209, 228; system of governmental authority in, 131

Packenham, Robert A., 252n

Paderewski, Ignacy Jan, 65

Pakistan, 25, 248, 269, 270

Palestine, 66, 68, 78, 255, 281

Palm, August, 86

Palmer, Robert Roswell, 73n, 85, 159n

PAN (Partido de Acción Nacional) of Mexico, 215

Paris Peace Conference (*1919*), 26, 60

Partido de la Revolución Mexicana, 213

Partido Revolucionario Institucional (PRI) of Mexico, 207, 212, 213, 216, 226n, 236

Peacock, Alan T., 76n

Peasants, 16; appropriation of land by, 75; migration to cities, 245

Peking-Moscow dispute. *See* Sino-Soviet conflict

Perón, Col. Juan Domingo, 196, 197, 198

Peru: military regime in (*1962-63*), 191; U.S. exercise of pressure against military junta, 252

Peter I of Russia, 16, 106, 112, 114

Petroleum: revenues from in preindustrial countries, 76n; exploitation of colonial economies by foreign companies, 218; political modernization resulting from discovery of, 243

Philippines, 53, 250, 254, 262, 263, 274; struggle between nationalist forces and a colonial ruler, 229

Plamenatz, John, 15

Plebiscites: question of forming nations by popular vote, 58-60

Poland, 24, 65, 252, 258

Polanyi, Michael, 102n

Political equality: the quest for in the modern nation, 79-82; pressures for and counterpressures, 80-82; contemporary theory of, 94

—participation for all social groups: subterfuges in prevention of, 81-82, 91; furtherance of, 84; effect of political organization on, 91, 92

—privilege and discrimination: control by a narrow social group, 89; ways of